Motorcycle Journeys Through

California
and Baja

**Other Touring Guides in
The Motorcycle Journeys Series**

Motorcycle Journeys Through the Alps & Corsica

Motorcycle Journeys Through the Appalachians

Motorcycle Journeys Through New England

Motorcycle Journeys Through Northern Mexico

Motorcycle Journeys Through the Pacific Northwest

Motorcycle Journeys Through the Rocky Mountains

Motorcycle Journeys Through Southern Mexico

Motorcycle Journeys Through the Southwest

Motorcycle Journeys Through Texas

Also From Whitehorse Press

Essential Guide to Motorcycle Travel

Motorcycle Journeys Through

California and Baja

Second Edition

by Clement Salvadori

Whitehorse Press
Center Conway, New Hampshire

Whitehorse Press books are also available at
discounts in bulk quantity for sales and
promotional use. For details about special sales or
for a catalog of motorcycling books, videos, and
gear write to the publisher:
   Whitehorse Press
   107 East Conway Road
   Center Conway, New Hampshire 03813
   Phone: 603-356-6556 or 800-531-1133
   E-mail: CustomerService@WhitehorsePress.com
   Internet: www.WhitehorsePress.com

ISBN-13 978-1-884313-60-8
ISBN-10 1-884313-60-4

5 4 3 2 1

Printed in China

Acknowledgments

A great many people helped in the preparation of this book, which includes both the original two books and this compilation, from my long-suffering wife to the CHP officer who stopped in the Mojave Desert to see if I were alright . . . I was, but the motorcycle had a flat tire, caused by a bent rim, so help was needed.

Some of these people gave me advice and information, good and bad, others provided a meal, a place to stay. Some took photographs, others recorded mileages, some kept me company on a ride or loaned me a motorcycle; a few suggested I get a real job.

I did enjoy a truly excellent year doing research for this book, and I rode roads in the Golden State and in Baja California that are on a par with good motorcycling roads anywhere else on this planet.

In alphabetical order, I thank: Joe Anastasio, Bruce Armstrong, Geraldine August, Steve Bergren, Terry Bowen, Buzz Buzzelli, Rich Cox, Craig Erion, David Fairchild, Kurt Grife, John Hermann, Larry Kahn, Reg Kittrelle, Clea Kore, Jenny "Mad Maps" Lefferts, Steve & Lise Posson, Jim Quaintance, Tod Rafferty, Bob & Jan Reichenberg, Ted Simon, Craig Stein, Calif Tervo, Mark Tuttle Jr., Bruce & Joan Webster, David Wells . . . and a great many others whose names escape me at the moment.

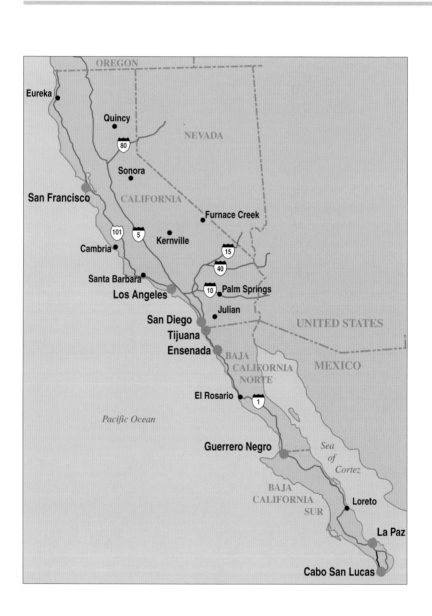

Contents

Foreword

Welcome to the two Californias, Alta and Baja. Alta (High) California is the old Mexican name for the American state of California, and Baja (Low) California is part of Mexico. While I have long maintained that Alta California offers some of the finest roads and scenery that any motorcyclist could wish for, the Baja offers an entirely different venue, easily accessible and quite wonderful in its own right.

Now, this is riding at its best—the Big Sur coast.

The dirt road to San Borja Mission goes through countryside populated only by various members of the cactus family.

This is really a combination of two books that Whitehorse Press requested I write, *Motorcycle Journeys Through California,* which first appeared in 2000, and *Motorcycle Journeys Through Baja,* which came out in 1997. Dan Kennedy at Whitehorse thought that combining the two would be interesting, and useful, as it would give a sense of possibility of riding Baja to a lot of readers who never thought of going there. Give the rider a taste of what lies south of the border, and he might well give it a try—and absolutely love the place.

Alta California is rather like your spacious, well-groomed front yard, while Baja California is the back lot you don't often think about. To clarify terminology, when I refer simply to California in this book, that will be the U.S. version; when I write just Baja, that will be the Mexican side of the border.

The California section describes 33 different day trips that you can take, as well as one 2,500-mile lap of the entire state, with not only directions but comments on a number of motels and restaurants, flophouses and greasy spoons, that you will pass along the way.

The Baja section is quite abbreviated from the original book, as I have geared this to the street rider, keeping the travels on pavement. There will be some references to various unpaved roads which are street-bike suitable, but the main intent is to get the rider from Tijuana to Cabo San Lucas without ever getting the tires dirty, noting the best places to sleep and eat along the way. And where to find gas to fill up your tank.

Enjoy.

Introduction: California

Welcome to California, which offers some of the best motorcycle riding in the world.

I know, I know, I know . . . great riding roads can be found all over this country, all over the world. I first rode the Alps when I was 17, on an NSU 250 Max, and have been going back regularly ever since—but they get snowed in for a good part of every year. Here in the semi-benign Pacific climate of California, many of the roads I write about can be ridden all year around, like the Big Sur Highway, or the Lost Coast road, or Death Valley. That is important—at least to me.

My biggest problem is always deciding: Where will I go today?

I first came out to visit this state in 1965, on a Velocette Venom Clubman, entering via Tioga Pass into Yosemite National Park. I fell in love with the park immediately, so much that I got a job and stayed for a month. Two years later I came back to California to get a graduate degree; I did not choose the school so much for its academic credentials but for its location—in Monterey, at the north end of the Big Sur. I returned several more times in the 1970s, and finally moved out permanently in 1980. No regrets.

THE WHERE OF IT ALL

It's far from being a perfect place. The cost of living is high, housing prices can be outrageous, and the occasional earthquake keeps us on our toes. But I get on a motorcycle every day, and I do have great roads to ride.

As I write this, it appears that the state of the state of California is pretty good. The economy is healthy, the natural environment is reasonably well-looked after, and thanks mainly to an overly zealous taxation program the population is actually diminishing a little. Or at least not growing very fast.

This is one big place. From Crescent City in the north to El Centro in the south is some 800 crow-flying miles, and the width averages about 200 miles. All told, the state encompasses over 155,000 square miles, which makes it the third largest in these 50 United States. If you don't know what the two biggest are, shame on you.

On the west side of the state are over a thousand miles of coastline, much of it bordered by California Highway 1, a truly scenic highway. All the way down the length of the state an irregular chain of low coastal mountains, from the Siskyou Mountains in the north to the Jamul Mountains in the south, keep the seaside climate rather separate from the inland weather. We will be doing a lot of coast riding.

In the middle of the state is the huge Central Valley, made up of the Sacramento Valley to the north and the San Joaquin Valley to the south. This is one of the most fertile places in the nation, thanks to the taxpayers picking up most of the tab for irrigating everything from cabbages to cotton. To be a farmer in that valley is to be rich. We shan't have much to do with the valley, because the roads are long and straight and rather boring.

Over to the east, coming down from Oregon, is the Cascade Range of mountains, which turns into the Sierra Nevada Range around Lassen Volcanic National Park. These mountains run all the way south to the Tehachapi, San Gabriel, and San Bernardino mountains, which provide superb riding for the Los Angeles area motorcyclists. Mountains are good, and we will see a great deal of them, from Mount Shasta in the north to Mount Palomar and the Laguna Mountains in the south.

Napa Valley welcomes visitors.

Down in the southeast of the state are the great Mojave Desert, which sits pretty high at 2,000 feet or more, and its cousin to the south, the Colorado Desert, a low desert. Choose the right roads and the riding in those wide-open spaces is superb, as there is nobody else out there. I can tear up a set of tires in a hurry on those roads, which has frustrated many a tire distributor who has been kind enough to offer a set of rim-protectors for "testing."

The tallest spot in the state is Mt. Whitney (named in 1864 for one Prof. Josiah Dwight Whitney of the California State Geographical Survey) in the Sierra Nevadas, at 14,494 feet; you can't ride up to the top, but you can get to Whitney Portal at 8,371 feet above sea level. And less than 150 road miles to the eastsoutheast is Badwater, in Death Valley, at 279 feet below sea level. So, in two to three brisk riding hours you can go from the highest to the lowest, which is sort of neat.

Criss-crossing California are about 170,000 miles of road: big roads like 12-lane freeways, little roads that wander through the national forests. The California Department of Transportation (known affectionately as CalTrans) maintains a lot of these highways and byways, and keeps them in pretty good shape. The condition of the county-maintained roads varies a great deal, depending on how much money a county has, and where it is willing to spend it.

THE PEOPLE

One interesting statistic is that fully 44 percent of the state is owned by us, the public. Along with country, state, and national parks there are thousands of square miles operating under the aegis of the National Forest Service (NFS) or the Bureau of Land Management (BLM), and most of the publicly owned lands have few or no inhabitants.

California's population is about 38,000,000, which averages out to more than 245 per square mile. However, if you go to Alpine county, covering 762 square miles of mainly national forest, its 1,000 year-around inhabitants each average almost a square mile to play in. Whereas the 46-square-mile San Francisco county is jam-packed with some 800,000 people. But who cares about the averages, as a third of all Californians are stuck in greater Los Angeles, another five million in the San Francisco Bay area, a few million more in San Diego, Bakersfield, Sacramento, and some other cities, which leaves relatively few to clutter up the roads we like to ride. There are not many people living along CA 36 between Red Bluff and Fortuna, and not a single gas station between Santa Margarita and Buttonwillow on CA 58. Our megalopolises are mega in size, but you don't even have to go near them if you don't want to.

THE ECONOMY

The economy of the state is worth about $5 trillion annually. If California were to secede from the union, as an appreciable minority in the population might wish, of the 195 or so countries in the world it would rank about 7th in wealth. And tourism, which we happen to be addressing in this little book, is a major factor.

Most of the state's money comes from agriculture, next is industry, including the sizable remnants of the military-industrial complex, a little oil, a lot of entertainment (Hollyweird), and the give and take of general commerce from the Halcyon General Store to Wal-Mart.

All of which business is taxed, of course, and that money goes to feed the bureaucracy, both in the state and in Washington. Lots of bureaucracy in the Golden State, with 58 counties and hundreds of towns and cities, all those b'crats striving desperately for womb to tomb financial security. Education chews up a whole bunch, with public schools going all the way from kindergarten to post-Ph.D. programs.

A LITTLE HISTORY

The pre-history of the state is a bit vague. Some say that the first people strolled in from Asia via the Bering Straits some 10,000 years ago, some say otherwise. A number of Indian tribes lived in the state before the Europeans came, and today many tribes are recognized as legal entities, which means they can build casinos on their land. Which irritates the Nevada gambling types greatly.

A Spanish explorer named Johnny Cabrillo made note of the coastline back in 1542, but the colonists didn't get around to building a permanent site until 1769, and that was in San Diego. Precisely when the Spaniards first began calling this stretch of Pacific coastline California is not known. The name comes from a 16th-Century Spanish novel, *The Adventures of Esplandian,* in which the hero finds an island of beautiful women run by Queen Calafia. This northern part of the West Coast was called Alta California, to distinguish it from Baja California, now part of Mexico.

The Mexicans threw out the Spaniards in 1821, and in an effort to populate Alta California, which was a long way from Mexico City, allowed foreigners to come in and settle. Unfortunately for Mexico most of these ingrates thought they would be better off as Americans than Mexican. The U.S. government, feeling the need to create its own destiny, threw the Mexican government out of Alta California in 1847.

Other than this disused railroad station, which is now a visitor center for the Mojave Desert National Preserve, there is a lot of nothing around this ghostly town of Kelso; I, for one, love all the nothingness that the deserts have to offer.

The next year a fellow named John Marshall found gold up at Sutter's Mill in the Sierra foothills. By 1849 the Gold Rush had begun, and the highway that connects many of the old mining camps is called, appropriately, CA 49.

After the gold madness subsided, while the East and Midwest developed factories and manufacturing, California stayed pretty much rural, with cattle ranches and lumbering and a lot of farming. An unscrupulous developer by the name of William Mulholland figured he could make a fortune selling land in the greater Los Angeles area if he could guarantee a steady supply of water, and built an aqueduct that drains the huge Owens Valley on the east side of the Sierras and brings the water 400 miles to the southwest. Bill got very rich as a result, but his family life was very dysfunctional.

Then the Great Depression arrived, and many people, starved out of their livelihood in the Dust Bowl, headed for the promised land. Read John Steinbeck's *The Grapes of Wrath* for more on that, and visit the Steinbeck museum in Salinas. World War II ended the Depression and boosted the population of southern California, as industries set up to do war work and needed laborers.

Since then California has been on a roll, business has boomed, population has soared, and CalTrans has constructed and taken care of a lot of fine byways in the more remote parts of the state. The money that goes into maintaining the Big Sur Highway or Feather River Canyon road is money well spent, to my admittedly selfish thinking.

Conversely, the police forces, from county deputy sheriffs to California Highway Patrol officers, create a lot of revenue for the local coffers by ticketing (presumed) speeders. But there are a lot of little-used roads with minimal surveillance, and those are the ones I tend to like to ride.

I've got a good mix of roads in this book, from the touristy, like California Highway 1 north of the Golden Gate Bridge, to the little-trafficked, like the Cecilville Road.

But every road in this book is a great road to ride.

General Stuff to Know

This is a book written for road-going motorcyclists, both for riders who like superbly twisty roads along the coast and in the mountains, and flat-out-hauling roads in the deserts, as well as for riders who like to take their time and smell the roses, or the orange blossoms, or whatever flowers are lining the road.

Any road that can be ridden fast can also be ridden slow, so I am appealing to both ends of the speed spectrum. I am not advocating excessive velocities, as the speed of a motorcycle on any road is determined by the rider's right hand, but there are some far-off roads in California which certainly do appeal to the sporting sense of many riders.

The focus of this book is on the road, on the ride. Getting there is far more important than being there—wherever "there" might be.

Add some spectacular scenery and interesting history, along with a few places to eat well and sleep soundly, and you have a motorcyclist's travel guide for California.

I spent many years riding around the state, covering tens of thousands of miles of pavement, riding every road you will read about in this book. And this was backed up by more than a quarter-century of living in California. I have seen bear, cougar, lynx, elk, antelope, deer, fox, coyote, rattlesnakes, and other undomesticated animals crossing roads, which shows that there are a great many rural miles to be covered.

I could fill up a huge appendix with the titles of books about California highways and byways. A few are good, most are pretty ho-hum. But there has never been a book quite like this one.

The whole purpose of this exercise is to get you on great roads. Do Disneyland if you want, go to the Palace of the Legion of Honor in San Francisco, or San Diego's Seaworld, Sacramento's Old Town, but dealing with those tourist hot spots is not really within the purview of this little tome. For those you can buy any of a hundred California guidebooks dedicated to the fly-and-rent-a-car crowd, the motorhomers, and the like.

This book is designed to be carried in your tankbag, and read before you go to sleep at night so dreams of high mountain passes and curling coastal byways will pleasure your night away. Or read about a Trip at breakfast, finish the coffee, and take off for an excellent day's ride.

MAPS

We are covering a rather large area in relatively few pages, and here I will explain how I'm going to do it. And you are going to have to use your own imagination, and get a good map(s), in order to create your own perfect journey. Any decent map of the whole state of California should have 99 percent of the roads that I mention; if the scale is 15 miles to the inch or more, you are in good shape. Of course, regional and county maps are even better, and if one is a AAA member, the California offices have some excellent detailed cartographic renditions of the roads I will describe.

Some people swear by those DeLorme books, with the whole state covered in page after page of excellent topographic rendering. I use those, but they are a bit large (11 x 15 inches) for tankbag work, and I am always having to turn to another page. I far prefer the folding paper map, which should be easily readable, and you can take a Magic Marker and plot your route.

CHAPTERS

For the purposes of this California section, the state has been broken into 13 general areas, each with its own chapter. You perspicacious readers may notice that the 13 areas are spread pretty much around the periphery of the state, so that you can easily go from one to another.

Plus there is a 14th chapter which covers the whole state at one whack. The "Been-There, Done-That" riders will probably go straight to that section, make the loop, and then go home and boast that they've seen all of California. Which they haven't.

Most chapters have a Headquarters, a town or city, each one offering at least two days of good riding in its own area, from Eureka in the north to Julian in the south. When I travel, I do like to unload the bike at a hotel and then spend a day or two riding without benefit of saddlebags.

From each Headquarters I take you on two or three Trips, loops which bring you back to your toothbrush. The Trips all have mileages, and I throw in a bit of history, and where to find a great burger or a plate of the freshest seafood.

Some feckless types might complain that in some chapters they have to use up part of a Trip just to get to the Headquarters, and that they find this to be very confusing. In that case my recommendation is to hire a helicopter which can pop you right into a motel parking lot at any given Headquarters, and you won't have to fret about this at all. Of course there is the occasional road-repetition, but you will notice that most times I have you go over the same road twice, you will do it in both directions. In truth, this book is best used by those riders who have good imaginations, who can read the book

This refurbished Victorian house sits in the little village of Westport, north of Fort Bragg.

and make their own minor adjustments to my programs.

Two of those 13 chapters deal with Linear Routes, like up CA 1 along the Pacific shoreline from the Golden Gate Bridge to the Lost Coast, or along the western Sierra Nevada through Kings Canyon and Sequoia national parks and along the Western Divide Highway. These are great roads which lend themselves more to a straightish shot than anything else, but I also include some excursions, places to stay, et cetera.

At each Headquarters I recommend a couple of motels, hotels, B&Bs, and then I will also suggest lodging in other places that I cover on each separate trip. For example, in the Central Coast section I suggest you bed down in Cambria. But some might want to go up to the Monterey Peninsula, which is perfectly fine, if a bit overly touristed. So there are also comments on what Monterey has to offer.

ROADS AND NAVIGATION

Roads are denoted as either Interstates (I-5), or US routes (US 395), or state highways (CA 168), or county roads (S2), or have no numbering, just a name (Santa Rosa Creek Road).

This couple is Halloween shopping along Santa Rosa Creek Road near Cambria.

I will include some very few bits of gravel and dirt, but 99.9 percent of the roads I will be dealing with are paved. The text will have big WARNING signs if I'm about to put you on gravel, and any non-paved stretch will be explained as to harshness. In dry weather all of them are Wingable. However, I know there are some riders who suffer a paralyzing phobia when it comes to lack of pavement, so they should just steer clear of such roads.

Each of the main Trips, loop or linear, will be well-explained, with mileage. These mileages are reasonably accurate, but not too precise—for good reason. One, if you and two friends go for a 100 mile ride, you may have three different readings on the tripmeters at the end. And two, I have found that a stretch of road on a map might be measured for one distance, the sign on the actual road might indicate another mileage, and the odometer show yet a third—Skyline Boulevard (CA 35) south of San Francisco between CA 92 and CA 9 being a case in point, in which the CalTrans sign reads 23 miles and the AAA map says 26, and a Harley tripmeter registered 26.3 miles.

Even with uneven mileages, there should be no way you will make a mistake with my directions; I make it pretty obvious where you are going to have to turn.

Sometimes the text will list a DETOUR, which would be a more pictur-esque/interesting way to get from Point A to Point B by other than the main route. There are also ALTERNATE ROUTES, which will veer you off in some other direction, but always with the same destination in mind.

And connecting the trips are CONNECTORS, routes you might con-sider to get from one Focal Point to another, let us say, Palm Springs to Julian. A CONNECTOR might appear in mid-Trip, just so if you want to head off to Death Valley from the town of Lee Vining, the book tells you how to do it.

ACCOMMODATIONS AND FOOD

Motels, hotels, from The Ritz down to flea-ridden, low-life joints will sometimes have prices, sometimes not. Pricing structures have become so complicated that a motel that charges $200 for a room on a weekend in high season, with a two-day minimum, can go for $50 on a Wednesday in low season. And some counties can charge a 10 percent "hospitality" tax, others do not. The best way to approach this is to call up and enquire, since a phone number goes with each place. I am covering a very few of the hos-telries that you will find along the road, and there are lots of others to choose from; if you want more choice, call the local Chamber of Commerce/ Tourist Bureau number that I have listed for the Headquarters in each chap-ter, and you will get a big packet in the mail.

That is "art" you are looking at, and this outdoor shop is to be found in Borrego Springs.

You will find that I have a weakness for rather old-fashioned, Fifties motels. The paint may be peeling, the faucet might drip, but I love them. Especially when each unit has its own little carport, and the place is out of the way as opposed to being on a major truck route. And they're cheap. I also like rather expensive places, for obvious reasons.

Food is where you find it, and out of the 25,000 (rough estimate) establishments which serve food in this state, from expensive lobster to a general-store sandwich, I list maybe a hundred. This is not a gastronomical guide, but I will try to keep you away from the fast-food chains. You can get precisely the same Whopper in your home-town or mine (Atascadero), which more or less defeats the basic notion of travel, which is to experience something different.

The town of Jacumba had a populaton of 15,000 in 1925; now it is about 300; this fireplace is all that remains of the old hotel.

This statue honors the fishermen who have sailed out of Humboldt Bay for more than 150 years.

CALIFORNIA'S NATIONAL FORESTS

In the chapters dealing with southern Californa (3, 4, 5, 14, and 15) I run Trips through four national forests, the Angeles, Los Padres, San Bernardino, and Cleveland, and as you enter these forests you will be greeted by a sign alongside the road saying FEE AREA. This means that you the public should pay yourself a fee of $5 a day, or $30 a year for using your own land. This bureaucratic idiocy, applicable to only those four forests, was established in 1997, but I have yet to purchase a Venture Pass, as the recreational fee is called. You only need pay the fee if you are going to stop and actually recreate in the forest; if you are only passing through, no need.

I'm sure that other things you see as you ride through California, and that I have not covered here, will perplex you on occasion; don't worry about it. Traveling should be enjoyable, and the best kind of travel is the simplest kind: point your front wheel in the direction you want to go, and let out the clutch.

With this book in your tankbag, you can ride the best roads that California has to offer, with a minimum of the boring in-between stuff.

Go forth, consume gasoline, wear out tires, and have a good time.

And remember, a journey without incident is a pretty dull trip indeed.

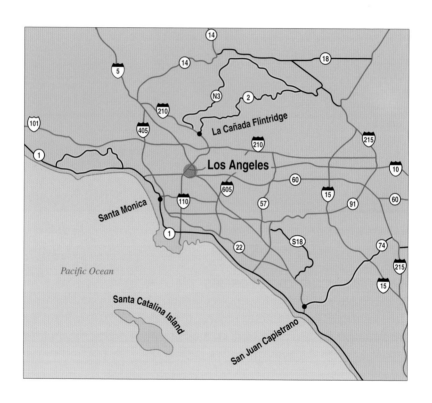

Los Angeles & Environs

Headquarters *Somewhere in Greater Los Angeles*
Los Angeles Bureau of Tourism *213-689-8822*
Getting There *If you can't figure that out for yourself, you will be in trouble; in which case my advice is to sell the bike and get a chauffeured limo. But just for the record, Interstate 5 is the main north/south route, with Interstate 10 coming in from the east. Or you can fly in by plane (ship, car, bicycle, hitch-hike) and rent a bike (see Appendix A).*
Ground Zero *There is none, can't be one, for the whole place. However, directions for the three trips I have planned for you will begin on one or another of the major highways that cut through Los Angeles, and with the help of a decent map you can figure your way around.*

I'm going to start the riding tour of California here, in the middle of Los Angeles, despite some minor misgivings on my part. Cities do not provide the best of riding venues, unless one is of the hooligan variety, but our geographic focus on any place often starts with a city, and from there we can spread out.

I had thought of beginning the book in Death Valley, a place unlike any other place in the world. However, in the end I decided that this urban environment would allow readers a proper appreciation for the realities of the Big Angel. Also because probably most out-of-staters would consider Los Angeles a place they would like to see, though they would have no idea what they want to see in it.

Here we are, in the biggest city in the U. S. of A.; those Big Apple guys will throw a fit, but if you take into account the population of Greater Los Angeles, and the amount of acreage covered, this is one helluva sizable town. Over ten million people live in Los Angeles county, most of them legal, some of them not. And you attach Orange county, which is really just a suburb of LA, and maybe some little bits of adjacent Riverside county, and you have a big land mass with a lot of people.

Believe it or not, and a lot of people who have never been out here do have, will always have, doubts, some superb riding is within an hour of LA City Hall. The Los Angeles basin has got the very rugged San Gabriel Mountains to the north, the Santa Monica Mountains to the west, and the

The muralists down in Venice have done a lot to pretty up some otherwise bleak views.

Santa Ana Mountains to the south. And each of these hilly places has great roads.

   Los Angeles is a very interesting city, a place unlike any other place, a vast collection of small urban enclaves which tries to function as a unit. The name has been substantially abbreviated from the original 18th Century Nuestra Senora la Reina de Los Angeles (Our Lady Queen of the Angels), when a one-legged man could get from one side of town to the other in half an hour. Today you must have your own transportation. Back in 1980, recently moved to the area, I thought I would drop my bike off for some repair work and take a bus home. It took me 20 minutes to ride to the dealer, four and a half hours to get back to where I lived. And things have gotten worse.

   Do get a map of Los Angeles county, not just the city. The whole place is based on freeways, or Interstates, or super-slabs, whatever you want to call those big highways that divide and re-divide the city. I-5 and I-405 are the major north-south routes, but you must not forget I-110 or I-710 or I-605 or CA 55 or CA 57. East-west roads include I-10, I-105, I-210, along with CA 22 and CA 60 and CA 91. Then there is US 101 which plunges right into the heart of LA—and disappears.

Concerning non-freeway roads, the only one I'll slip in here is CA 1, running more or less along the coast from Dana Point to Malibu. Taking fast freeways I can do those 80 miles in a little over an hour; taking the scenic CA 1, figure four hours.

Los Angeles has always been a car-conscious place, and the **Automobile Club of Southern California** was founded there in 1900. In 1915 LA had 55,000 registered cars; no mention of motorcycles, but I bet there were a bunch.

Along the Ortega Highway is Caspers Wilderness Park, which has a few miles of horse-riding trails and a corral to keep the horses in.

Down in Venice, you could sit at an outdoor cafe and cheerfully watch people all day long; in this case, Bob Reichenberg is the fellow being watched.

There is no conventional "Downtown" to LA. **City Hall** is roughly where I-5 and I-10 cross over each other in a gloriously complicated intersection. A clump of more high-rise structures can be found over in **Century City,** about ten miles to the west, just south of Beverly Hills. The rest of the city just sprawls, thanks to the automobile, mostly in bungalows and two-story apartment buildings.

Where to stay. Not easy. If you want a cheap motel, try around Los Angeles International Airport, or Disneyland in Anaheim in Orange County. Figure out your favorite hotel chain, be it Motel 6 or Radisson, call up the 800 number and see if they have some suitable digs where you want to be.

For my recommendations, with safe motorcycle parking, try the following. If you want old-fashioned high class, the **Chateau Marmont** at 8221 Sunset Boulevard in Hollywood, with 63 rooms and bungalows with prices ranging from a modest $350 to an immodest $3,000 (323-656-1010, 800-242-8328). The place opened in 1929 as a very sophisticated spot where movie stars could live and be indiscreet, and the reputation holds. Best Western, Holiday Inn, Comfort Inn, Days Inn, Ramada—they all have Hollywood hostelries.

Down in **Venice,** where watching buff bodies is at its best, try the **Best**

Western Marina Pacifica Hotel at Pacific Avenue and 17th Street, right in the very heart of Venice, a half-block off the Boardwalk—which is really asphalt, not wood, but the pedestrians and roller-bladers are definitely worth seeing. And the place is less than five minutes' walk from **Restaurant Row** on Main Street; the hotel has 88 rooms and rates start at $150 (800-421-8151, 310-452-1111). If you wonder why there are no canals in Venice—there were when Venice was created in 1904; however, 25 years later California's mad passion for the automobile caused them to be filled in and paved over.

For a really nice spot a little outside of mainstream LA, think of the 47-room **Malibu Beach Inn** on the beach smack dab in the middle of Malibu town, priced from $200 on up (22878 Pacific Coast Highway, 800-4-MALIBU, 310-456-6444).

There are ten thousand things of interest in LA, whether it is the **Los Angeles County Museum of Art,** or the **Petersen Automotive Museum** for fine motorcycles. But if I start getting into "city sights," we will never get out on the good riding. Although I should mention that one of the primary cultural attractions in the area, the **Getty Center,** is motorcycle friendly; just ride up along the I-405, and between the I-10 interchange and the US 101 interchange is the Getty exit. For automobiles the Getty has a reservation list for the limited parking weeks long, while for motorcyclists there is no waiting and the parking in the museum's garage is also free; good, decent people run this outfit, who understand that we take up little space.

LA is noted for its "weekend motorcycle venues," and I will include the three most notorious in this chapter, the Rock Store, the Crest, and the Ortega. During the week hardly a bike is to be seen on these roads, unless it is ridden by some moto-mag editor flogging the latest and fastest, but come Saturday morning, the picture changes, as the $40,000 store-bought customs and $400 junkers tear off to the rendezvous of choice.

A curiosity in California, and especially in SoCal (as southern California is abbreviated) where the weather is generally sunny, is the fact that relatively few of the half-million motorcyclists appear to commute on their machines. Maybe when gas hits $4 a gallon that will change.

Trip 1 Rock Store

Distance *64 miles*

Highlights *This is Profiling Paradise. On a sunny Sunday morning you will see the rich and famous, the poor and infamous, and everybody in between up there in the Santa Monica Mountains above Malibu.*

The Rock Store itself is a defunct gas station and country grocery store on Mulholland Drive to the west of the village of Cornell, and a functioning cafe that is the destination of a thousand motorcyclists every weekend. There is lots of good riding in these mountains, but the purpose of most attendees is just to see and be seen, to discuss the latest carbon fiber license-plate holder or chromed brake disc. And to check out the celebrities.

That's Veronica Savko on the front steps of the Rock Store; she and husband Ed (who was taking a nap) own the place.

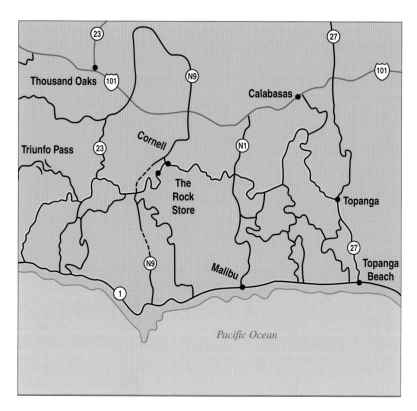

Ground Zero for this trip will be on CA 1 between Santa Monica and Malibu, right at Topanga State Beach—which is just six miles west of where I-10 turns into CA 1, a mile or so west of where Sunset Boulevard runs into the sunset at the ocean's edge. Between Sunset and Topanga you pass from the LA city limits into LA county.

0 Miles   TRAFFIC LIGHT—TURN RIGHT onto Topanga Canyon Boulevard, a/k/a CA 27. Forty years ago this place was rustic; today it is high priced, with a few elderly hippies still trying to hang on, and the two-lane road is jammed with new SUVs.

4+ Miles   TURN LEFT, going across the bridge, onto Old Topanga Canyon Road. On your left you have just passed the **Topanga Creek General Store**, providing nourishment from eight in the morning to whenever (310-455-1250), and the Topanga Post Office; right opposite the turn, on the right, is the Topanga Central Auto Service.

Old Topanga Canyon Road twists and turns for a bit, past the Mill Creek Dressage & Equestrian Center and other signs that the earth people are on the losing end of possession.

12 Miles STOP sign—TURN LEFT onto **Mulholland Highway,** and you have gone up a thousand feet since leaving the beach. You are actually in the suburbs of the "rapidly growing" (an understatement) town of **Calabasas,** but also in the **Santa Monica Mountains National Recreation Area,** where the government and the property owners go toe to toe. The amount of open, publicly owned land within the 4,000 square miles of Los Angeles County is quite impressive, more than 35 percent.

16 Miles Off to the left goes Stunt Road, which leads to Saddle Peak Road and Tuna Canyon Road, and other roads where the weekend morning sporting riders like to test their lean angles. Mulholland itself is a trifle on the tame side, and is regularly cruised by the sheriff and the CHP.

17 Miles Cold Canyon Road goes off to the left, down to **Monte Nido** and Piuma Road and La Flores Canyon Road. But for my money, and pleasure, the better canyon riding is in the western part of the Santa Monica Mountains, so I recommend you GO STRAIGHT along Mulholland Highway. For the geologically inclined, these mountains got tossed up out of primeval ooze less than two billion years ago, in Precambrian times.

20 Miles TRAFFIC LIGHT—GO STRAIGHT, crossing over Las Virgenes Road/Malibu Canyon Road, a/k/a County Road N1, and entering **Malibu Creek State Park.**

23 Miles STOP sign—GO STRAIGHT, crossing over Cornell Road/ Lake Vista Drive; watch it, as cross-traffic does not stop.

25 Miles The Rock Store, appearing on your right. On any sunny Saturday or Sunday morning, the place should have several hundred motorcycles in front.

The Rock Store on Mulholland Highway, a semi-sacred shrine for Los Angeles-area riders, is a very worthwhile Sunday destination for anyone visiting on two wheels.

The Rock Store

The original store, not surprisingly, is made of rock. Outside sit two gas pumps which have not pumped gas for a good many years. And it has become the most singularly focused destination in California—all you see are motorcyclists, from all rides in life, be it Jay Leno on a Black Shadow or the average stud or studette on what he or she can afford. The motorcycling life is a great equalizer, and while at The Rock Store, all are equal.

Back in the Fifties the Rock Store was simply a store that served the nearby community of **Cornell,** and the venturesome types coming out from Los Angeles for a day in the mountains. Which included groups of motorcycle riders, who would stop, sit in the shade of the trees, and knock back a Pabst or NuGrape.

In 1961 Ed and Veronica Savko bought the store, which the local tax assessor lists at 30354 Mulholland Highway, and life continued pleasantly enough. And the number of motorcycles in the Los Angeles area began growing considerably, thanks to the Japanese invasion. This place was an ideal destination for a day ride. A little cafe was added, and business boomed on the weekends. Ed soon stopped selling gas, as it was more of a convenience to his customers than a profit center; his decision was helped along one fine day after his tanker truck lost its brakes when he was at the wheel.

Then the store became less important, as Cornellians could just as easily buy from the malls along the burgeoning US 101 corridor in the **San Fernando Valley,** just three miles to the north. And catering to the increasing motorcycle crowd became the profitable way to do business. The cafe expanded, and Ed added on a patio with an outdoor grill. The food that the Rock Store serves, from eggs and bacon to double cheeseburgers, is not *haute cuisine* but rather good, solid stuff. The coffee is hot, the sodas are cold.

As a sideline the Savkos would rent the Rock Store to movie companies for location shots. And it appeared that Hollywood wanted the place during the week, the motorcyclists came on the weekends, so for the last ten years the cafe has operated on Friday from 11 o'clock, Saturday and Sundays from seven o'clock, generally closing after dusk. Try calling 818-889-1311 to check on things; even better yet, just show up. ∎

26 Miles The road winds away from the Rock Store, climbing, and comes into a sweeping left-hand, uphill turn—and a pull-off spot to the left that is the official **Volcanic Landscape Lookout of the Mulholland Scenic Corridor**—or at least that is what the sign says. Mostly it is referred to as the **Squid Spotting place,** because a lot of overly zealous riders come tearing along Mulholland, knowing that ten to a hundred people are looking at them, and stage fright freezes them at an inopportune spot. Whenever a TV crew wants to do some blood 'n' gore shots they set up a camera here, and the squids come out in force, and oblige the cameramen by tearing up a lot of expensive bodywork.

29 Miles STOP sign—GO STRAIGHT across Kanan Road/N9.

30 Miles ANGLE RIGHT, staying on Mulholland, as Encinal Canyon Road drops off to the left; Encinal is a good ride, and will take you back to the coast in a most curvaceous manner.

32 Miles STOP sign—TURN LEFT onto Decker Road/CA 23, which also serves as Mulholland.

34 Miles STOP sign (three-way)—TURN RIGHT on Mulholland, as Decker goes straight.

34+ Miles A barely noticeable road, Yerba Buena, goes off to the right, being a rather rough stretch of pavement that will take you down to the coast in 11 miles, over **Triunfo Pass,** at 2,777 feet it is the highest paved road in the Santa Monica Mountains.

Mulholland itself is dropping fast down through Arroyo Sequit; those huge dishes off to the right belong to AT&T. Do not get cocky as the road nears the sea, as there are a couple of turns which regularly catch a silly rider, possibly causing grievous damage to mind, bike, and spirit.

41 Miles STOP sign—TURN LEFT; you are at CA 1 at **Leo Carrillo State Beach.** Be quite aware as you breeze along, mountains to your left, ocean to your right, that it took a lot of work to build this road along the shore. It was begun in 1921, finished in 1929, and still manages to get itself closed down by mudslides if there is a very heavy rain.

If you are looking for properly cooked fresh fish, take a right at that STOP sign, heading up the coast, and in a mile you will come to **Neptune's Net,** a very rustic surfing and motorcycling hangout that serves up excellent seafood and has superb views of surfing and wind-surfing action across the road. Opens around 10:30 a.m., closes early evening (310-457-3095).

44 Miles Going east on PCH, off to the left is Decker Road/CA 23.

45 Miles To the left is Encinal Canyon Road, a very fine way to get back to Mulholland.

48 Miles **Zuma Beach** off to your right, where, for a fee, you can park

Neptune's Net, right along California's Coast Highway near Malibu, is a motorcycle hang-out and fish 'n' chips provider.

your bike and eat beach food and stare at out-of-shape humans in skimpy bathing suits. Have you ever stopped to consider how absurd the term "suit" is when applied to what we wear when going for a swim?

50 Miles At a TRAFFIC LIGHT, Kanan-Dume Road/N9 goes off to the left, while CA 1 becomes a four-laner.

53 Miles **Latigo Canyon** up to the left, another marvelous way to return to Mulholland.

56+ Miles Past the well-manicured campus of **Pepperdine University**, past Malibu Canyon Road/N1, you drop down a long hill and at the bottom is a TRAFFIC LIGHT. To the right is the **Malibu of Movie Legend.** The city actually stretches for more than 25 miles along the coast, but here, right off Webb Way, is Malibu Road, which leads to the **Malibu Colony.** If you go left, and then a quick right, you will come to the Cross Creek Center, with a large food court in the middle, where many Rock Store types migrate to later in the day.

Malibu Colony

In 1927 some movie types wanted to get away from the hustle and bustle of Hollywood, and the newly opened road gave them access to this remote stretch of beach. A small colony grew, with severe gate-guards to keep hoi polloi away. Malibu Colony has grown to cover over a mile of coastline, and though anybody can use the low-tide beach, it will take some walking, either from **Malibu Lagoon State Beach** to the east, or **Amarillo Beach** to the west. It is much better to know some-body famous (or merely rich) who lives there and go in through the gate. Then watch the sun set from some of the most expensive real es-tate on earth.   ▪

57 Miles Cross over **Malibu Creek** and you are in the main part of the Malibu business district, with the **Malibu Inn** (310-456-6060) serving up very good food all day long, and the Malibu Pier a good place to walk off the lunch. The aforementioned Malibu Beach Inn is not far from the pier, if you are so taken with the scene that you wish to spend the night.

Just west of the Rock Store, at a lookout above a sweeping 180-degree turn, blood-sport enthusiasts gather to watch the squids scrape metal, plastic—and sometimes leather.

Headed for the Rock Store, a couple of scratchers are coming up Latigo Canyon, the Harley hot on the heels of the BMW.

60 Miles **Las Flores Canyon** off to the left, leading up to Mulholland, through a maze of other roads; don't worry about getting lost, as eventually you will be back at either Mulholland or CA 1.

63 Miles Tuna Canyon comes down to meet CA 1—in recent years it was made one-way down to the sea, rumor having it that local residents objected to snarling bikes going up the hill.

64 Miles Arrive back at **Topanga Beach.**

Trip 2 Crest Highway & Newcombs Ranch

Distance *123 miles*

Highlights *This loop can be ridden slowly by the gentlemanly touring type with trailer in tow, but it is best enjoyed by the serious sporting rider, as it is a superb, and occasionally tricky, loop that starts down in the valley, goes up to nearly 8,000 feet, swings back on the south side of the Mojave Desert, then back via low canyons through the mountains.*

Starting point is where the northern segment of CA 2 and I-210 meet in La Canada Flintridge, just north of Pasadena; the exit sign reads CREST HIGHWAY. *You are about 1,300 feet above sea level here, and the Santa Monica beaches are a mere 25 miles away. Technically CA 2 starts in Santa Monica, but unless you really love crawling along with urban traffic through many traffic lights, you will freeway over to La Canada Flintridge.*

When there is heavy winter rains, the Big Tujunga River can tear up a thin strip of asphalt in a hurry.

Ground zero for this trip is where CA 2 starts north from Foothill Boulevard, which parallels I-210 on the south side. Right there on Foothill is the Hill Street Cafe, open from 6 a.m. to 11 p.m daily, a meeting place for riders who want to fortify themselves with caffeine before heading up the mountain.

0 Miles Intersection of Foothill Blvd. and Angeles Crest Highway, with a 76 station on your left, Shell on your right; next gas, 60 miles. If you wish, and many a sport-rider does, you can do those 60 miles in less than an hour, which will cause adrenaline to course through your veins like the oil passing through the pump in your engine.

First-timers, be wary. There are some deceptive curves on this road, and an error in judgement just might have you running off a mountainside with nothing to stop you for the next 2,000 feet.

Crossing over I-210, heading up the hill, the road is four-lanes for two miles, running through suburbia, past the country club, and then all signs of dwellings stop, the road narrows to two lanes, and you are in the **Angeles National Forest,** climbing up through the **San Gabriel Mountains,** passing a ranger station, Slide Canyon, Dark Canyon, twisting higher and higher. This is a serious road, and all the black tar stripes that CalTrans puts in the cracks (or snakes, as these are unaffectionately called), can put your lean angle on alert.

9 Miles GO STRAIGHT at the Clear Creek intersection, staying on CA 2. N3, a/k/a the **Angeles Forest Highway,** goes off to the left; you will be on the northen end of that road in about 80 miles.

14 Miles GO STRAIGHT at the Mt. Wilson intersection, or **Red Box Gap** as it is officially called. If you want a really, really twisty nine-mile (up and back) sidetrip excursion, do go up to **Mt. Wilson Skyline Park** and the observatory. The observatory tends to be open only on the weekends, but the ride up, and the view from the top, amidst a huge antenna field, are stupendous. I might add that skate-boarders like this little stretch, and try to outfox the rangers and come slithering down at outrageous speeds—and no brakes.

18 Miles GO STRAIGHT on CA 2 as Upper Big Tujunga Canyon Road goes down to the left. If you have very limited time, or are suffering from vertigo, take Upper Big Tujunga and in nine miles you loop back down to the Angeles Forest Highway.

20 Miles You are already at 5,000 feet, and the views of the Los Angeles valley are receding as you enter the middle of the mountain range, going past **Charlton Flats,** and still climbing into the forest. Much of the road is open, some of it is wooded, and the transfer from bright sun to shade can be a trifle unnerving.

26 Miles Past the turn-off to the **Chilao,** in the woods, **NEWCOMBS RANCH** appears on your left.

Newcombs Ranch

On a sunny weekend upward of a hundred bikes will be parked out front, riders tire-kicking or inside eating, while others go screaming by on the road. The restaurant is open every day from eight o'clock on (626-440-1001, or newcombsranch@aol.com if you wish to check).

As I said before, this is a serious road, and riders tend to take themselves quite seriously, with all the go-fast stuff that can be bolted on a bike. And they dress accordingly, too, with expensive and colorful leathers. And then feel a bit humiliated as some old codger on an aged 750 Nighthawk stays right with them as they continue up the mountain at great rates of speed. Experience is the real key here.

I remember well the morning years ago, when video was relatively new, and a small group of us went up the mountain with Jim Wolcott having a camera mounted on his rear seat, pointing backward. We chased him up the mountain, and then back down to Newcombs, where Jim plugged the camera into the TV, and we all sat and watched what we had just done while eating breakfast, and everybody came in from outside to watch, as well. Here we were, watching what we had all just done, and would then go out and do it all again—motorcyclists are a strange breed, as any golf addict will attest. ■

31 Miles   You are coming up to the **Waterman Ski Area** and **Cloudburst Summit** (7,018)—and you are barely an hour from the beach. This is one reason why SoCal is as close to being a motorcyclist's paradise as you can reasonably hope to find. Go past the **Krakta Ridge Ski Area,** and the road is high, open, and can be exceedingly fast. Here you are paralleling the Pacific Crest Trail for a few miles, if you would care to park the bike and take a hike.

37 Miles   You see a short, straight tunnel ahead of you, which turns out to be two short, straight tunnels, but there is a slight curve at the far end, and if you have just whacked it up to 120 mph, you can be in for a surprise. Be cautious.

Do stop at the **Jarvi Overlook** just beyond the tunnels, to admire the view and to contemplate your mortality. Mr. Jarvi was a U.S. Forest Service manager who did a superb job in keeping this place just as motorcyclists love it to be.

Now you are getting huge views of the **Mojave Desert** off to the left. Up and over **Dawson Saddle** (7,901 feet, the high point on the road), and off to the right you can see **Mt. Baldy** (a/k/a Mt. San Antonio), over 10,000 above sea level. Then it is up to **Blue Ridge Summit** (7,386 feet) followed by a steady descent taking you down to a wide spot in the road called **Big Pines**.

39 Miles   After the first big winter storm Caltrans generally closes the road between here and Big Pines.

56 Miles   TURN SHARP LEFT onto N4, marked PALMDALE, JACKSON LAKE on the sign. Not much in **Big Pines,** but there is a stone tower and a ranger station, and if you have passed them, you missed your N4 turn.

Back to Big Pines: ANGLE RIGHT, heading northwest, downhill, on N4, a/k/a **Big Pines Highway,** with that aforementioned sign reading PALMDALE, JACKSON LAKE. Nice road, as it curves down through the foothills, past Jackson Lake.

62 Miles   GO STRAIGHT on Big Pines Highway, while N4 cuts sharp right. At the corner is **Mile High Cafe** (661-261-3154), open every day except Wednesday, serving breakfast from eight o'clock Friday through Sunday, 11 a.m. the rest of the time.

As you whizz along Shoemaker Canyon, Pinyon Ridge is to your left, while the Mojave Desert is becoming more apparent on your right.

67 Miles   STAY STRAIGHT as Big Pines Highway becomes Valyermo Road, and Big Rock Creek Road goes off to the left.

67+ Miles   STAY LEFT on Valyermo Road, going over a bridge, while Bobs Gap Road goes off to the right.

71 Miles   TURN LEFT at the sign reading LITTLE ROCK DAM 11, onto Pallet Creek Road—and a hundred yards along TURN RIGHT onto Fort

Wrightwood

Four miles beyond Big Pines on CA 2, past the **Mountain High Ski Area,** is the mountain community (6,000 feet) of the Wright brothers' wood, a family who ranched up here about a hundred years ago. Arco and Shell both sell gas.

A lot of motorcyclists come here to eat, though the number of eateries is limited. **The Grizzly Cafe** (760-249-6733), right on CA 2, serves a great breakfast every day of the week. **Cinnamon's Bakery,** on CA 2, is open at 5 a.m. every day, but that is a bit early, even in June, for a dedicated motorcyclist to have arrived. On Park Street, the main street in town, which runs at right angles to CA 2, is the **Evergreen Restaurant & Racoon Saloon** (760-249-4277). If you want to enquire about taking motorcycle trips to Australia or Zimbabwe, stop in at **Tri-Community Travel** on CA 2, opposite Park Street, which is the official U.S. representative for **Edelweiss Tours** (800-582-2263); the owner, Mary Etta Horne, is both a motorcyclist and a skier, and has the best of both worlds up here.

If you are so taken with the place that you wish to stay, the **Mountain View Motel** on CA 2 offers an assortment of rooms, some with jacuzzis (760-249-3553). ■

Tejon Road. This good asphalt will whistle you along through the foothills at a great rate.

78 Miles TURN LEFT where the sign reads ANGELES FOREST HWY 10, LITTLE ROCK DAM.

81 Miles STOP sign at a four-way intersection out in the middle of nowhere, and the other traffic, running between **Pearland** and **Little Rock Reservoir** does *not* stop. CONTINUE STRAIGHT, and you are on Mt. Emma Road, circling the northwesterly portion of **Mt. Emma Ridge.**

88 Miles STOP sign—TURN LEFT onto Angeles Forest Highway (N3), with the sign saying HWY 2 21. Pointing to the right the sign reads PALMDALE 10.

90 Miles To the right goes Aliso Canyon Road, which runs into **Soledad Canyon,** and another way out of these mountains.

93 Miles You are up on **Mill Creek Summit** (4,910 feet) with a small intersection, the right turn going to **Mt. Gleason,** the left back up to **Chilao** on a dirt road.

99 Miles To your left is the well-marked turn to Upper Tujunga Canyon Road, which can take you back to CA 2 in nine miles.

100 Miles **Hidden Springs Cafe** is on your right, open from roughly 10 a.m. until roughly dark, with Elva Lewis's family running the operation; Otis is often at the griddle, and he turns out a fine hamburger.

104 Miles TURN RIGHT onto Big Tujunga Canyon Road, leading to Sunland. You could go straight and hit CA 2 in four miles, and backtrack to La Canada Flintridge, but this is more fun.

The Big Tujunga Canyon Road makes a steep descent into Big Tujunga Canyon, past the Big Tujunga Dam, built in 1931, over several old concrete bridges, then flattens out as it runs alongside the river; it is generally dry, but when winter rains come the river can fill up in a hurry and the road can be closed.

115 Miles Enter **Sunland** from the north, go through several STOP signs, always following your nose.

116 Miles TRAFFIC LIGHT—TURN LEFT at intersection with Foothill Boulevard, and you go seven miles east on Foothill. Or pick up I-210, if that is in your plans.

123 Miles Back at the **Hill St. Cafe** and the start to the Angeles Crest Highway.

That is Elva Lewis, proprietor of the Hidden Springs Cafe, about to change all those CLOSED *signs to say* OPEN.

Trip 3 Ortega Highway & Lookout Roadhouse

Distance *44 miles (if you just go up to the Lookout and come back)*
Highlights *This is not really a loop, as 90 percent or more of the riders who go up the Ortega Highway come back the same way. CA 74 is a good road and has superb views—on a clear day. And the destination, The Lookout Roadhouse, always has a bunch of motorcyclists eating breakfast, drinking coffee, kicking tires, and exaggerating the truth.*

When I first went up it in May of 1980, I thought this was one outlandishly great ride, and it began just ten miles from where I was living in Laguna Beach. Life couldn't get much better. Then, long after I had moved from Laguna to Atascadero the county made the highway a "double fine zone." So if you adhere to the speed limits, you have no worries. This is the Orange County Racer Road, which, unfortunately, is becoming a tad too civilized for a lot of riders.

To get there, come south down I-5 past El Toro and Mission Viejo to San Juan Capistrano.

Ground zero for this trip is at the ORTEGA HWY/CA 74 *exit.*

That's the new church in San Juan Capistrano, in a lot better condition than the old mission.

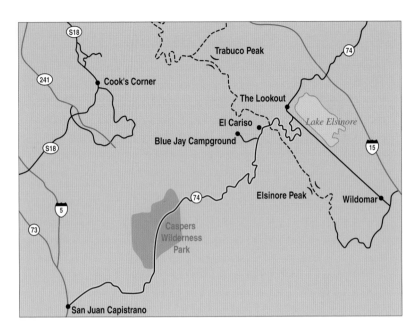

0 Miles TURN LEFT at TRAFFIC LIGHT after exiting I-5 at ORTEGA HIGHWAY/CA 74 exit, crossing over I-5, heading east. Several gas stations are there to do your bidding.

1 Mile If you are historically minded, you will pass the **Parra Adobe & Harrison House** site on your right, now in the middle of San Juan suburbs; these are two of the oldest buildings in the county, though there is nothing of great visual note to recommend them unless you are a student of 19th Century California architecture.

3 Miles You are beyond the San Juan city limits, crossing over **San Juan Creek,** passing through a tid-bit of the fast-vanishing crop-land in Orange County, and through the TRAFFIC LIGHT where the Antonio Parkway goes off to your left, La Pata Avenue to the right. Now the road becomes pleasantly curvy, sliding over low hills and down into dales, paralleling the San Juan Creek off to your left for a ways.

8 Miles The entrance to **Caspers Wilderness Park** (949-923-2210) is to your left. This is a county park, some 8,000 acres, and can be genuinely wild; every few years somebody gets mauled by a mountain lion here—which makes it all the more exciting. The fact that this wilderness is just a few minutes from gross over-population makes it even more astonishing. For anybody who wonders who the namesake was, Mr. Caspers was an Orange County politician in the 1970s who is responsible for the park's existence; we must commend a man with such foresight.

San Juan Capistrano

If you wish to soak up a bit of California history, TURN RIGHT at that TRAFFIC LIGHT and you will be in front of the old **Mission San Juan Capistrano** after 300 yards. Construction on this mission began in 1776 and was completed some 15 years later. A few years went by and the padres decided that an even bigger church was needed to glorify the Almighty, and nine years were spent building a more noble edifice— which an earthquake knocked down in 1812; God does work in wondrous and mysterious ways.

A minor historical note is that after the Mexican revolution of 1821, in which the Catholic church sided with the Spanish losers, the mission and its property was secularized by the new government. It was President Lincoln who gave it back to the church in 1865.

The town is a tourist trap, but a nice one. **Sarducci's Cafe,** at Capistrano's train depot on the west side of the mission, serves good food all day (949-493-9593). If you want a place to stay down in these parts, you can do worse than the **Best Western Capistrano Inn,** just on the east side of I-5, and walkable to all the sights and sites (27174 Ortega Highway, 800-441-9438, 949-493-5661). From here you can get an early start on the Ortega.   ■

10 Miles You have a long straightaway, out in the middle of absolutely nowhere, and half way along is a traffic light. That is the entrance to the **Nichols Institute,** which is some sort of bio-medical research outfit, and how the place got permission to build out here in the middle of the wilderness beats me. I like to think the place does top-secret work for the goverment, handling potentially extremely dangerous biological and extraterrestrial stuff, and thus its remoteness. Though I doubt it.

12 Miles The road winds along past the **San Juan Hot Springs,** which was a hedonistic hangout until the place burned down a few years back. Over a little bridge, and a small road on the left leads to a church-sponsored camp called the **Lazy W Ranch.** Then it is by the forest-service fire station and you are now in the **Cleveland National Forest,** where the good part of the Ortega starts.

For the next 12 miles you are climbing up the **Santa Ana Mountains,** which divide the super-heated inner valleys from the cool coast. When you hear someone saying that "the Santa Anas are blowing," it means a hot wind is coming from the east, and this is the time of year (usually the fall) that keeps the firefighters well employed.

The road runs along the south side of **San Juan Canyon**, with a lot of curves and bends that should be ridden with caution. An hour after dawn on a weekend morning, the brightly leathered boys and girls will be dashing up and down on their -R bikes. You cross into **Riverside County**, pass a picnic area and a campground, come around a 180 sweeper, and up a hill to . . .

18 Miles . . . the **Ortega General Store & Old Candy Shop**, on your right, with a small commercial campground. Not much of a motorcycling hangout.

Then dash down the hill a bit, crossing **Decker Canyon**, and a superbly fast "S" runs you up high; this road was reconstructed in 1990, and whoever engineered the place had to have had a racetrack in mind. The road straightens a bit as it goes past the turn to **Los Pinos Camp** (for wayward youth) and the **Blue Jay Campground;** After the Blue Jay you can take a left onto a long, rough dirt road that goes past **Trabuco Peak** (4,604 feet), and eventually drops down to **Silverado Canyon**, or stay on the rough pavement as it curves back to the Ortega.

21 Miles Into **El Cariso**, a small mountain community with **El Cariso General Store** on the right side, the **Hell's Kitchen** is on the left, which caters mostly to the cruiser crowd, open early on the weekends, a bit later during the week (951-609-3390, www.hellskitchen-ca.com).

Past the forest-service fire station, and an intersection, with pavement leading off to the left and right. The left road connects with Blue Jay and the Trabuco Peak, while to the right the road runs past some upscale housing, then turns to dirt as it goes by **Elsinore Peak** and drops down to **Wildomar.**

21+ Miles Come over the crest of the highway, which is about 2,600 feet above the Pacific that lies just 21 condor-flying miles away, swing down a couple of bends, curve right—and the whole of **Lake Elsinore** and the surrounding valley are 1,500 feet below.

22 Miles The **Lookout Roadhouse** (951-678-9010) is on your left; if you want to see this view before you get there turn on your computer and punch in www.LookoutRoadhouse.com. And on a weekend many, many motorcycles are parked in the lot. The knee-grinders are here from dawn to nine or ten, followed by the more laid-back types throughout the rest of the day. The Lookout has been in business since 1945, and was bought by **Barbara Sheahan** in 1968; this delightful woman keeps the place open from eight in the morning to seven in the evening seven days a week, and serves up a rib-coating breakfast.

That's Tim Denardo, manager of the Lookout Roadhouse, showing me how tall he is.

Lots of riders come here just to fraternize, compare notes on the latest sticky tires, and discuss the latest ups or downs of H-D stock.

28 Miles   You have just looped down and down the mountain to the STOP sign at the intersection with Grand Avenue. Taking a left keeps you on CA 74, which, as I said at the beginning, will run you over the next set of mountains and down to **Palm Springs;** A right will run you south down to Mount Palomar, or a windy trip through the **Walker Basin** via De Luz to Fallbrook. Or you can return from whence you came; as I always maintain, no road is ridden properly until it is ridden in both directions.

Connector

The Ortega does provide a great connection to other motorcycling venues, like the **San Jacinto Mountains** above Palm Springs (just follow CA 74), or **Mount Palomar** down in San Diego County (see Chapter 15).   ∎

Cooks Corner

On any weekend short of a rainy one, a hundred or more bikes will be pulled up in front of this Orange County hang-out, mostly Harleys, but everything else is there as well.

Cooks, a bar and a grill, has been around in roughly the same state of disrepair since 1947, and used to be a reasonably rural hangout when I began going there in 1980. Locals who lived in the hills and bikers were the mainstay of the business. A number of patch-holders (1-percenters) used to show up, but the then-bartender, **Big Mac,** was large enough to maintain the peace. The clientele has changed somewhat as suburbia surrounds the place, but even though the sawdust on the floor is now imported, the place has its charm. The place opens at seven o'clock for the breakfast crowd, and continues well on into the night, 365 days a year. Beer and booze are the money-makers, the food is just a convenience so serious drinkers don't have to go home.

Easiest way to get there is to be on I-5, and as it enters El Toro, take the El Toro Road exit and head east on what is also referred to as Orange County S18. It is a large suburb you are going through, becoming lightly wooded as it runs alongside Aliso Creek. After nine miles you are unmistakably at Cooks, with Live Oak Canyon Road going off to the right.

After your glass of root beer, you can go back the way you came or follow S18 up Santiago Canyon, past lots of new housing developments, until it connects with a CA 55 in the city of Orange.   ■

On a pleasant Sunday, several hundred motorcycles will show up at Cook's Corner, in eastern Orange County.

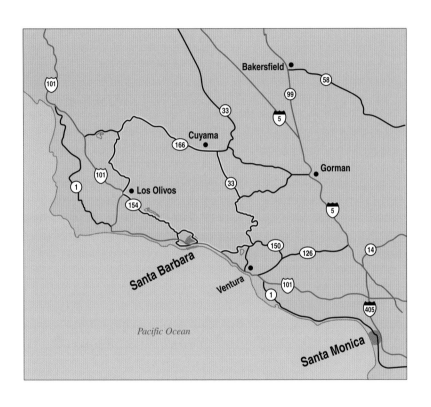

Santa Barbara County

Headquarters *Santa Barbara*
Chamber of Commerce/Visitor Center *805-965-3021 or 805-568-1811*
Best Time to Visit *All year*
Getting There *US 101 is not only the road of choice—it is virtually the only road. It is a freeway, so you have to choose your exit. If you are coming from Los Angeles and want a peaceful seaside approach, take the CABRILLO BLVD exit, and you will ride in along the beachfront. And you pass right by the Visitor Center, at the corner of Garden Street, should you want to collect an armful of literature and maps. If you want Downtown, take the GARDEN ST exit and stay on the inland side of US 101.*
Ground Zero *This will be where State Street butts into Cabrillo Boulevard at Stearns Wharf. If you are coming north (west, really) on US 101, you can take the above-mentioned Cabrillo Blvd. exit, or from either direction take the GARDEN ST exit and head for the shore, just a quarter-mile away. That will put you on Cabrillo, turn right, and a block down is State.*

This place is within easy access from the City of Lost Angels, just a hundred miles away, but it has an entirely different atmosphere. Civilization, such that it is, is wedged in along a narrow coastal strip, and everything else in the county is close to the 21st Century definition of wilderness (no houses and a lot of trees), thanks to the presence of the **Los Padres National Forest.** And it does provide two good loops, one being big, the other small.

Very nice city, the city of **Saint Barbara.** Charming. Almost too charming, especially since the City Fathers chased most of the homeless people out of the place; rumor has it the local authorities gave them all bus tickets to Bakersfield.

The town of Saint Barbara occupies a narrow east/west strip of land backed by the **Santa Ynez Mountains,** fronted by the **Pacific Ocean,** and a lot of expensive people live here, most of them discreetly tucked into the hills above the city. They know that the tourists throng to the coast, and prefer to keep their distance.

It takes a bit of figuring to get geographically organized in this town. The main street is **State Street,** which runs from Stearns Wharf, under US 101, for about four miles all the way west to meet up with US 101 again. This was the old 101, and the west end has a lot of the older (inexpensive) motels.

Santa Barbara became an active mission in 1786, but the building you see today was completed in 1820, after the original was destroyed in an earthquake.

About ten blocks of State right downtown have been turned into a strolling paradise, with sidewalk cafes, restaurants, bookstores, all the ways to spend money. One lane of traffic still moves along in each direction, but there is no parking in those blocks; lots of spaces and garages on the side streets. On Tuesday afternoon two blocks are closed off for a farmers' market. Central Santa Barbara has been built on a grid pattern, with a lot of one-way streets, so circling a block or two will usually get you to where you want to go.

The city has several key tourist destinations, the primary one being **Stearns Wharf** (where, by the way, you can ride out and park your motorcycle *for free*—cars pay), the **Mission Santa Barbara**, founded in 1776, and the **Presidio**, the old Spanish military headquarters.

Where you stay is up to you and your budget. The **first Motel 6 in the country** is a two-minute walk from **East Beach,** at the east end of Cabrillo Blvd., and when it opened in 1962 rooms cost $6; now they go from a low of $62 to a high of $140, depending on the season. You can see that the company down-sized the rooms after building this one, which has 51 rooms (443 Corona del Mar, 805-564-1392, 800-466-8356); note, this is one of five M-6s in the area, so make sure you get the Santa Barbara Beach M-6. Smack dab in front of the Motel 6 is the **Radisson Hotel Santa Barbara,** at

901 East Cabrillo Blvd., which is a bit more pricey and has more than three times as many rooms (805-966-2285). If you want to stay right by Stearns Wharf, the **Harbor View Inn** has 96 rooms, ranging from "non-view" chambers for $220 to "luxury ocean view" suites for $1,000 (805-963-0780).

For a slightly different, and more elegant approach, try the 60-room **Montecito Inn,** built in 1928, some 35 years before the US 101 freeway separated it from the sea. Legend has it that **Charlie Chaplin** was involved in its construction, so his presence is made known in the establishment (1295 Coast Village Rd., 805-969-7854, 800-843-2017).

Sustenance. You will have to stroll out on Stearn's Wharf, which has several restaurants and cafes, and, like all good tourists, you will have a meal in which where you eat is more important than what you eat. Perfectly adequate, but uninspired; I have been told that at one well-advertised restaurant the clam chowder comes right out of a can. More interesting, and generally less expensive food can be found among the shops at the marina, less than a mile west of the wharf.

For more rewarding gastronomical experiences, I would recommend **Esau's Coffee Shop** at 403 State (805-964-4416), near the intersection with Gutierrez Ave.; the breakfast is excellent. Or go up State for 13 blocks to 1701, which has the nicest **IHOP** I have ever eaten at, with patio dining. For lunch I would go to the **Fresco Cafe** (805-967-6037) at the west end of State Street, in the Five Points Plaza at the intersection with La Cumbre Road; the gorganzola and walnut salad is delightful, as is the double-chocolate mousse pie. Seaside ambience can be had at the **Breakwater Restaurant** down at the harbor, with the biggest anchor I have ever seen decorating the front lawn (805-965-1557). For dinner, the **Montecito Cafe** at the Montecito Inn does itself proud, or **Chad's,** at 625 Chapala (parallel to State).

Trip 4 Big Loop

Distance *207 miles*

Highlights *This loop covers some territory, going east from Santa Barbara to Ojai, north over Pine Mountain Summit to Cuyama, west on CA 166 along the Cuyama River, south on Tepusquet and Foxen Canyon roads, and then east on CA 154 over San Marcos Pass.*

0 Miles Head east on CA 225/Cabrillo Blvd., going past the **Tourist Information Office** at the corner of Garden Street.

2+ Miles TURN RIGHT to access US 101 SOUTH/LOS ANGELES, though technically this is an easterly direction, passing **Montecito, Summerland,** the **Santa Barbara Polo Club,** and into **Carpinteria.**

14 Miles EXIT RIGHT at CA 150/OJAI sign, and TURN LEFT, heading for Ojai. After a little over a mile you pass the east end of CA 192, which was Foothill Road in Santa Barbara, Casitas Pass Road in Carpinteria.

Along CA 54, Lake Cachuma, a mighty reservoir fed by the Santa Ynez River, caters to boaters.

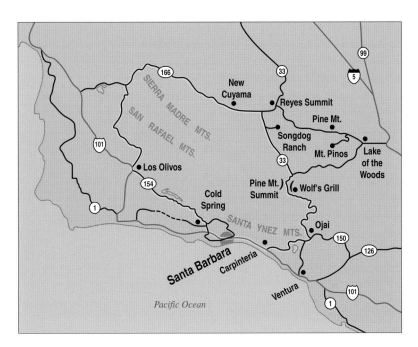

21 Miles Cross over **East Casitas Pass** at 1,143 feet and come down by **Lake Casitas.** This stretch is all rather uncluttered, and has a nice curvy highway, quite suitable for a "recreation area," although the police might disagree as to just what the definition of recreation is. Drop out of the hills and into **Ojai Valley.** Off to the north you can see the **Santa Ynez** and **Topatopa Mountains,** and the discerning eye can spot the opening created by the **Ventura River.**

29 Miles TRAFFIC LIGHT—TURN LEFT (on green light) onto CA 33/ 150.

31 Miles TRAFFIC LIGHT—TURN LEFT, following CA 33, letting CA 150 run into Ojai. **Ojai** itself is a charmingly overpriced town, with a lovely main street and delightful places to spend money.

31+ Miles A 76 station on your left is the last gas for 65 miles.

32 Miles STOP sign, and CONTINUE STRAIGHT on CA 33, also known as the Maricopa Highway.

32+ Miles The **Deer Lodge** (805-646-4256) is on your left, established in 1932 and proclaiming in its ads: "Feeding Hungry Bikers for 70 Years"; the place puts on a pig roast every weekend. Leaving The Deer Lodge the road runs through orchards, soon coming alongside the Ventura River (such that it is) and then following Matalija Creek through **Wheeler Gorge,** and the road gets seriously twisty.

39 Miles   A blind tunnel (i.e. it has a curve in it so you don't see through it to the end), and then a quarter-mile beyond that two short straight tunnels, *followed by a slight left curve and often water on the road, which can turn to ice when really cold.* You have been officially cautioned.

The road ascends for several delicious curves, then drops back down into the valley of **Sespe Creek,** going through **Sespe Gorge** (very nice!) and follows the creek, going upriver, for a good ten miles, up into a broadening valley. A lot of weekend motorcyclists are out here, as this is primo country.

59 Miles   A small white and red house on your right, looking rather decrepit, with WOLF'S GRILL on the sign. Whether it reopens (summer 2006) is anybody's guess.

63 Miles   You are at **Pine Mountain Summit** at 5,084 feet, not bad considering you are a mere 20 miles from the ocean. And you start to wiggle downhill, all the way to the **Ozena Forest Service Station.** Watch out on the downhill, as some of the corners can be sandy.

69 Miles   STAY STRAIGHT on CA 33, as Lockwood Valley Road goes off to the right. This is a fast piece of asphalt, curving along the east bank of the **Cuyama River.**

Around Mt. Pinos

If you take that right turn at Mile 69, this will add an additional 44 miles to the route, but is well worth your while. You begin by zipping up along a flat valley; after about 3.5 miles a sign pointing to the right indicates Camp Scheideck, an old-fashioned (no telephone) resort a mile off the road with a good cafe. Then the road goes over the 5,516-foot summit, into **Lockwood Valley,** and on to the STOP sign at **Lake of the Woods** (21 miles). TURN LEFT and go five miles up Cuddy Valley Road, and do not miss the right turn to **Pine Mountain** (nothing to do with the previous Pine Mountain Summit)—otherwise you will dead-end up on top of Mt. Pinos. Head into the summering community of Pine Mountain on Potrero Road, which turns into Cerro Noroeste Road, and it is a stunning run along the edge of the **San Joaquin Valley** to the intersection with CA 33/166 at **Point Reyes Summit** 2,968. At the STOP sign TURN LEFT on 33/166, and in 4.6 miles you are at the intersection with CA 33, on the main loop.   ■

71 Miles   In the less-than-wide spot in the road is the **Halfway House Station,** better known for beer than burgers, although if whoever is behind the bar is willing, he might put a pattie on the griddle.

81 Miles   Another wide-ish spot in the road, with **The Place Restaurant** on your left.

86 Miles   Slow, look carefully, there on the right is Ballinger Canyon Road and a sign reading SONGDOG RANCH.

90 Miles   STOP sign, TURN LEFT onto CA 166.

Songdog Ranch

A mile up the road is the palatial country estate of Jim Reveley, at 680 Ballinger Canyon Road (nice big number, although there are only two houses in the canyon). JR is best known for the **Rev-Pak** motorcycle luggage he has been making for the last quarter-century, though he actually lives a few miles away, while his daughter Jenny and husband Steve Stith keep the ranch going. They love company, so just drop in if you're passing by (661-766-2454).   ■

Out at Songdog Ranch, a motorcycle-oriented campground, Jim Reveley will make you feel right at home . . . and he'd be happy to sell you some of his Rev-Pak motorcycle luggage, as well.

On Foxen Canyon Road you will find 10 wineries—but you should forego sampling all their wares if you are riding.

95 Miles Cross over the Cuyama River and enter **Cuyama** (Pop. 160), with the Old Cuyama Store as the focal point. You are now in the Cuyama Valley proper, and will follow it for a good many miles.

99 Miles You are in **New Cuyama**, with about ten times the population of Cuyama. There is even the **Buckhorn Motel,** with 22 rooms (661-766-2591), the **Buckhorn Saloon,** and the **Buckhorn Restaurant,** specializing in buffalo burgers, and a hundred yards away is a Mobil station—the first gas since Ojai.

Leave town, and it is a delicious ride along the Cuyama River for the next 39 miles—except that this very rural section of two-lane highway has had a lot of accidents (mostly stupid drivers running off the road) in recent past, and the CHP sees fit to patrol it quite heavily. With radar. The road slips and slides and curves along the river, and is a beaut. Hardly a house to be seen until you get to the **Pine Canyon Forest Station,** and then be prepared to slow down.

138 Miles TURN LEFT onto Tepusquet Road, which winds into **Buckhorn Canyon.** The road was repaved in 2005 and is a pleasure to ride.

140 Miles Cross over **Buckhorn Creek** and begin a steep climb.

141 Miles You are at the summit, and begin a long descent along the **Tepusquet Creek.**

153 Miles STAY LEFT (STRAIGHT) at the Y, right after the **Byron Vineyard,** unless there is a sign reading ROAD CLOSED. In which case you bear right.

153+ Miles Since there is not much traffic along this road, there has never been a bridge over the **Sisquoc River;** in the dry season the crossing is made over two hundred feet of gravel. However, after the first winter storm the gravel gets washed out and the road is closed until spring. Recently, local wine-tasting rooms have objected to the decreased traffic when the road is closed, and promises have been made to build a bridge in 2007—don't hold your breath.

Detour

This forces the rider to go back to the Y and go right along Santa Maria Mesa Road to the STOP sign, left on Foxen Canyon Road, and follow that as it ends up on the far side of the Sisquoc River, meeting up with the beginning/end of Tepusquet Road.

■

---

154 Miles STOP sign at end of Tepusquet Road, TURN LEFT on Foxen Canyon Road.

155 Miles The **Sisquoc Winery** and the church are right ahead, while Foxen Canyon Road swings to the right.

156 Miles The **Foxen Winery,** with tasting room, made somewhat famous in the movie, *Sideways.* Old man Foxen was an English fellow who settled here in the 1840s, married a Mexican woman, and then decided to throw in with the Americans when they came marching through in 1846.

165 Miles You are on top of **Zaca Mesa,** with wineries all around; this is serious grape country.

168 Miles TURN LEFT, staying on Foxen Canyon Road, while Zaca Station Road continues straight.

172 Miles STOP sign, TURN LEFT onto CA 154.

173 Miles The town of **Los Olivos** is off to your left, along with **Mattei's Tavern,** a good place to eat. If you take the GRAND AVE turn to your right, you will be in Los Olivos, and in the middle of that little village is what is claimed to be the first gas station in California, at least according to owner Bob Cole, a garage since 1901, pumping gas since 1912. The EPA forced him to shut down in January of 1999, due to old tanks, but he was looking

It's a hazy day, but from the East Camino Cielo road, Kurt Grife can look out over Santa Barbara Channel, almost 4,000 feet below.

for somebody to buy the place who would keep it as a gas station; no luck. Nearest gas is in Santa Ynez, about five miles south.

173+ Miles   The **Los Olivos Grocery** (805-688-5115) is on your right, a splendid place to stop and have a sandwich; there is a fine deli in the back, and great seating on the deck out front.

178 Miles   CA 276 goes off to the right.

185 Miles   The entrance to the 6600-acre Cachuma **Lake** Recreation

Solvang Vintage Motorcycle Museum

If you want to see some lovely old motorcycles—and newish as the collection includes a Britten—go due south from Los Olivos to Solvang, a pleasantly touristy place made to look like a mythical Danish town, and you will find the museum at 32 Alisal Road. It is open on weekends from 11 to 5, and by appointment (805-686-9522).   ∎

Area is on your left, with camping available. No swimming, just boats polluting the water with gas.

191 Miles On your left is Stagecoach Road, the old way over the pass. The much newer CA 154 is far less interesting, except for the **Cold Springs Bridge**, which was recently reinforced for protection against earthquakes— good luck when an 8.1 hits.

Stagecoach Road and Cold Springs Tavern
Take the turn to the left and follow Stagecoach crossing over Paradise Road, and then under the arching **Cold Springs Bridge**— way up above you. Then deep in the shadows of the trees lies **Cold Springs Tavern** (805-967-0066), a motorcycling mecca on the weekends, quiet the rest of the time. This is where the stage-coaches of yore would stop to rest the horses and liquor up the passengers so they wouldn't notice the bumps so much. After your sarsaparilla, continue on up the road, take your first left, and you are back on CA 154.   ■

195 Miles You are on **San Marcos Pass** (2,224 feet), and only seven linear miles from the sea. To the left goes East Camino Cielo (Trip #2), and in front of you is a superb view of the ocean, with the **Channel Islands** off in the distance, about 25 miles offshore. And a few oil rigs set up in the channel to remind you where that stuff in your gas tank comes from. On a clear day you can see the 70 miles to the Palos Verdes Hills in Los Angeles.

195+ Miles To the right is the start of West Camino Cielo, 20 miles of bliss, of which about half is unmaintained dirt; a d-p bike is recommended.

197 Miles A discreet intersection, with Painted Cave Road going off to the right, the left, the old San Marcos Pass Road down to the right; that latter is a twisty delight, and you have to wonder how the stagecoaches made it up. Or down. Slowly, I suppose.

CA 154 winds down the south face of the **Santa Ynez Mountains.**

201 Miles Cross over CA 192, a/k/a Foothill Road, which goes along the backside of Santa Barbara.

202 Miles TRAFFIC LIGHT—TURN LEFT after crossing over US 101, merging into 101 going south (east, really).

206 Miles Exit at GARDEN ST—RIGHT TURN, toward beach.

206+ Miles STOP sign, TURN RIGHT onto Cabrillo Blvd.

207 Miles Arrive back at Ground zero, at Stearns Wharf.

Trip 5 Mountain & Beach

Distance *41 miles*

Highlights *This is a very short, very, very tasty little circle, cruising along the crest of the Santa Ynez Mountains behind Santa Barbara, which is a pretty rough section of asphalt, and high, at 3,500 feet, and then plummeting down to town and back along the waterfront, past the beaches to Stearns Wharf.*

0 Miles Head west along Cabrillo Blvd.

0+ Miles STOP sign, GO STRAIGHT along Shoreline Drive, as CA 225 turns off to the right. This takes you past the harbor, where you can turn in and admire how yachtsmen spend lots of money.

The road wends along the bluffs for a bit, and I bet those houses on the sea-side of the 1600 block are really, really expensive.

3 Miles TRAFFIC LIGHT—TURN LEFT onto Cliff Drive/CA 225.

Accelerate, brake, turn—again and again and again—on the winding East Camino Cielo road in the Santa Ynez Mountains.

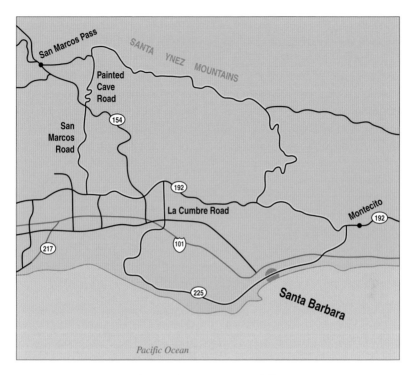

San Marcos Pass

SANTA YNEZ MOUNTAINS

Painted
Cave
Road

154

San
Marcos
Road

192

La Cumbre Road

Montecito

192

217

101

225

Santa Barbara

Pacific Ocean

4 Miles STOP sign, STAY STRAIGHT on Cliff Dr. as CA 225 turns to the right on Las Positas. Past the **Brown Pelican** restaurant (805-687-4550), Cliff turning into Roble de Marina Drive, and winding past **Hope Ranch** (where the working rich live) on Las Palmas Drive, past the **La Cumbre Golf & Country Club,** and finally over the top of US 101 and straight, the name changing from Las Palmas Drive to La Cumbre Road.

8 Miles TRAFFIC LIGHT—STAY STRAIGHT on La Cumbre. On the left corner is **Five Points Plaza** shopping center, with the aforementioned Fresco Cafe to calm your appetite.

9 Miles TRAFFIC LIGHT—TURN LEFT onto Foothill Road, which you follow as it passes beneath CA 154 and name-changes to Cathedral Oaks Road.

12 Miles TRAFFIC LIGHT—TURN RIGHT onto San Marcos Road, which seems to be going off into some suburbia. After less than a mile the road moves out of the tree-shaded houses and begins some serious climbing, with really tight 300-degree turns marked at 5 mph.

15+ Miles STOP sign at intersection with CA 154; look both directions carefully before crossing over and continuing along what is now Painted Cave Road.

19 Miles STOP sign—TURN RIGHT onto East Camino Cielo Road. Straight ahead may be a sign which reads: CAUTION STORM DAMAGE. East Camino Cielo Road has a lot of potholes, but virtually no traffic, and unbeatable views. For the next nine miles you go slowly, and stop a lot, as you run right along the ridge of the Santa Ynez Mountains. To the left you look down into a great, long valley of the **Santa Ynez River,** part of the **Los Padres National Forest** and the **Dick Smith Wilderness;** to the right it is down to the rooftops of Santa Barbara, the **Pacific Ocean,** and a bunch of oil rig platforms out in the channel. You will be close to 4,000 feet above the sea, just six miles away.

28 Miles STAY RIGHT at the fork in the road, heading for Santa Barbara. If you go left you will end up in **Big Caliente Hot Springs** down in the Santa Ynez River valley.

Now you drop quickly, into Rattlesnake Canyon, past a hang-gliding take-off, the road changing names, becoming Gibraltar Road.

34 Miles STOP sign—TURN LEFT onto El Cielito Road, another STOP, GO STRAIGHT across Mountain Drive.

34+ Miles STOP sign—TURN LEFT onto CA 192.

The aquarium out on Stearns Wharf is a focal point for Santa Barbara tourists.

Hang-gliding off the Camino Cielo behind Santa Barbara is popular—though the glidist sometimes wonders where he will end up.

36 Miles STAY STRAIGHT on CA 192 as CA 144 goes off to the right. CA 144, to my thinking, may be the shortest State Highway in all of California, running for just two miles down to US 101; why a few short city streets become a State Highway like that baffles me—except Santa Barbara must like it as the CA rating makes the state responsible for maintenance costs.

38 Miles TURN RIGHT onto Hot Springs Road, keeping right again on Hot Springs after half a mile, and now past the **Montecito Country Club.**

39 Miles Go under US 101 as Hot Springs turns into Cabrillo Boulevard, past the **Santa Barbara Cemetery** (prime real estate!) and puts you right along the shore by the **Santa Barbara Zoological Gardens.**

41 Miles Arrive back at Ground Zero, **Stearns Wharf.**

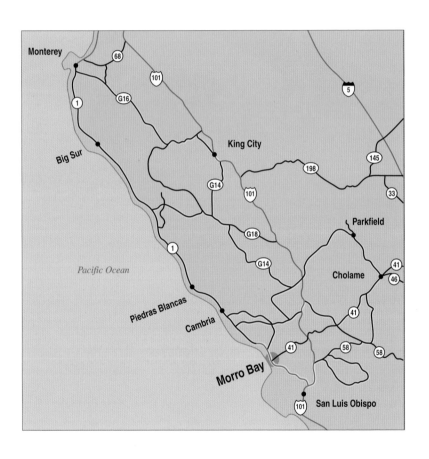

Big Sur & Central Coast

Headquarters *Cambria*

Chamber of Commerce *805-927-3624 This organization will provide you with long lists of motels and B&Bs in the area, and I promise that there are many of them, since this is the southern gateway to Big Sur and, more important for the tourist business, the Hearst Castle.*

Getting There *CA 1 is the way, either coming north from San Luis Obispo, or south from Monterey. Or take CA 46 going west from Paso Robles and meeting CA 1 just south of Cambria. Coming from the south you climb a longish hill which is crowned by a traffic light, and a sign reading CAMBRIA pointing to the right. This takes you along the old Coast Highway, dropping down into East Village and the center of activity. At the north end of town is another TRAFFIC LIGHT on CA 1.*

Ground Zero *That TRAFFIC LIGHT on CA 1 at the north end of town, where Main Street goes off inland, Moonstone Drive toward the ocean.*

In Monterey, the tourist action is always heavy on Cannery Row, but the motorcyclists come in droves during the races at Laguna Seca.

This is my backyard. And the reason I dwell in this part of the Golden State is, in my humble estimation, that the local roads make for the best motorcycling in the world, taking into consideration that I wish to ride all year around. You can talk enthusiastically about the Alps, you can wax eloquent about the Rocky Mountains, but I will exchange high passes for a 12-month riding season.

And I also have high passes in the **Sierra Nevada** mountain range just half a day away.

A motorcyclist cannot go wrong in this part of California. Unless he arrives right after a big storm and CA 1, the Big Sur Highway, is shut down

A troop of motorcyclists come south along the Big Sur Highway, a road that every motorcyclist should ride at least twice in his or her lifetime— once in each direction.

due to landslides. But in that case there are the other places, like Pozo and Parkfield and Carmel Valley Road, which will be fine destinations.

I was rather undecided as to where to place the focal point, the Headquarters, for this chapter. It could have been at the county seat of **San Luis Obispo** (SLO), a college town with lots of activities and much to recommend it, but I decided to take a very different approach and put you up in the small coastal town of Cambria, which is really my preference; it is 30 miles north of SLO-City, 100 miles south of the **Monterey peninsula.**

Cambria was named by some homesick Welshman who lived in this little valley along the **Santa Rosa Creek,** or at least that is the romantic side of the story. The old part of town, called **East Village,** is over a mile from the ocean, with Main Street and a few offshoots. Here is a worthy bar, **Camozzi's,** a selection of eateries from a bakery to excellent restaurants, and half a dozen motels. Farther along Main is the much newer **West Village,** occasionally prone to flooding during very rainy winters, which is why the old-timers did not build there. It has a row of quaint-looking tripper-traps selling everything from olive oil to toy soldiers to used books.

My primary recommendation for a place to lay your head is in the old part of town, at the **Blue Bird Motel,** which is nothing special, a wooden one- and two-story affair with 37 rooms (with no phones) that is just plainly and simply nice (805-927-4634; 1880 Main St.). And it is walking distance to **Linn's** for breakfast (805-927-0371), and to **Robin's** (805-927-5007) or **The Brambles** (805-927-4716) for dinner. And to Camozzi's for the evening's entertainment, which means live music on most weekends, from blues to rock to folk.

Down on the seashore is Moonstone Beach Drive, with another dozen or more motels packed in cheek by jowl, earnestly portraying their romantic possibilities, and trying to capture the tourist trade, with names like **Best Western Fireside Inn By The Sea** (800-528-1234, 805-927-8661). The catch here is that there is a road between these motels and the sea, and that the motels are usually built on narrow lots at right angles to the coast, so the views are limited. But you can always go out to walk.

If you like the sea air while you are eating, try the **Moonstone Beach Bar & Grill,** with patio dining, serving from eight in the morning until nine in the evening (805-927-3859).

Trip 6 **Pozo Loop**

Distance *193 miles*
Highlights *From Morro Bay to San Luis Obispo to Pozo, with a bit of seaside, a touch of town, a good deal of ranching country*
0 Miles Head south on CA 1
5 Miles STAY STRAIGHT as CA 46 goes off to the left.
7 Miles The village of **Harmony** is off to your left (Pop. 18, Alt. 175), where a couple of dozen craftsmen try to earn a living by selling to the tourists. The whole place, such that it is, is owned by one man who threatens to turn it into some sort of theme park. We hope he fails.

Come over a rise on CA 1 and the whole of **Estero Bay** is before you, with the houses of Cayucos about five miles in front of you, **Morro Rock** another seven miles beyond that. On a clear day this is a damned fine view . . . except for the three great smokestacks of the Morro Bay power plant, a fossil-fuel generator. We all need and use electric power, but making it is never a pretty sight.

Morro Bay is the only safe mooring at the south end of Big Sur; that is Morro Rock in the background.

16 Miles TURN RIGHT into **Cayucos,** down Business CA 1, which parallels and will put you right back on CA 1 in about two miles. Stop at the cheerfully retrograde **Old Cayucos Tavern** on Ocean Avenue, the main street, and have a Virgin Mary. If you are there on January 1st you can partake in the **Polar Bear Dip.**

Morro Bay

The Spanish explorer Juan Cabrillo thought that the big rock which protects the harbor reminded him of a moor's turban, hence the name. That was before the major quarrying that took place on the rock in the early part of the last century, which has substantially altered the moorish look. The town used to have a reasonably sized fishing fleet, but while several dozen boats do still fish out of there, the main business is now tourism.

Down on the waterfront, the **Embarcadero,** there is a long strip of restaurants and tripper-traps (a/k/a souvenir shops). You can get reasonable fish at the **Great American Fish Company,** right down on the wharves (805-772-4407), but I prefer **Dorn's Original Breakers Cafe** (805-772-4105), on Market Avenue, up on the low bluffs above the Embarcadero. And kitty-corner across Market, on the corner with Morro Bay Boulevard, is the **Breakers Motel** (805-772-7317).

The local action in MB is at the intersection of Harbor and Main streets, with two bars competing for the beer-buck, **Legends** and **Happy Jacks Tavern.** ∎

Dirt riders will gather at the Pozo Saloon, in San Luis Obispo County, for a hit of sarsaparilla after a grueling day in the forest.

32 Miles Pass the turn for CA 41, which you will be coming back on later.

32+ Miles If you want to go into Morro Bay exit right at the MORRO BAY, MAIN ST sign.

36 Miles CA 1 freeway, a/k/a Cabrillo Highway, is now running through the Chorro Creek valley alongside a row of smaller versions of Morro Rock stretching off to the east. Pass Cuesta College on your right, California Men's Colony (a white-collar prison) on your left. As you approach San Luis Obispo, passing several traffic lights, Cabrillo turns into Santa Rosa Street. Pass CalPoly (California Polytechnic University) off to your left, and intersect with US 101. You might want to fill your tank before you get on US 101, as there is no gas available in the next 100 miles.

45 Miles TRAFFIC LIGHT—RIGHT TURN right after crossing over US 101, following US 101 NORTH signs.

54 Miles EXIT RIGHT off US 101 onto CA 58/SANTA MARGARITA. You have just climbed over the Cuesta Pass, the highest spot on US 101 between Los Angeles and San Francisco, as the road climbs over the **Santa Lucia Range**. At 1,522 feet it does not sound like much of a climb, but after miles and miles of flat, it is an impressive, and picturesque ascent. The road into Santa Margarita is called El Camino Real, The Royal Road, which was the Spanish name for the dirt track that ran from San Diego to San Francisco 200 years ago.

San Luis Obispo

Nice town, a college town and the county seat. Head on into town on Santa Rosa, and at the fourth TRAFFIC LIGHT TURN RIGHT on Higuera Street, one-way, the main drag in town. The center of the action is about three blocks down, between Chorro and Broad streets. Find a place to park, and there are even a few motorcycle parking slots scattered about—at less than half the rate cars pay.

Mother's Tavern, The Library, and the **Frog & Peach Pub** and other bars and restaurants are spread out over this stretch of downtown. A block away is the old **Mission San Luis Obispo de Toloso** (Saint Louis, Bishop of Toulouse . . . which is in France, for those weak on such trivia), begun in 1772, and still holding services in the restored chapel; it is a beautiful place just to wander about.

For breakfast, I like **McClintock's Dining House** at 686 Higuera (805-541-0686); for ribs, **Mo's Smokehouse BBQ** at 970 Higuera (805-544-6193). If you are in town on Thursday evening you will find five blocks of downtown Higuera closed off for a large farmers' market, with lots of food available.

If you are looking for a singular place to stay, SLO-City has many offerings. I cannot help but recommend the **Madonna Inn,** at 100 Madonna Road off US 101 on the south side of town. You cannot miss it, as bright pink was the late Alex Madonna's favorite color, and it advertises itself as having "109 unique rooms and suites." Unique is right, as they all have a different decor, from Caveman to Hawaiian, Old West to Fifties Funk. It is an experience; whether you wish to miss it or not is up to you (800-543-9666, 805-543-3000, Madonna Road exit off of US 101). Much more conventional, and at the other end of town, is the **Apple Farm Inn,** at the Monterey Street exit off of US 101, with 68 rooms (800-255-2040, 805-544-2040); the Apple Farm is full of old-fashioned goodness, from chicken and dumplings to brownies and apple pie. The Apple Farm is also owner of, and next to the **Motel Inn,** whose claim to fame is that it was the first motel in the world—or the country, or the state, or something. It opened in 1925 as the **Milestone Motel,** a contraction of Mo(tor) and (Ho)tel. Unfortunately all that remains of this historic Motor Hotel is the sign and the old towered reception area.   ■

55 Miles You are in downtown **Santa Margarita,** a small town whose original reason for existing was to service the railroad which came through here in the 1880s. The Union Pacific still has a dozen trains a day passing along these tracks, but the need for personnel has been greatly reduced. On your left in town is **Tina's Cafe** (805-438-3828) which serves good breakfasts and burgers seven days a week, shutting down after lunch.

55+ Miles TURN RIGHT, following CA 58, crossing railroad tracks.

57 Miles GO STRAIGHT, though CA 58 goes off to the left, staying on Pozo Road.

Good road, Pozo, recently surfaced. Pass La Pilitas Road to your left, pass the left turn at Rinconada to **Lake Margarita,** past River Road to your left, all the time hurtling along straightaways, around bends, over hills. This is 16 miles of very good riding.

73 Miles Arrive in **Pozo,** which is a great Saturday or Sunday destination, albeit very quiet the rest of the week. There is a forest-service fire station, a few houses, the old **Pozo Saloon** (open Saturday and Sunday, 805-438-4225), and that is about it for the town of Pozo. A hundred years ago this place was a stage-stop on the San Luis Obispo to Bakersfield run, but them days is long gone. On the weekends their might be a couple of dozen bikes outside, from cruisers to dirt bikes.

A rough dirt road runs south out of Pozo, past the forest-service fire station, called Hi-Mountain Road, which goes back over the Santa Lucias to **Arroyo Grande** and San Luis Obispo. East of Pozo in the **Los Padres National Forest** is **Turkey Flats** and a big ORV area.

74 Miles STAY STRAIGHT, on Park Hill Road, as Pozo Road goes off to the right. You can follow Pozo Road out to CA 58 if you wish, but there are about ten miles of unpaved going; I took a ZX11 through there, but I can't say I recommend it for the sporty brigade.

77 Miles STAY STRAIGHT, on Park Hill Road, as a sign points to the right, indicating Turkey Flats and Black Mountain. The road to the top of **Black Mountain** (3,625 feet) is paved, albeit a bit roughly, since the FAA has all sorts of instruments up there, and it is the highest spot in the western part of the county, so it makes a nice, if gnarly, sidetrip.

Continue along Park Hill Road, which, depending on recent weather, is sometimes clean, sometimes a bit dirty, especially the section along the **Yaro Creek.** Take it easy, as there are a couple of deceptive turns.

79 Miles This being one of the deceptive turns, as River Road runs off to the left, Park Hill to the right, and if you go straight you will find a big ditch.

84 Miles Big curve in the road, Las Pilitas Road goes off to the left, a hundred yards further on Huerhuero Road goes to the right, and you stay on Park Hill.

92 Miles   STOP sign, TURN RIGHT onto CA 58, going up a hill in an absolutely wonderful series of tight curves; second gear, stay on the throttle.

94 Miles   CURVE RIGHT, staying on CA 58, as CA 229 goes off to the left.

Via Creston

If you want to add a few extra miles and a lot of extra fun, take CA 229, which twists very tightly over a low range of hills, down to the **Huerhuero Valley,** and after eight miles you come into **Creston** (Pop. 270). You pass the **Loading Chute** restaurant (805-237-1259) on your left, and then the **Long Branch Saloon** (805-238-1152), also on your left. Opposite the Long Branch, O'Donovan Road goes off to the right; take that. It tears flatly along the **East Branch Huerhuero Creek** for a little over five miles, and then rejoins CA 58. Good little excursion.   ∎

99 Miles   O'Donovan Road comes in from the left; CA 58 is whistling along some rolling countryside, round some curves, past La Panza Road going off to the left.

108 Miles   TURN LEFT onto Shell Creek Road. It is easy to miss this, as there is a paucity of signage, but a watertank and windmill on your left should alert you. If not, crossing the bridge over **Shell Creek** should tell you you have gone a hundred feet too far.

Shell Creek Road, for my limited money, is one of the most fun roads in the state. No traffic worth mentioning, lightly curved, and as fast as you want it to be. Of course, there is a bit of open range along the way, so watch out for the beef. And for the antelope, which disregard all fences but generally stay away from the road.

At the north end of the valley the road hugs the east wall, and the going is a bit slower.

118 Miles   TURN LEFT onto Truesdale Road. If you inadvertently go straight you will find yourself fording **San Juan Creek,** which is usually dry, but can be flooded.

121 Miles   Truesdale Road makes a right-angle turn to the right, and enters a large grape-growing area, all part of the wine-drinking mania that has infected these United States in the last 15 years. Of which I approve.

122 Miles   TURN LEFT onto Clark Road, in the middle of the vineyard, at an intersection with no STOP signs anywhere.

123 Miles   STOP sign—TURN LEFT onto CA 41. The next 10 miles are very nice indeed, as the road winds through the hills, gets up to 1,500 feet, and drops back down to Huerhuero Valley.

134 Miles   STAY STRAIGHT on CA 41, as CA 229 goes off to the left, to Creston. Follow CA 41, which will come down the **Atascadero Grade** with all of the **Salinas Valley** and the town of **Atascadero** spread out in front. A long bridge will take you across the Salinas River and into town. The Spanish word "atascadero" loosely translates to "a place to get stuck in," as wagons in the 19th Century would ford the river here and would sometimes get stuck.

145 Miles   TRAFFIC LIGHT—STAY STRAIGHT CA 41, going under

The Motel Inn in San Luis Obispo opened up as the Milestone Mo-Tel (motor-hotel) in 1925, and it is credited as the first establishment to use the word "motel."

US 101 and becoming Morro Road. This heads west, leaves the valley, and climbs up the Santa Lucia Range to the 1,438-foot summit, then down through **Devil's Gap,** past the **Half-Way Station** (open most weekends with food and music), into the **Los Padres National Forest,** past the forest-service fire station, **Cerro Alto Campground,** and then the winding descent into **Morro Creek Valley.**

161 Miles   STOP sign—TURN RIGHT onto CA 1 going north.

165 Miles   TRAFFIC LIGHT—TURN RIGHT, the sign reading OLD CREEK ROAD (right) STUDIO DRIVE (left). Old Creek is a back way to Cambria, and very much worth it. There might still be a sign saying: LANDSLIDE, LOCAL TRAFFIC ONLY, but it has become a fixture, and the road is fine; if the road is actually unusable, a barrier will stop you.

Follow Old Creek up the hill, around the top of the **Whale Rock Reservoir,** and down the hill.

169 Miles   STAY STRAIGHT; at the bottom Santa Rita Creek Road (dirt) goes to the right, eventually getting back to US 101. Then a bridge crosses over Old Creek, and Cottontail Creek Road goes off to the left, a dead end.

Old Creek Road wiggles along, runs under a magnificent bower of oak trees—followed immediately by a very steep, very sharp right-hand turn, and up and over the Santa Lucias, hitting a 1,415-foot summit.

174 Miles   STOP sign—TURN LEFT onto CA 46, which will lead to CA 1 and the coast. Back in the Sixties, if you wanted to come from Paso Robles, a small city on US 101 to the east, and go down to the coast, you came along to this intersection, with Santa Rosa Creek Road going to Cambria, Old Creek to Cayucos. Neither of these were easy roads, but the tourists all wanted to go see **Hearst Castle.** In the early Seventies the project was approved to build a highway from this intersection to meet up with CA 1, and it opened in 1974. Now it carries a lot of traffic. About two miles on is the summit, at some 1,500 feet, and then it is a scenically inspiring tenmile drop down to CA 1.

186 Miles   STOP sign—TURN RIGHT onto CA 1

191 Miles   Arrive back at Ground Zero.

Trip 7 Parkfield Loop

Distance *214 miles*

Highlights *Via Santa Rosa Creek Rd, Shandon, Parkfield, San Miguel, Hunter Liggett, the Nacimiento Road to the coast, and south on CA 1*

0 Miles Head back through **Cambria** along Main Street, past the **Blue Bird** and **Camozzi's**, right out of town.

2 Miles TURN LEFT onto Santa Rosa Creek Road; remember that this used to be a main road into town back in the Sixties, but it has now become a rustic paradise. Go past the high school, and then it is just good fun. The first five miles are quite easy.

7 Miles STAY RIGHT, as Curti Road goes off to the left. Now the road gets a good deal twistier, finally entering a very shaded stretch, and then emerging in a valley. At the end of the valley the road makes a 180-degree turn and climbs up to make a second 180-degree turn, and if you stop to look you will see that you have seen this road many times before—it is a favorite place for motorcycle magazines to photograph bikes.

Many of the photographs you see in motorcycle magazines are taken on Santa Rosa Creek Road, running from Cambria toward Paso Robles.

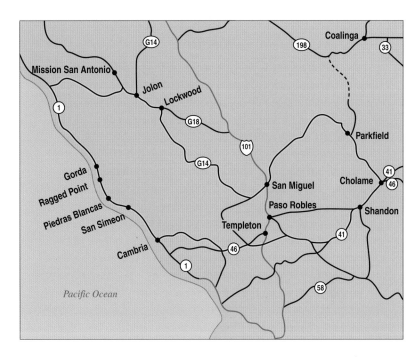

Climb up, past Cypress Mountain Road (dirt) going to the left, and up to the summit at 1,860 feet. You have crossed the **Santa Lucia Range,** and now head down the east side, along **Rocky Creek.** It is a superlative stretch of road, but not necessarily a fast one.

18 Miles STOP sign—TURN LEFT onto CA 46. This two-laner is wide, smooth, and fast, and very well patrolled by the CHP.

20 Miles York Mountain Road is off to your left. If you would like to purchase a bottle of wine from the original (1882) vineyard in this part of California, take this little road and stop at the **York Mountain Winery** tasting room. You can continue along York Mountain Road to get back to CA 46.

24 Miles TURN RIGHT onto Vineyard Drive, past the **Mastantuono Winery** and tasting room.

27 Miles Cross over US 101, having gone past the **Pesenti** and **Creston Vineyards** tasting rooms—or maybe you stopped.

27+ Miles TRAFFIC LIGHT—GO STRAIGHT, onto El Pomar Drive. If you take a left at the light you will be on Main Street in Templeton, an un-incorporated, one-street town that has several good places to eat. For breakfast and lunch try **Joe's Other Place** (805-434-JOES), for dinner **McPhee's Grill** (805-434-3204), and for steak, **A.J. Spurs Saloon** (805-434-2700).

Wineries

San Luis Obispo county is working very hard to compete with Napa Valley, by the way, and we have over 150 commercial wineries in the area, along with a large number of private little vineyards whose owners have not gone to the hassle of legitimizing their product with the authorities so that the wine can be sold.

Part of the grape growing is just south of San Luis Obispo in the **Edna Valley,** but the major portion is around **Paso Robles** and **Templeton.** California has over 400,000 acres of land dedicated to wine grapes (as opposed to eating grapes or raisins), and the dream of every vintner is to develop a following that will pay $50 a bottle or better. San Luis Obispo county has more than 15,000 acres under vines.

Historically, the padres brought the first grapes to the region in the late 18th Century to make sacramental wine. In 1882 a gent from Indiana, Andrew York, set up the first commercial winery. And then the wine-crazed 1970s had everybody turning rough ranchland into expensive vineyards, doubling and tripling the price of land.

Many wineries have tasting rooms. In the good old days if you showed up at a winery you would be rewarded for your diligence by getting to sample the best that they had, and then you would buy a few bottles and be off. Nowadays, touring wineries has become a major tourist attraction, and many wineries charge you for the privilege of tasting. The reason is that the wineries know that most of these visitors have no real knowledge of wine, and no intention of purchasing an '87 cabernet, and that a small profit can be made off these samplers. As well as sell them a T-shirt or corkscrew.

For local wines, a **Wild Horse Merlot** is usually a good bet.   ∎

Keeping on El Pomar Drive, crossing over the **Salinas River,** the road winds through the countryside.

34 Miles STOP sign—GO STRAIGHT, continuing on El Pomar.

37 Miles STOP sign—TURN LEFT, as El Pomar T-bones into Cripple Creek Road.

38 Miles STOP sign—TURN RIGHT onto Creston Road, curving around to your right and going alongside an exquisitely expensive horse-breeding place called **Creston Farms.**

40 Miles   TURN LEFT at end of horse farm railing onto Camp 8 Road.

43 Miles   STOP sign—TURN LEFT onto CA 41; you are about to do that gorgeous winding stretch again, as you did in Trip #1, only going the other way.

53 Miles   STOP sign—TURN RIGHT, following CA 41 through **Shandon** along Centre Street.

55 Miles   STOP sign—TURN RIGHT, as CA 41 merges with CA 46, becoming a four-laner, and double-fines if you are caught speeding. Be cool.

61 Miles   On top of the rise, to the left, is what remains of the town of **Cholame**, with the **Jack Ranch Cafe** (805-238-5652) offering sturdy trucker food, and a memorial to the late James Dean.

62 Miles   TURN LEFT (cautiously) onto Cholame Valley Road, a large sign along CA 41/46 reading: PARKFIELD, and pointing to the left . . . as well as indicating that the next left goes to Fresno, the straight to Bakersfield. The road heads straight up the valley, and has no traffic to speak of, but there is a lot of open range, which means a lot of cattle. The road crosses into Monterey county and every now and then it chooses to change course and move to the other side of the valley via a right-angle turn.

About ten miles along the road goes past a farm, crosses **Cholame Creek,** and starts winding a bit. Informational signs tell you that you have arrived at the **San Andreas Fault, Pacific Plate** side. Turkey Flat Road goes off to the right, dead-ending in a couple of miles, then you cross through a girder bridge and Ranchito Canyon Road (dirt) goes off to the left.

Death of James Dean

A mile to the east of the memorial Dean met his end in 1955 when he crashed his Porsche into a Ford coupe, where CA 41 and CA 46 split. That intersection has been substantially altered since then, but you can see the possibility for disaster, with Dean driving west into a setting sun. The poor fellow, with the uninspired name of Turnipseed, driving east in his car probably did not even see the low-profile Porsche as he made his left turn onto CA 41.

Who knows where Dean's career would have taken him had he lived. We do know that he was a motorcyclist, and had a Triumph T100C. A Japanese fan of Dean paid for the Jack Ranch Cafe memorial some years ago, and the CA 41/46 split was officially designated, in 2006, the 50th year since Dean's death, as the James Dean Memorial Intersection. A heckuva way to be remembered. ■

77 Miles TURN RIGHT, over the little bridge, the sign reading: PARKFIELD 1/2, COALINGA 29. Not much in **Parkfield** but a small school, a forest-service fire station, and the **Parkfield Inn & Cafe**. Which is a great spot. If you want an uninterrupted night (sort of; Parkfield is known as The Earthquake Capitol of the World), check into the six-room inn (805-463-2421). The cafe is closed on Wednesdays, opening at 11:30 the rest of the week, shutting the door about when everybody goes home.

If you choose to take the road on past Parkfield, it turns to dirt in about six miles, as it climbs over the hills and drops down to CA 198 near Coalinga.

To continue on our planned route, you will need to go back to that little bridge, TURN RIGHT at the STOP sign, which puts you on Vineyard Canyon Road, and San Miguel is 24 miles away.

81 Miles TURN LEFT, staying with Vineyard Canyon, while ahead is a sign reading: NOT A THROUGH ROAD. Believe it.

In two miles you climb up to the 2,602-foot summit, and then it is a fast 15 miles down along the valley. By early 1999 the road had been resurfaced in some of the rougher stretches, and a goodly pace could be maintained. Considering that the sheriff might come this way once a month, you don't have much to worry about.

98 Miles STOP sign—CONTINUE STRAIGHT, merging with Indian Valley Road. You can see San Miguel in the distance.

99 Miles STOP sign—TURN RIGHT, and in a hundred feet is another STOP sign, TURN RIGHT again, crossing over the Salinas River on River Road.

100 Miles STOP sign—TURN LEFT onto Mission Street, and you are in downtown **San Miguel**. This used to be a tough-guys town back in the hey-day of World War II, when GIs from Camp Roberts and **Fort Hunter Liggett** would pour in to spend their money on bad booze, card games, and good women. That is all long since cleaned up, and San Miguel is a pretty sleepy place.

Down at the south end of town is the large **Mission San Miguel Arcangel**, founded by Franciscan padres in 1797, and secularized (sold to civilians) in the 1840s. The mission returned to the Catholic church in 1878, and a hundred years later had been restored to its original glory. Unfortunately the church building itself got a major shaking in the 2003 earthquake, was closed to the public, and is currently awaiting a very expensive retrofitting.

Lunch and dinner can be found at **Dos Padres Mexican Restaurant** (805-467-0033) on 14th Street, while the tiny ten-seat **Country Diner**

Cold Springs Tavern (See Trip 4) began as an old stagecoach stop in the 1850s, and remains popular to this day.

(805-467-3681) at 1289 Mission Street serves breakfast and lunch. The only gas station in town is at 10th and US 101.

101 Miles MERGE with US 101 going south.

102 Miles TURN RIGHT onto San Marcos Road.

107 Miles STOP sign—TURN RIGHT onto County Road G14/ Nacimiento Lake Drive.

109 Miles TURN RIGHT, following G14/Nacimiento Lake Drive.

117 Miles Cross the **Nacimiento Dam** at the east end of the lake, and then climb the hill.

119 Miles TURN LEFT, following G14, which has become Interlake Road. Great riding for the next 20 miles. Drop down into **Bee Rock Canyon,** then whisk along **Harris Valley,** across the **San Antonio River,** and out through **Tule Canyon** to **Lockwood.**

139 Miles STOP sign—TURN LEFT, following G14, now known as Jolon Road. At that little intersection is a store which sells cold sodas and the like.

Fort Hunter Liggett

If you GO STRAIGHT, instead of making that Nacimiento-Fergusson turn, you will pass the barracks and transportation areas, and then will see a large, red-roofed building on the hill to your right, **The Hacienda Restaurant & Lodge.** This is the old officer's club, and before that it was one of Willie Hearst's many houses on his far-flung spread, designed by Julia Morgan, the same architect who drew up the plans for Hearst Castle. It is now a restaurant serving lunch and dinner most days, and a guest lodge that used to be the old **Bachelor Officers Quarters** (831-386-2900).

If you continue on past The Hacienda you will come to the **Mission San Antonio de Padua,** which was begun in 1771. It was a profitable mission (the church was interested in making money as much as in saving souls) and in 1830 the valley had over 8,000 cattle and 12,000 sheep, but it was abandoned in the 1880s. Time and earthquakes knocked it down, but today the place looks as it did in the early 1800s, having been completely reconstructed. ∎

144 Miles TURN LEFT, after seeing the sign that reads FORT HUNTER LIGGETT 5, MISSION 6, to the left; if you go straight on G14 you will be in King City in 18 miles. Several years ago you would be in the middle of downtown Jolon at this point, except there is nothing there. In 1997 there was a small town, with a large trailer park, big store, gas, restaurant, and then one day it all vanished. Had to do with the down-sizing of the military at Fort Hunter Liggett.

144+ Miles STOP, definitely stop, at the gate entering the fort. **Fort Hunter Liggett,** named for the general who took over the command of American forces in Europe in World War I after General Pershing left, is mainly used for training purposes, and has a very small permanent party. The fort used to be an open base, so access was not controlled, but following 9/11 all that changed. Federal police now guard the gates, and you will have to show a driver's license with motorcycle approval, current registration, and current insurance. If you do not have those three items, forget about entering.

147 Miles TURN LEFT, following the sign that reads: NACIMIENTO-FERGUSSON ROAD/CA 1. This is not a well-marked turn, but it is the first turn to the left.

Stay on the Nacimiento-Fergusson Road.

148 Miles   Cross over the **San Antonio River** on a girder bridge. Or you can ford it at the tank crossing, just 100 feet downstream; much more fun, especially if the river is high.

150 Miles   Road to the right, which will run up to Del Venturi Road, which becomes Indians Road, turns into dirt, and eventually stops at a barrier keeping you out of the Ventana Wilderness Area.

STAYING STRAIGHT you are coming out of the woods and into a rather treeless area. Now you are prancing over the open range, having a good time, and the U.S. Army Corps of Engineers does believe in laying good asphalt, as the road dips and winds around the folds in the land.

156 Miles   Leave the military reservation, where another federal cop will stop you, and head up along **Nacimiento River,** with several campgrounds in the **Los Padres National Forest.** Start a steepish climb and pass a ranger station.

165 Miles   At the very top, sort of in the woods, you have an intersection, of sorts, with dirt roads going off to the right (north) and left (south). To the right, the dirt Cone Peak Road goes up to 4,500 feet—if it is open to vehicles—and dead-ends. To the left, the rough dirt South Coast Ridge Road goes down to the coast—again, good d-p riding, although I have struggled up on a standard motorcycle on more than one occasion.

Move forward a hundred feet and the Pacific Ocean is far away in front of you, and you begin a very twisty seven-mile descent to the Big Sur Highway/CA 1. Go easy, as the corners can be dirty. And stop a lot to marvel at the views.

167 Miles   Ah, a grand view of the coast still way below you, and of the road you are on twisting away way down there. No guard rails; be cautious, enjoy, stop, and take pictures.

171 Miles   TURN LEFT after meeting up with CA 1; right goes up to Monterey. Since I will run you all the way up the coast from Cambria to Monterey in the next trip, Trip #3, I am not going to run you quickly back to Cambria, touching on just a couple of places. If you want more information on this southward journey, just go forward a couple of pages, find the Nacimiento-Fergusson turn-off at Mile 43, and start reading backward from there.

179 Miles   **Gorda,** with gas, food, lodging (805-927-1590).

192 Miles   **Ragged Point,** with gas, food, lodging (805-927-4502).

206 Miles   San Simeon, and the **Hearst San Simeon State Historical Monument**

214 Miles   Arrive back at **Cambria,** Ground Zero

Trip 8 Big Sur Highway

Distance *251 miles*

Highlights *Run up the Big Sur coast and down Carmel Valley, then along the west side of the Salinas Valley. This will also serve as a CONNECTOR, taking you into the Monterey peninsula. The hundred miles between Hearst Castle and Carmel is in the top half dozen roads in the world for a motorcyclist to ride. Except you want to do it when the traffic is low and the coast is clear. Which usually means starting early in the morning in spring or fall. The road is officially the Cabrillo Highway/CA 1, but popularly known as the Big Sur Highway.*

For those not familiar with pre-American California, the Spaniards used Monterey as their capitol, and to them that big wilderness to the south, which was virtually impossible to traverse, became known as El Sur Grande.

Or, as the Kingston Trio sang in the Fifties, "The south coast, the wild coast . . . "

Looking north from Hurricane Point to Bixby Bridge—this is the Big Sur at its best.

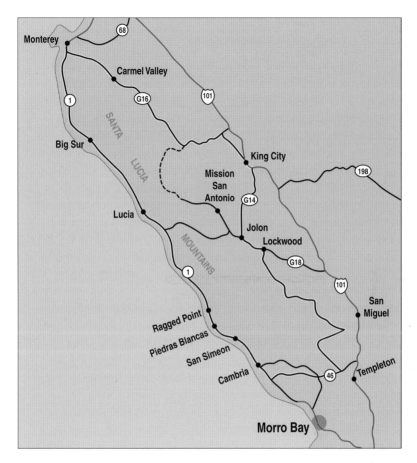

0 Miles Traffic light; head north on CA 1. Road starts running along the edge of the flatlands that stretch from the Santa Lucia foothills to the sea. Good for cattle, long curves okay for very fast motorcyclists.

4 Miles The so-called community of **San Simeon**, which is nothing much more than a dozen motels scrunched in on each side of the highway. Its only reason for existence is its proximity to Hearst Castle.

7 Miles If you look up on the ridgeline to your right, you will see the towers of **Hearst Castle**. And the big sign indicating you should turn to your right in order to get a closer look at this marvel.

14 Miles Coming up on **Piedras Blancas** (white rocks, thanks to the guano on the rocks). There is usually a huge crowd bothering the elephant seals on the beach. The old lighthouse is just beyond, but casual visitors are not welcome. The road develops a couple of straightaways, then comes around a vicious curve to drop down to . . .

Hearst Castle

William Randolph Hearst's dad, George, made a lot of money from mining interests in the late 1800s and bought most of the land around the little seaside community of **San Simeon.** Willie got his father to buy him a failing newspaper, the **San Francisco Examiner,** and turned it into a sensationalist paper, using lurid headlines and pictures, much as the tabloids by the check-out counter at the supermarket do. He made his money a quarter cent at a time, selling his newspapers, but he sold a lot of papers. He got to be very rich and very powerful, and when he was 50-something he fell madly in love with a showgirl named Marion Davies, who just happened to be more than 30 years younger than he was; how predictable. He built his castle on the coast so his mistress could throw great parties, and the work went on from 1919 to World War II. He called the place **La Cuesta Encantada** (The Enchanted Hill), but it is now better known as Hearst Castle; the main section has a mere 40,000 square feet of living space in over 100 rooms.

Mrs. Hearst, his official wife, was an understanding woman and stayed in New York, spending lots of his money and having her own version of a good life. In 1958, the Hearst heirs, realizing they had a great white elephant on their hands, gave the place to the state, and it has since become a serious money-maker as thousands of tourists troop through every week ($20 to $24 a head, depending on the season; evening tours are more).

The castle is worth a visit, if only to see what excess wealth can do to good taste. You ride in, park the bike, get a ticket, get on a bus, go up the hill, walk around for an hour or more, and think how nice it would be to have all that money. You should allot a half day to this little adventure, and there are different tours you can take. Including a night-time one. To get more relevant information, call 800-438-4445.

Opposite the castle, on the sea side, is the actual remnants of the whaling station of San Simeon, with a small store and sandwich shop. ∎

21 Miles . . . **San Carpoforo Creek,** with a house belonging to the National Forest on the right just after you cross the bridge. Now the **Santa Lucia Mountains** are coming straight down to the ocean. This is the beginning of serious riding, the road climbing sharply, steeply, twistily.

23 Miles **Ragged Point,** with a very pleasant lodge (805-927-4502) and a very good restaurant, coffee shop, hamburger joint, and small store that also sells gas.

From here the road gets occasionally fast, occasionally hazardous. If you are a first-timer, take great care with the posted 15-mph signs you will see. My theory about the Big Sur Highway is that one should ride it slowly in one direction to admire the view and get the feel of the road, ride it slowly back the way you came . . . and then you can ride it at any speed you wish.

The real hazard on this road is not the road itself, but the gawping tourists who are constantly wandering over the center line, slowing abruptly for no reason other than to gaze out to sea, and driving in and out of scenic viewpoints.

34 Miles Gorda, with gas, food, and half a dozen cabins to lodge in. Beyond Gorda a mile is the turn onto Los Burros Road (dirt) which scrabbles up to the South Coast Ridge Road (dirt), and then a couple of miles further on Plaskett Ridge Road (dirt), which also climbs up to South Coast Ridge Road. There is a campground at **Plaskett Creek,** and then the fast open **Pacific Valley.** Drop down to **Mill Creek Picnic Area,** start back up and . . .

43 Miles . . . there is a sign for NACIMIENTO-FERGUSSON ROAD, with a 300-degree turn back to your right, over a cattle guard. **Kirk Creek Campground** almost across the road. Even if you did not do Trip #2, it is definitely worth going up Nacimiento Road for a couple of miles, as there are stupendous views of the coast in both directions. Remember, you are in no hurry.

45 Miles Cross over the bridge at **Lime Kiln Creek State Park.**

When William Randolph Hearst wanted to impress his mistress and friends, he did it in a big way, building a veritable castle at the south end of the Big Sur.

47 Miles The not-so-bustling community of **Lucia,** with nought but a small store and restaurant, usually open for early lunch, breakfast on the weekends, and the ten motel rooms of **Lucia Lodge** sitting in a row, one out on the edge of the cliff over the sea, the rest coming inland. You want #10, right at the end; expensive, but worth the extra pennies to get a fireplace and a view (831-667-2391).

More fast road, often improved by CalTrans in an effort to defeat the landslides of the winter.

55 Miles Pass the **Esalen Institute,** BY RESERVATION ONLY. This place is a very pleasant hangover from the Sixties, one of these holistic feel-good resorts where you can check in for a couple of nights, eat vegetarian food, attend soul-searching seminars, and, best of all, hang out in the natural hot springs that are on the cliff high above the water (831-667-3023).

59 Miles Coming up on the **Julia Pfieffer Burns State Park.** Good hiking, and a wonderful waterfall falling into the ocean.

Just north of here, in 1983, a landslide came down from **Partington Ridge** and closed the highway for over a year. The road tends to sweep around the outside curve of a hillside, then cut inland for an even tighter curve around a watercourse, and on and on.

Bixby Bridge, the keystone to the success of the Big Sur Highway, was completed in 1932 and made briefly famous in the opening shots of the TV series, "Then Came Bronson."

Soon, however, you see signs of civilization, like art galleries and inns and even the **Henry Miller Museum**. You are approaching the community of **Big Sur**.

67 Miles Nepenthe—loosely translated from the Greek as "the place to lose oneself in." This is probably the nicest lunching spot on the coast. Go up on the high terrace and order an ambrosiaburger; ten bucks but it is worth it for the view.

Crest the rise, and the two fanciest places on the Big Sur coast are at the top, the **Ventana Big Sur Inn** is inland (831-667-2331, 800-628-6500), the **Post Ranch Inn** on the edge of the sea. Take the latter if you have a spare $1000 to spend (408-667-2200).

Down in the stretched-out community of Big Sur are other options, the **Pfeiffer Big Sur State Park** having the **Big Sur Lodge** (800-424-4787, 831-667-3100), and half a dozen commercial places to stay along CA 1.

Just south of the entrance to the state park is the turn down Sycamore Canyon Road to **Pfeiffer Beach;** it used to have free access, but in 1998 the state began charging five dollars.

71 Miles My favorite sleeping spot, when not staying at the Post Ranch, is the **Ripplewood Resort,** with a dozen cabins down by **Big Sur River** that were built to house workers back in the Thirties (831-667-2242). Ask for number 8 or 9, right on the river's edge.

76 Miles **Andrew Molera State Park** is on the left, which gives pedestrian access to four miles of unblemished beach; worth the hike. Opposite the park, off CA 1 a dirt road goes up to the right, the Old Coast Road, with a sign reading: IMPASSABLE IN WET WEATHER. Truth, but a great ride on a dry day.

Move past the **Point Sur Light Station** (begun back in 1887) which is now a state historic landmark and guided tours are run on weekends (831-625-4419), down to **Little Sur Creek,** with a curving bridge that begs speed—except for those concrete rails.

83 Miles **Hurricane Point,** where it can get righteously windy.

84 Miles Over **Bixby Bridge,** made mildly famous in the opening credits of the Sixties TV show, "**Then Came Bronson.**" On the north side of the bridge the Old Coast Road reconnects with CA 1. This bridge, finished in 1932, was built with the help of prisoners who would get time off on their sentences. That is good use of prison labor, and we should do it today.

The road straightens out a bit as it tears over **Rocky Creek Bridge,** past Palo Colorado Road, over **Garrapata Creek,** past **Garrapata State Park,** crosses **Malpaso Creek** and enters **Carmel Highlands**. The show is almost over.

95 Miles   Off to the left is **Point Lobos State Reserve,** a very nice, but very crowded park, where the hordes from Monterey come to see a bit of wildlife. Then it is down past the **Carmel River State Beach** and the **Carmelite** nunnery.

99 Miles   Cross **Carmel River** and come to a traffic light. You are now on the southwest edge of the **Monterey (King's Mountain) Peninsula.** Take a left and go into Carmel, or GO STRAIGHT up the hill and into Monterey. If you want lots of info, go directly to the Visitors Center at 380 Alvarado Street in downtown Monterey (831-649-1770).

Monterey Peninsula

The Monterey Peninsula is a Tourist Destination, which is why I'm not too keen on it. There is lots to do, lots to see, but it is not really motorcycling. Except for the national and international motorcycle races that are held every year out at the **Laguna Seca Raceway,** a few miles east of town on CA 68. Then you do have to go to Monterey.

The big show pieces on the peninsula are **Cannery Row,** with the **Monterey Bay Aquarium** at the west end, and a dozen restaurants serving over-priced food. And **Fisherman's Wharf,** which is a glorious tourist-trap, and very picturesque. Then there is the gated community called **Pebble Beach** and the overly rated **17-Mile Drive**—and motorcyclists cannot pay the tab at the gate and cruise the 17 miles unless they have dinner or room reservations somewhere inside the fence. Or have a friend who will buzz them in.

For food, it's everywhere. Down on Cannery Row every second business is food. On Fisherman's Wharf I gravitate to **Abalonetti's Seafood,** which does have the most scrumptious fried calamari. However, I would go over to the Wharf #2, the working wharf a quarter-mile north of Fisherman's Wharf, where all the boats unload, and go to the **Sandbar & Grill** (831-373-2818). If someone else is picking up the tab, try **Club XIX** at **The Lodge** in Pebble Beach.

For fine accommodations, check in at the **Monterey Plaza Hotel** on Cannery Row, with 290 rooms and suites, prices starting around $200 and going up to $3,500 (800-334-3999, 831-646-1700). On the more economical end you can go along to North Fremont Street, where a long line of mid-range motels await your business, like the **Best Western De Anza Inn** (2141 North Fremont, 800-858-8775, 831-646-8300). ∎

99+ Miles TRAFFIC LIGHT—TURN RIGHT onto Carmel Valley Road/ G16, sign pointing toward CARMEL VALLEY.

109 Miles STAY STRAIGHT as Los Laureles Grade/G20 goes off to the left, a good way to get to Laguna Seca Raceway.

111 Miles You are in **Carmel Valley Village,** last chance to gas up for a while. Great riding for the next 40 miles, right down Carmel Valley, over a rise, and down toward the **Salinas Valley.**

140 Miles STOP sign—TURN LEFT following G16, as to the right you go into **Arroyo Seco.**

147 Miles TURN RIGHT, heading down to the girder bridge, the sign reading GREENFIELD; cross the bridge over the **Arroyo Seco River** and keep going, now on Elm Avenue, running flat through farmland.

151 Miles TURN RIGHT onto Central Avenue, a hard to anticipate turn right out there in the middle of flat, flat fields; you are now headed south, paralleling US 101.

158 Miles TURN RIGHT onto US 101 as Central Ave. ends.

161 Miles EXIT RIGHT onto G14/Jolon Road, where there is gas and a convenience store.

177 Miles Pass the turn to Fort Hunter Liggett and the **San Antonio Mission** (where you were in Trip #2), staying on G14.

182 Miles RIGHT TURN opposite the **Lockwood Store,** following G14 down Interlake Road.

202 Miles STOP sign—TURN RIGHT, following G14 and dropping down to the **Nacimiento Dam.**

212 Miles STOP sign—TURN RIGHT, leaving G14 and going onto Chimney Rock Road, a very nice piece of under-utilized asphalt.

218 Miles LEFT TURN at **Adelaida Cemetery** onto Adelaida Road.

219 Miles STAY LEFT on Adelaida Road as Klau Mine Road goes off to the right.

220 Miles TURN RIGHT onto Vineyard Drive.

229 Miles STOP sign—TURN RIGHT onto CA 41.

246 Miles STOP sign—TURN RIGHT onto CA 1.

251 Miles Arrive back at Ground Zero.

Connector

If you are in Monterey, and want to keep going north toward San Francisco, the next chapter, just stick on CA 1.   ■

6

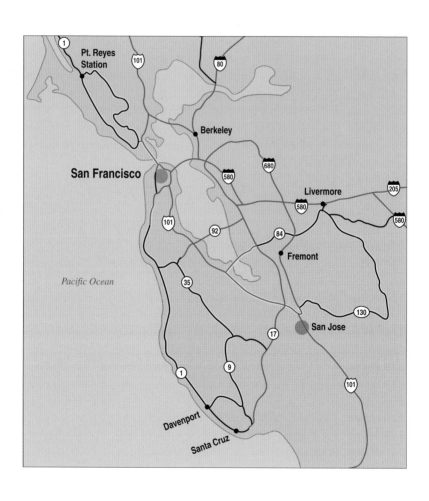

San Francisco & Bay Area

Headquarters *San Francisco, The City By The Bay*
San Francisco Visitors Bureau *415-391-2000*
Getting There *The main north-south route is US 101, or you can come up I-280 from San Jose in the south, which connects with I-80 coming from the east across the Bay Bridge, making an arc from south to east. Or vice-versa.*
Ground Zero *There isn't one. Again, like Los Angeles, you will have to do a little work for yourself and figure out where a couple of Interstates and freeways are, and take the trips from there. For the two southern loops I will have to rely on you, the faithful, competent, geographically aware reader, to make your way through the city to pick up either I-280 or US 101 (it's not very difficult, I promise. Van Ness Avenue south from Fort Mason comes to mind, or 19th Avenue from Golden Gate Park to Daly City).*

Alcatraz Island, out in the bay, is now a tourist destination; many people think the government should return the place to its original use, rather than building new prisons.

This is author Jack London's house that burned down before he could move into it, now part of the Jack London State Historic Park north of Sonoma.

This is a broad sweep of land and water, the *terra firma* cluttered with millions of people, but there is great riding in the area. How many times have I used that expression, "great riding"? But I mean it. The Bay has a lot of hills around it, and they provide the under-populated riding venues we all seek. And San Francisco is the finest big city that California has to offer.

Nice city, the City of Saint Francis, which also constitutes the smallest county in California, about 46 square miles, a lot of it hilly. And the better part of a million people living there. **San Francisco,** as the locals like to refer to the name, though the good old boys from Modesto are apt to talk about "going to Frisco," offers a great deal in the way of entertainment, from tawdry thrills in North Beach strip joints to good museums.

San Franciscans have managed to prevent any interstate from carving a great swath through their fair city. The standard way through the city is via US 101; the freeway ends downtown, putting you on Van Ness Avenue going north, hang a right on Lombard Street, and, Bob's your uncle, you are at the **Golden Gate Bridge.** Choice #2 is to come up CA 1, which merges with I-280 in **Daly City** for a few miles, then leaves and cuts north through San

Francisco on 19th Avenue and Park Presidio Boulevard to meet with US 101 at the bridge. The third choice is I-280, which connects CA 1 and US 101, and eventually just ends in the downtown area.

I've chosen three noteworthy rides out of SF, one to the Santa Cruz mountains and Alice's Restaurant, another to Mt. Hamilton east of San Jose, and a third to Marin County, on the north side of the Golden Gate Bridge. That last one will be dealt with in the next chapter, 7, the North Coast, or the Marin to Mendocino Road, CA 1.

Exploring San Francisco itself is not really within the intended scope of this book. There is an official **49-Mile Scenic Tour** which most maps you buy in the city will show; that will take a day. If I try to direct you in this brief guide, it will take 30 pages, so I will leave you more or less on your own, with a good map on top of your tankbag or in your pocket.

On a limited basis, I recommend **Coit Tower** on Telegraph Hill, the wiggly bit of **Lombard Street** between Hyde and Leavenworth (one way from Hyde), **Chinatown, Ghiradelli Square, Palace of the Legion of Honor in Lincoln Park, Twin Peaks,** and for those of us who remember the '67 Summer of Love, the **Hashbury** (those 20 blocks around the intersection of Haight and Ashbury streets) though it is much, much changed. And a trip to **Alcatraz Island;** why on earth the California authorities don't reopen that place instead of building new prisons is beyond me.

Also **Fisherman's Wharf** and **Pier 39** (which has an official Welcome Center with lots of maps), near where one can put up at the **Best Western Tuscan Inn** (800-648-4626, 415-561-1100), with 221 rooms. The Tuscan Inn is as good a location as you can find, within walking distance of just about everywhere. If you are looking for less expensive digs, there are a whole bunch of motels along the west end of Lombard Street heading for the Golden Gate bridge. Of course, it would be much nicer to stay at the Fairmont Hotel (415-772-5000), on top of Nob Hill, which has great views and good cable-car access if you want to leave the bike in the garage.

For me to try to suggest places to eat—too much to choose from. Though I always go to **Chinatown.** And if you want to soak up the local motorcycling milieu, head to **Farley's Coffee House** at 18th and Missouri, or **Zeitgeist,** a bar at Valencia and Duboce.

Trip 9   Santa Cruz Mountains & Alice's Restaurant

Distance   *Roughly 144 miles from and to I-280*

Highlights   *A ridge of big hills comes up the San Francisco Peninsula, the Santa Cruz Mountains, which run from Salinas all the way up to South San Francisco, and right behind the seaside city of Santa Cruz. And along the crest in the northern portion is Skyline Boulevard, a glorious stretch of wooded, two-lane road running some 26 miles. CA 35/Skyline Blvd. technically begins in the southwest corner of San Francisco, right by the zoo, but that initial stretch is pretty urban and boring, so I shall get you to the good parts in a hurry.*

    Come south on I-280, past the CA 1 SOUTH exit, then CA 35 flows in going south, continue down I-280/CA 35, with Crystal Springs Reservoir appearing on your right, to where the big green exit sign says: CA 35, CA 92 HALF MOON BAY.

0 Miles   EXIT RIGHT to the STOP light, TURN RIGHT onto CA 92/35, crossing between the upper and lower reservoirs, and head up the hill, or the east side of the **Santa Cruz Mountains,** to be precise.

Not much happens at Alice's Restaurant on weekday mornings—but just wait until the weekend.

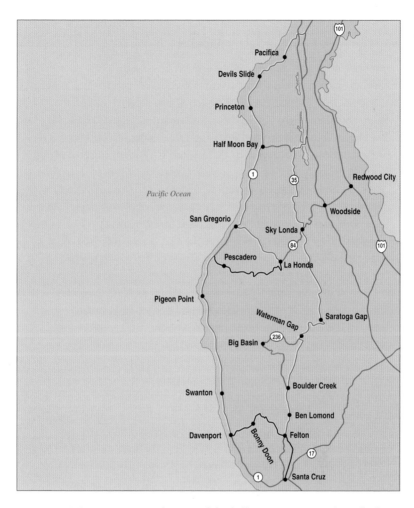

2 Miles   TURN LEFT at the top of the hill, on a major road marked CA 35. A sign reads: JUNCTION 84 13, JUNCTION 9 23; the latter is some three miles short of the mark, but who is to argue with the CalTrans mileage counter. Now, this is the good part of **Skyline Boulevard,** where leather-clad *Ducatisti* (with one-piece Dainese) and Harley riders (Brando jacket by First Gear, chaps by MotorClothes) collide . . . sometimes literally, so watch out.

It is a short run uphill, then into the woods. In the summer a lot of fog hangs out here, so if your vision is limited, watch out. And remember that on a weekend a lot of riders who ride this road week in and week out, year in and year out, will be hustling along at speedy speeds, because they know all the turns.

Alice's

Nobody other than the post office ever seems to refer to this intersection as Sky Londa; it is always Alice's. On any Sunday there are motorcycles all over the place. A short stretch of low buildings sits on the east side, and on the right side is **Alice's Restaurant** (650-851-0303), which had to do with a lady named Alice and not a singer named Arlo (his Alice had a restaurant in western Massachusetts), and an angled parking lot. Occasionally you will see a row of motorcycles fall over, as parking is dodgy on the slope. Leave your bike in gear and use your sidestand.

Alice's is the **classic hangout,** having a small deck with a few tables out front, and a dozen tables inside; open for breakfast at 7:30 on weekdays, 8:30 on the weekends. Right next door is **Alice's Station,** pumping gas for those with tiny, tiny tanks, or those who forgot to fill up before coming here.

Across the road, where the parking is flat, and all the spaces have faded signs reading: CAR PARKING ONLY, is the **Mountain Terrace** (659-851-1606), open for lunch and dinner. It has no tables out front, so one cannot admire the motorcycle scene, but once inside there is a big deck overlooking a grassy stretch with a volleyball court. The place can seat 350 people, according to the fire marshal, with probably another 200 standing around. A general store and real estate office are also in the line.

Taking a left down CA 84 will put you in **Woodside** after seven miles, a very upscale community best known for **Buck's Restaurant** (650-851-8010) and **Robert's Market.** Buck's is where you go for breakfast and to eavesdrop on all the venture capitalists talking about where to put money, and Robert's is where you go to buy the makings of a picnic lunch. If every town had a market as nice as Robert's, the world would be a far better place; it is a glorious establishment, with a lovely produce department, and a meat counter to die for.

Back at Sky Londa, taking a right (heading west) on CA 84 takes you down to the little intersection at **La Honda** after seven miles. More on that later.

GO STRAIGHT on CA 35. The road runs right along the ridge of the mountains, rising a little, very pleasant, with lots of open space preserved by San Mateo County.   ■

It is smooth two-lane, and as you cross over **Kings Mountain,** a pricey rural community with the **Kings Mountain Country Store** on your right, the **Bella Vista** restaurant (dinner) on your left, the **Mountain House** restaurant (dinner) on your right. This last is at the corner of Henrik Ibsen Road, and what cultured type came up with that literary resource I know not.

9 Miles A small crossroads, with Kings Mountain Road going down to the east, Tunitas Creek Road going to the west, which is a good ride in itself. KEEP STRAIGHT.

15 Miles The road descends into a wide open area, and crossroads with CA 84 going east-west to the CA 35 north-south, called **Sky Londa.** And the infamous Alice's Restaurant.

22 Miles Another intersection, with Alpine Road dropping off to the right, Page Mill Road down to the left. Alpine will run you back down to **La Honda,** so do not be afraid to explore.

28 Miles STOP sign—TURN RIGHT at the junction with CA 9 at the **Saratoga Gap,** 2,634 feet above the Pacific Ocean, or San Francisco Bay, as the case may be. Skyline Boulevard continues straight, turning very narrow and twisty, while to the left Congress Springs Road goes down to the town of Saratoga; you want to go right on CA 9, down toward Boulder and Santa Cruz.

34 Miles STAY LEFT at **Waterman Gap,** where CA 236 goes off to the right, ending up in the same place as CA 9—Boulder Creek.

Detour
CA 236 is a beautiful if slowish ride, 17 winding miles through the **Big Basin Redwoods State Park,** California's first state park; take it if you want to loiter a bit. And loitering is good, despite what the forces of law and order are apt to say when you do it on Main Street.

But we'll stick on CA 9, heading south along the **San Lorenzo River.** ■

42 Miles Enter **Boulder Creek.**

44 Miles The **Brookdale Lodge** is on your right, and I recommend a stay there (831-338-6433). It's old, it's nice, it's recently refurbished, and a real live brook runs through the dining room; you can't beat that with a redwood tree. This area was all timbered in the 1870s and 1880s, and by the turn of the last century the railroad was being turned to tourist purposes. The lodge was originally built in the 1920s, and has undergone a lot of adjustments since then, but it is reputed to have ghosts.

Hemp History

Many inhabitants of the Santa Cruz Mountains are in the forefront of environmentally correct thinking, and farming. And one of the more profitable crops is hemp. Back in 1937 the passage of the **Marijuana Tax Act** made criminals of anyone growing hemp. However, hemp is a legitimate crop, and has very strong fibers, making it an excellent material for knapsacks and rope and thousands of other products.

Did you ever see an old movie about life at sea on a sailing ship, and some sailor cuts off the end of a bit of rope and stuffs it in his pipe? That's hemp.

An outfit called **Californians for Industrial Renewal** tried to put an initiative on the state ballot in 1998, saying that hemp plants with less than 1 percent THC content (the stuff that gets you stoned) could be legally cultivated. Didn't happen.   ■

46 Miles   Enter **Ben Lomond.** You see **Henfling's Firehouse Tavern** (831-338-8811) on your left; if you reach the TRAFFIC LIGHT you've gone 100 feet too far. Henfling's, a rowdy bar and grill, usually has motorcycles in front on a weekend; it opens at 9:30 on Sunday mornings, for those who like to pray over a pint of **Boulder Creek Brewing Company's** best and a plate of ham and eggs, 11 o'clock the rest of the week.

Go through the traffic light, heading down CA 9.

50 Miles   STOP light—TURN RIGHT, going up Felton Empire Road.

At this light you are in the middle of **Felton,** home of the **Roaring Camp Railway;** if you take a left at the light you will find the entrance to the railroad yards a half-mile up the road. Where, for a reasonable sum of money, you can chuff along on behind a steam engine. You can even take it all the way down to the **Santa Cruz boardwalk,** which is probably the best way to get to that benighted spot.

Felton Empire Road takes you uphill, on narrowing asphalt.

54 Miles   STOP sign—GO STRAIGHT, as Felton Empire meets **Empire Grade;** GO STRAIGHT, Felton Empire turning into **Ice Cream Grade.** No one I spoke with claims any knowledge of how that name got attached.

56 Miles   STOP sign—TURN LEFT onto Pine Flat Road.

58 Miles   KEEPING STRAIGHT, Pine Flat becomes Bonny Doon Road.

62 Miles   STOP sign—TURN RIGHT at intersection with CA 1; you are going north up the coast, past the remains of Davenport on **San Vicente Creek,** with a store and cafe.

63 Miles **Davenport** is a small community with store and eateries, and the 1915 St. Vincent de Paul church set back off the road. It was founded in 1867 by a shore-whaler named **John Davenport**, who set up a business going out and harpooning grey whales as they migrated from Alaska to Baja. The whaling is long done, but a big cement plant is just up the road, and is the main employer in town; a live railroad is still in occasional use to service the plant.

67 Miles CA 1 goes straight, Swanton Road angles off to the right.

Detour
The old inland road is a tad longer than the newer CA 1, as Swanton Road runs up **Scott Creek,** past what passes for the town of **Swanton,** over the ridge and drop back toward the sea, connecting with CA 1 after five miles. It's fun, and a pleasant respite from all those waves.   ∎

71 Miles Northern end of Swanton Road.

76 Miles Just after passing into **San Mateo County,** the 400-acre **Coastways Ranch** is on your right; nice place to live. And to sell produce. Between the road and the sea is the **Ano Nuevo State Reserve,** which is the best place to see what the coastline looked like before the road and the automobile arrived.

79 Miles CA 1 continues straight, Gazos Creek Road angles off to the right, opposite the coastal access.

Alternate Route
Onto Gazos Creek Road. You wind in, the road's name mysteriously changing to Cloverdale after two miles, past **Butano State Park,** and then down into the **Pescadero Valley.** TURN LEFT at the STOP sign to get into Pescadero proper.   ∎

82 Miles Pass **Pigeon Point Lighthouse & Youth Hostel**; it's worth getting a hostel membership just to stay there, and do not forget to make a reservation (650-879-0633).

88 Miles TURN RIGHT at the hand-painted PESCADERO sign, onto Pescadero Road.

90 Miles The town of **Pescadero,** where a flashing overhead light tells you that you are at the intersection with Stagecoach Road, and downtown Pescadero. A very worthwhile stop is at **Duarte's** (pronounced do-arts, with a silent "e") for excellent food since 1894, be it fried calamari, menudo, or a steak; they have everything from crab cioppino to PB&J sandwiches (650-879-0464). Definitely recommended, and you can eat in the bar as well. Just a hundred yards up from Duarte's, on the other side of the road, you can buy artichoke bread at the **Country Bakery & Grocery.**

Staying on Pescadero Road you are heading east into the Santa Cruz Mountains.

101 Miles   KEEP LEFT at the intersection, with Alpine Road going off to the right.

102 Miles   STOP sign—TURN LEFT onto La Honda Road and head downhill.

If you TURN RIGHT at the STOP sign onto La Honda Road and go up a few hundred yards, into the center of the village of La Honda, on your right is **Apple Jack's Inn** (circa 1879), a weekend hangout for the biker crowd (650-747-0331). Good sarsaparilla. Continue on another hundred yards to a little shopping center on the left side of the road, you will find the **Merry Prankster** (650-747-0660), where the Dainese crowd tends to loiter on weekends, comparing carbon-fiber license-plate holders.

109 Miles   La Honda Road has descended 400 feet in the last few miles, and you are in **San Gregorio.** In 1880 the town had two churches, a school, a hotel, and a saloon. All it has now is the **San Gregorio General Store,** on your right, with a pleasantly eclectic collection of "stuff" for sale.

110 Miles   STOP sign—TURN RIGHT onto CA 1.

117 Miles   Tunitas Creek Road goes off to the right, if you wish to get back to Skyline Boulevard, it is a great, twisting, tree-shaded nine miles, and a great way to get back up on Skyline. But we will continue along CA 1 just to give a couple of other choices.

After a few miles you begin to enter **Half Moon Bay,** a fishing village gone tourist and going residential.

125 Miles   You are in the middle of **Half Moon Bay.**

Alternate Route

TURN RIGHT onto CA 92; this will take you back over the ridge to connect with the crowded bay side of the peninsula and I-280. However, it tends to be a heavily trafficked road, with commuters on the weekdays, tourists on the weekends. If you choose to go this way, after five miles you pass the intersection with Skyline Boulevard/CA 35, that you were at 117 miles ago, and two miles further along you are back at I-280.

■

That's Pigeon Point Lighthouse & Youth Hostel, along CA 1, a very nice place to spend the night.

A better suggestion is to STAY STRAIGHT, going north, on CA 1.

130 Miles You go past **Princeton** and the Half Moon Bay airport, and in two more miles see the **Point Montara Lighthouse & Youth Hostel**. . . fully booked most every weekend, so call for reservations (650-728-7177).

135 Miles Past the **Devil's Slide,** which is where the road is often blocked during winter rains, as it is cut into the ocean side of **Mount Montara** that runs 1,900 feet above sea level. CalTrans continues to do battle with Mother Nature on this steep section, and the lady always wins. Keep this in mind when you are coming through here on a stormy day, 500 feet above the crashing waves.

137 Miles Drop down sharply to **Pedro Valley** and **Rockaway Beach** and a bit of congestion. A couple of miles further on CA 1 becomes a freeway as it enters **Pacifica,** a suburb of San Francisco with some 50,000 residents.

144 Miles Now you merge with I-280, heading north into **San Francisco.** You are on your own.

Trip 10 Mt. Hamilton

Distance *94 miles from getting off of I-880 to getting on US 101*
Highlights *You will be riding through some unexpected wilderness at the southeast end of the Bay.*

If you found I-280 for the Alice's Restaurant loop, you can find it again for this one. Go south of the CA 92/35 exit about nine miles, and take CA 84 going east (if you go west you get back to Sky Londa and Alice's), heading toward Redwood City and US 101. Follow 84 south with US 101 for two miles, then exit on CA 84, always east, going for the Dumbarton Bridge and Fremont.

Cross the south end of the Bay on Dumbarton (no toll in this direction), and keep on CA 84 as it slides into I-880 going south.

That is the Lick Observatory atop Mt. Hamilton.

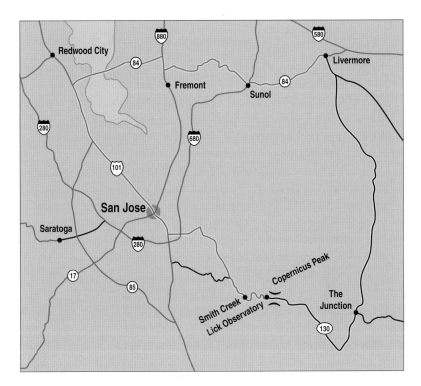

0 Miles   EXIT I-880, following signs for CA 84 to Fremont and Livermore.

1 Mile   TURN RIGHT onto Fremont Blvd., following CA 84.

1+ Miles   TURN LEFT onto Peralta Blvd., following CA 84.

4 Miles   TURN LEFT onto Mission Blvd., following CA 84.

4+ Miles   TURN RIGHT at traffic light, following CA 84, onto Niles Canyon Road. If you want a sugar and fat rush, **Niles Doughnuts** on the corner will provide it.

Finally you are breaking loose of the megalopolis that is the Bay Area and getting into a bit of the unbuilt-up. CA 84 winds up along **Alameda Creek**, along with an old railroad, so various bridges are crossing time and again as this two-lane road goes east.

9 Miles   The community of **Sunol** is off to your left, a short loop off of CA 84; not much there but the **Sunol Lounge** on Main Street, a motorcyclists' hang-out on weekends, and the **Old Towne House Cafe** (925-862-2374) by the railroad tracks.

9+ Miles   STOP sign—TURN RIGHT at **Sunol Corners**; a Greek-looking temple is off to your right, some sort of self-congratulatory symbol built by the water department to celebrate the bringing of water from the **Hetch Hetchy Reservoir** in the Sierra Nevadas to this bit of the world.

Overpopulation

If you are doing this at rush hour, you will appreciate how many people now live well beyond the 80 towns and cities that make up the **Association of Bay Area Governments,** which include 5.5 million inhabitants, as a steady stream of cars are constantly moving back and forth. Around 1990 the Bay communities more or less put a moratorium on building new housing—but people were still flocking to the area for high-paid, high-tech jobs. So developers went to communities outside the Bay area, like **Livermore,** and began putting up houses as quick as they could drive nails, but the highway arteries did not follow suit. Now many previously lightly trafficked semi-rural roads are packed with cars. One solution has been the establishment of a commuter train running through **Niles Canyon** from Livermore to San Jose—but that is a bandaid on a gaping chest wound.   ■

10 Miles   GO UNDER I-680 and immediately curve 270 degrees to the right to get on the Interstate, going north, and you stay on less than a quarter of a mile.

10+ Miles   GET OFF I-680 at first exit, marked CA 84, LIVERMORE. You are on Vallecitos Road, going along the **Vallecito Valley** past the **Vallecitos Nuclear Center;** do not forget that scientists have been doing lots of atomic research in Livermore these past 50 years. It is a nice road rolling through the hills, but was a lot less crowded ten years ago.

20 Miles   You are in downtown **Livermore,** going east on 1st Street. Ahead you see a tall flagpole, almost as though it is in the center of the street.

20+ Miles   TURN RIGHT at the flagpole; you see 1st Street curving off to the left; you want to go right on South Livermore Avenue, also known as County Road J2, though there is no indication of that. Best to gas up along here, as there is nothing for the next 70 miles. You will be clearing town in just a mile or two.

23 Miles   TURN RIGHT onto Mines Road, just as you pass the **Concannon Vineyards;** the sign indicating Mines also reads: Del Valle Regional Park. Old Jimmy Concannon began his vineyard here back in 1883, and established the fact that good wine grapes could be grown in California.

Now you are getting into the back of beyond. And you are only some 20 crow-flying miles from the Bay area.

27 Miles   TURN LEFT, staying on Mines Road, marked for MT. HAMIL-
TON, while Del Valle Road goes to the park. Mines Road will be following
the **Arroyo Mocho** for the next 20-some miles.

35 Miles   A cautious county bureaucrat has mandated a sign saying ONE
LANE ROAD, which means that rather than have a yellow line down the
middle, it has a white line down each edge. The road is a reasonably good
road, not a real one-laner at all, and since you are seeing one vehicle every
five minutes or so, you are not worried about width. You cross from
Alameda in **Santa Clara County.**

52 Miles   Arrive in the **San Antonio Valley,** with several scattered houses,
a sign outside a small trailer reading RUTHIE'S MALL (makes you want to go
see what Ruthie's Mall is all about, doesn't it?), the Sweetwater forest-service
fire station on your right, **The Junction Cafe** (925-897-3148) on your
left—which should be open by 11 a.m. every day except Wednesday. Mines
Road ends, turning into San Antonio Valley Road, and Del Puerto Road
goes off to the east, the sign reading: PATTERSON 31.

GO STRAIGHT, with a small notice that San Antonio Valley Road is
officially called County Road West 130—with SAN JOSE 38.

Great wilderness out here, and just a very few ranches hidden off in the
valleys. Cross **San Antonio Creek,** make a sharp turn to the right and go up
the **Arroyo Bayo,** and soon start a serious climb up to 4,200 feet, in the
Diablo Range of mountains, with great views looking down into the valleys
below.

71 Miles   A complex of observatory buildings appear, with **Copernicus
Peak** (4,373 feet) on the north side of the road, **Lick Observatory** south of
the road on top of **Mt. Hamilton** (4,209 feet).

This place was built in the 1880s, as part of the **University of California,**
long before the Bay area grew up and light pollution intruded. But it is still
an active place with lots of astronomy students making use of all the telescopes, including the 120-incher installed in 1959.

CA 130, as opposed to County Road 130, starts from here and heads
downhill in a precipitous fashion.

78 Miles   Cross over **Smith Creek,** with a fire station on your left, and enter **Joseph Grant County Park.**

82 Miles   Quimby Road goes off to the left, a short-cut down to south San
Jose.

90 Miles   STOP sign—TURN LEFT onto Alum Rock Avenue.

93 Miles   ACCESS US 101 going north; San Francisco is just 50 miles
away.

Trip 11   Up The Coast & Back Over Mt. Tamalpais

Distance   *83 miles*

Highlights   *Much of this will be covered in the beginning of the next chapter, the North Coast, which deals with CA 1 from the Golden Gate Bridge to the Lost Coast.*

First off, you have to get to the Golden Gate Bridge. Find US 101 or CA 1 going north through the city, and they will take you right there. Or just look for the bridge towers, if the day is reasonably clear.

The south end of the bridge has a Vista Point on the east side, which means the access is off 101 going north. From the Vista Point you can either get back on US 101 North, or go down to the Marina section of San Francisco, or take a subway passage under 101 that will put you on US 101 South. Good view of foggy towers on most days, though if the weather is clear, the place certainly offers a Kodak Moment (see Golden Gate Bridge sidebar).

The Golden Gate Bridge

The idea of a suspension bridge across the entrance to San Francisco Bay first came around in the 1870s, when such technology was still in its infancy, and getting to San Francisco from the north meant a rough ferry ride. Bad weather could ground the whole operation, and if you were prone to seasickness, it was especially unpleasant. Around 1918 the notion of bridging that gap called the Golden Gate (think of the setting sun) began to be taken seriously, and 15 years later construction began.

The two towers stretch 760 feet above the water—with 420 feet between them, and the cables, moored in solid rock and concrete at each end of the bridge, are 7,650 feet long. The roadway is some 260 feet above the water, high enough to let the biggest ships pass beneath. The bridge was opened in April, 1937.

Today more than 30,000 vehicles use the bridge on a daily basis, and tolls pay for its maintenance. To simplify matters and expedite the flow of traffic, the toll is charged only when going south ($3 for motorcycles, and cars, which is grossly unfair, though during rush hours motorcycles are waved through). That adds up to roughly $90,000 a day; not bad. ∎

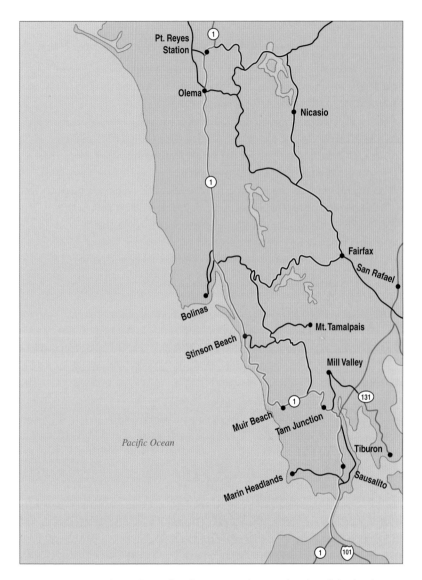

0 Miles   Begin the mileage for this trip at the south side of the bridge, at the non-functioning toll booths. Cross over the bridge, and there is the North Vista Point, again on the east side of the road. If it is a clear day you will have a great view of San Francisco . . . but there are not many of those kind of days.

2 Miles   Just up from the northside Vista Point is the Alexander Avenue exit from 101, which will run you down to **Sausalito.**

Marin Headlands

If you have an extra hour take the Alexander Avenue exit but do not go to Sausalito. Instead, go left through the underpass, marked SAN FRANCISCO US 101 SOUTH, emerge on the west side, hang a right (this will all be clear as you do it) at the brown and white sign reading MARIN HEADLANDS, part of the **Golden Gate National Recreation Area (GGNRA);** 550-0560 for the ranger station and information. The trip out to the headlands on Conzelman Road is about five miles, and you won't get lost; you can loop back to Alexander Avenue on Bunker Road, which has a long tunnel. If the day is clear, it will be a delight. The whole area was part of the defense complex protecting the entry to **San Francisco Bay** from the Spanish-American War to World War II. Great views, and you can clamber all over the old gun positions. ■

Back on US 101, now officially called The Redwood Highway, you go through the **Rainbow Tunnel,** and then start down the hill.

6 Miles   Take the freeway exit that reads CA 1/STINSON BEACH, going back under 101 and heading toward **Mount Tamalpais Junction.**

6+ Miles   STOP light—TURN LEFT, onto the road marked STINSON BEACH. This is **Tam Junction,** and MILL VALLEY is to the right. An ARCO gas station on the corner, run by genial, turbaned Sikhs, is a well-known Sunday meeting spot for Bay Area motorcyclists for nearly 50 years.

9 Miles   STAY LEFT on CA 1 at the fork in the road, which will occur after several miles of climbing and arriving at a slight rise. The road going up and to the right, the **Panoramic Highway,** goes to Mt. Tam and on to Stinson Beach; you want the one to the left, starting a steepish, twisting, winding descent down to the shore. This is not for the agoraphobic nor those suffering vertigo, and on the Sunday morning run this is considered the most hazardous stretch. This byway did originate as a stage road back around 1870, and I can imagine many a passenger preferring to walk.

13 Miles   On the corner, at the left turn to **Muir Beach,** sits the **Pelican Inn,** a romantic retreat for those taking a short trip from the city. It does the whole English bit, with grassy lawn, rose bushes, the building with beams and mullioned windows, Guinness and Watney's on tap, all pleasantly camp. With only seven rooms, it is a bit selective (415-383-6000); the management does include a decanter of sherry and a big breakfast with the price of a room.

14 Miles   You will pass the **Muir Beach Overlook,** off to the left. And CA 1 continues along a spectacular cliffside route. Screw up on a corner along here . . . you do not want to think about it. Next you will see **Bolinas Lagoon,** and the long spit of land that runs out from Stinson Beach, which is where you would want to have a house if you lived in that part of the world.

18 Miles   Pass the north end of Panoramic Highway and enter Stinson Beach, founded by one Nathan Stinson in 1880 as a resort where the city folk could refresh themselves. In "downtown" Stinson the **Sand Dollar Restaurant** (415-868-0434) and **Stinson Beach Grill** (415-868-2002) sit on opposite sides of CA 1; the latter offers a dozen tasty "Cajun" pan-fried oysters for $17.25. On a Sunday morning, early, there is often a group of motorcyclists who come in from Tam Junction early and meet at the **Parkside Cafe,** which is to the left a hundred yards at the only STOP sign in town.

Leaving Stinson Beach the road weaves along the edge of the **Bolinas Lagoon,** flat and fast, occasionally luring an overly exuberant rider who ends up in the drink.

The Sunday Morning Run

If you happen to be at Tam Junction at 7:45 on a Sunday morning, you may see anywhere from ten (on a rainy day) to 100 (sunny) or more motorcycles at the ARCO; this is the start of the infamous weekly run, one of America's longer-lived and firmly established unofficial motorcycle events, going on since the 1950s. The bikes gather here, and then at eight o'clock head off north along CA 1 to Point Reyes Station. If you wish to partake, feel free, but I very much recommend hanging back toward the rear of the pack. The guys up front go really, really fast, and they know the road as well as they know the number of their bail bondsman.

The more sensible riders stay at the rear, and are out to enjoy the ride and the camaraderie, and not risk life, limb, and losing the old driver's license.

Over the years there have been a small number of bad accidents, but that has not diminished the pleasure of the run. Occasionally the forces of law and order will descend with helicopters and patrol cars to arrest a bunch of people for speeding, at which point all the lawyers along on the ride will volunteer their services, and the state gets to spend a lot of money for little result.

Should you be in the area on a Sunday morning, I do recommend this little fraternal adventure.   ■

22+ Miles At the north end of the lagoon will be a small crossroads, hardly marked at all; the road to the left goes to Bolinas, the road to the right goes to Fairfax on the old, little-used Fairfax-Bolinas Road (you will be in Fairfax in another 26 miles, getting on the east end of that road). The privacy-loving inhabitants of Bolinas are noted for destroying any sign on CA 1 that indicates the town's whereabouts, and this has actually had the precise opposite effect, as San Franciscans think it is a lark to go out and visit this place that the inhabitants do not want visited.

Detour
Bolinas

Do go out to **Bolinas,** a little throwback to the Sixties. Go up the road a mile, take a left at the STOP sign, and soon you will be in the town. The Bolinians love where they live, and seem to hate that strangers come to enjoy their little town, even though places like **The Shop Cafe** and **Smiley's Schooner Saloon & Hotel** (Est. 1851) make their living off of visitors. If you are interested in deceased literary types, this is the town where author Richard Brautigan did himself in in his own house, and his body was not found for a week.

When leaving Bolinas, retrace some of your steps, but there is no need to make a right and retrace your entire route, as you can GO STRAIGHT along Horseshoe Hill Road to reconnect with CA 1. Take care as you speed along under the imported Eucalyptus trees; these quick-growing rascals come from Australia, and tend to leave slippery bark on the road in shedding season. Note that you are running right along the **San Andreas Fault Line** as it runs between Bolinas Lagoon and Tomales Bay.

■

32 Miles Enter **Olema,** with several Hippie-Era merchants surviving quite well. The **General Store,** on the right, has excellent spinach and feta stuffed bread. At the flashing red light (which means STOP) the Sir Francis Drake Boulevard will go off to the right, heading southeast to Fairfax, San Anselmo and US 101. This is a major access road to **Point Reyes National Seashore,** and it can get downright crowded on Sunday afternoon. At the intersection is the **Olema Farmhouse Restaurant,** open for lunch and dinner, breakfast on the weekends, and next door is the **Point Reyes Seashore Lodge** (415-663-9000) which has rates starting at $85 plus 10 percent (off-season, weekday, creek view), going up to over $200).

34 Miles Continuing from Olema on CA 1 you will see the sign indicat-

Point Reyes National Seashore

This national seashore is 70,000 acres of pretty nice real estate, and developers would dearly, dearly love to get their greedy hands on just a little bit of it. If the San Andreas were to creak a little, this could be one fine island. **TURN LEFT** off CA 1 (now Sir Francis Drake Blvd.) just after the blinking light in Olema, onto Bear Valley Road, which runs by the **Bear Valley Visitor Center,** and onto the road (Drake Boulevard again) to **Inverness,** a small town on Tomales Bay.

There are several places to stay, a couple of restaurants, but the main glory of Point Reyes National Seashore is out on the beaches. Sixteen miles beyond Inverness the road ends at **Point Reyes Lighthouse,** and it is a beaut ride. On the way you will pass the turn to **Drake's Beach,** and supposedly Sir Frank careened his ship in the vicinity in 1579, which means he ran it on the beach at high tide so the sailors could clean the bottom. Whether or not this was the place remains open to debate—but it makes a good story.   ■

ing Sir Francis Drake Boulevard going left to Point Reyes National Seashore, while you GO STRAIGHT, crossing Lagunita Creek.

34+ Miles When you are in downtown **Point Reyes Station,** you will see **The Station House Cafe** on your right. Yes, a railroad, the **North Pacific RR,** did run between here and Sausalito from 1874 to about 1935. On a Sunday morning the cafe is crowded with leathered motorcyclists who have just raced these last 29 miles from Tam Junction at speeds most motorists would consider unconscionable. Sensible riders who want to avoid the crowd will go up to the end of Main Street, where CA 1 turns right on Fourth Street, and look left to the **Pine Cone Diner.**

Point Reyes Station is the apex of this loop, and from here you have a variety of ways to get back to San Francisco. Including retracing these previous 34 miles, which is not a bad idea. However, given my druthers I would go north out of town half a mile, and then head back toward SF on a different route, which will go over Mt. Tamalpais.

35 Miles TURN RIGHT on Petaluma-Point Reyes Road.

41 Miles TURN RIGHT on Nicasio Valley Road.

48 Miles STOP sign—TURN LEFT onto Sir Francis Drake Boulevard.

53 Miles TRAFFIC LIGHT in downtown **Fairfax;** TURN RIGHT onto a commercial frontage road, leading onto the Fairfax-Bolinas Road; this becomes a nicely twisty road as it disappears into the Marin Water District watershed.

This twice-lifesize truck sits outside the Calistoga water bottling plant.

61 Miles Cross **Alpine Dam,** and the road will start to climb steeply.
63 Miles At the crest TURN LEFT onto West Ridgecrest Boulevard, which leads to Mt. Tam. If you continue straight on the Bolinas-Fairfax Road you will end up at the Bolinas/CA 1 junction that you passed at Mile 22+.
67 Miles GO RIGHT at Rock Spring Junction, which is a huge parking area.
69 Miles STOP sign—TURN LEFT onto **Panoramic Highway.**
74 Miles STOP sign—TURN LEFT onto CA 1.

To the Top of Mt. Tamalpais

If the day is clear (Ha ha!) you should definitely go to the top of Mt. Tam, which has unparalleled views of the San Francisco Bay. At the **Rock Spring Junction** take a left onto East Ridgecrest Boulevard and that will take you to the top of Mt. Tam in three miles. ■

Napa Valley

Napa Valley and the surrounding area is undoubtedly the most romanticized region of California, and it covers the narrow valley that was formed by the **Napa River** eons ago. In 1850 Napa became a California county, and it was a productive agricultural area until the wine-making industry took off some 30 years ago. Now over 200 wineries are in the valley, along with many good restaurants and a dozen hot springs.

The riding opportunities are not all that great, as the roads tend to be narrow, straight, and crowded, very crowded. With diligent enforcement of the law. However, since many readers may want to go see this place for themselves, here are a few hints.

The heart of the valley is only 75 miles from San Francisco, and you could do a long day trip, but I think you would have much more fun if you spent a night in the town of **Calistoga.** The place is small enough to be enjoyable on foot, has good food and places to stay. And has many hot springs, thanks to the extinct (?!) volcano, **Mt. St. Helens,** just to the north.

The oldest place in town for a room and a soak is **Indian Springs,** 1712 Lincoln Avenue (707-492-4213), which opened up a thermal pool in 1862, probably to give the miners in the area a place to get clean. Today it is family owned, rather than by some anonymous corporation, and offers both bungalows and regular rooms for sleeping, a big pool for swimming, and mud baths a specialty.

For food I gravitate to the **Calistoga Inn,** 1250 Lincoln Avenue (707-942-4101), which has a patio right next to the Napa River (more like a stream, most of the time), where the food is excellent, and, for a break from the incessant wine-drinking, they have a commendable brewery on the premises.

The activity in the area mostly revolves around tasting wine, buying wine, drinking wine. The first vineyard was planted back in the 1860s, and for the next hundred years wine was made and consumed, but no big deal. Until 1976, when at a blind tasting at a prestigious wine competition in Paris, Napa wines won first place in both reds and whites. The boom began, and now anybody who has a half acre of land in the valley has his own label.

I like wine, dry reds being my preference, but I certainly do not suffer a sophisticated palate. If somebody wants to spring for a $100 bottle, that's fine, and I will enjoy it. But if I'm spending my own money . . . much less. **The Wine Garage** in Calistoga has some 250 different wines in stock, and there will be something there to suit both taste and wallet.

A bit of history has been preserved in the valley, and one of the best places is the old **Bale Grist Mill State Historic Park,** about five miles south of Calistoga on CA 29/128 in the **Bothe-Napa State Park.** The mill was built by Mr. Bale in 1846, when the place had newly become American, with mill-stones imported from France, and a huge "overshot" wooden water wheel that powered the place. Impressive.

For riding purposes, on the west side of the Napa River is CA 29/128, and on the east, the **Silverado Trail.** The Silverado is the better, less-trafficked of the two, and is the start of a nice loop, which I'll just rough in. From Calistoga go south nine miles on Silverado, at the intersection with CA 128 go east (left) for 12 miles, then north 13 miles on Berryessa-Knoxville Road, which brings you alongside **Lake Berryessa.** At the north end of the lake TURN LEFT on Pope Canyon Road, which after 11 miles runs into the garage, general store, and post office that is the community of **Pope Valley.** From there you can take the short way back to Calistoga via Howell Mountain Road, or the longer run via Pope Valley Road and **Middletown.**

Chamber of Commerce Numbers

Calistoga: 866-306-5588, www.calistogachamber.com
Napa: 707-226-7455, www.napachamber.org   ■

77 Miles Traffic light—TURN RIGHT at **Mt. Tam Junction.**
83 Miles Arrive back at the **Golden Gate Bridge.**

Napa Valley vineyards are nothing if not neat—all the better to attract the tourists.

The water-powered Bale Grist Mill, originally built in 1848, sits along Mill Creek in Napa Valley.

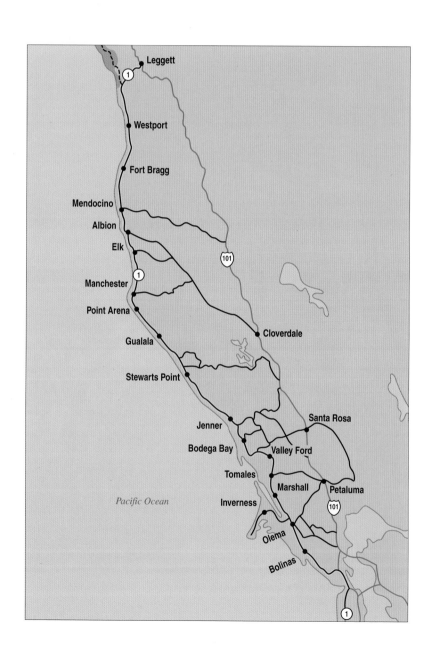

North Coast

From the Golden Gate to the Lost Coast, this is a straight stretch of winding road, CA 1, running for 207 miles up the California coast through Marin, Sonoma, and Mendocino counties. At the end you can either continue north to Humboldt county and Eureka (Chapter 8), or, if you have become obsessed with looping, once you hit the end of CA 1 at Leggett you can ride south on US 101 and be back in San Francisco in less than four hours.

This coast road is one of the great rides in California, if not the world. I have thrown in a number of little detours and alternatives and miniature loops, and I truly hope that most of you rider/readers will not stick just to CA 1. The ocean is backed by the Coastal Range of low mountains, and to dash in and out of these mountain valleys is downright good fun, good riding.

The first part of the chapter is a repetition of the first 35 miles of Trip 12, so I will only reiterate the main points.

You can do the whole stretch from the Golden Gate Bridge to Leggett in one long day, but that is about as bright as buying a $150 bottle of Johnny Walker Blue Label and mixing it with Coke. Savor this ride.

Trip 12   A Linear Route up the Coast

Distance *207 miles*

0 Miles Begin at the south side of the **Golden Gate Bridge,** at the non-functioning toll booths, and head north on CA 1/US 101.

6 Miles Take the freeway exit that reads CA 1, STINSON BEACH, which will go back under 101 and wind around to Mt. Tamalpais Junction.

6+ Miles **Tam Junction** is a STOP light, where you will TURN LEFT onto the road marked STINSON BEACH.

9 Miles STAY LEFT on CA 1 at the fork in the road.

32 Miles Enter Olema, where the flashing red light indicates you should stop, and then CONTINUE STRAIGHT.

34+ Miles Arrive in downtown **Point Reyes Station.**

35 Miles The Petaluma-Point Reyes Road goes off to the east, CA 1 goes straight. The next dozen miles are splendid, rolling along beside **Tomales Bay,** curving, bending, magnificent views, idyllic farms (at least to the city boy who doesn't understand the work involved), riding at its best.

Almost makes you want to move to Mendocino and open up a B&B.

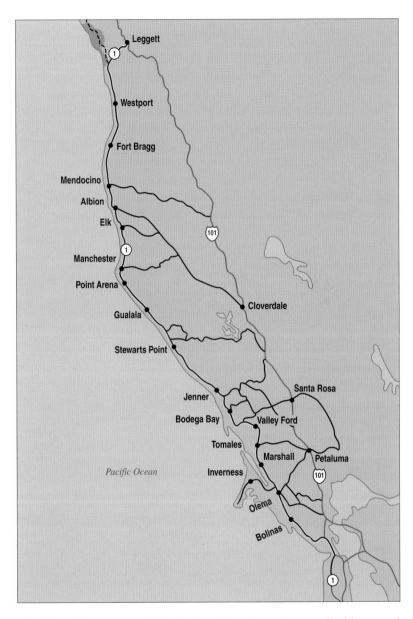

44 Miles The town of **Marshall,** with a few decaying buildings and boarded up businesses on the narrow bit of land between the road and the bay. However, if you are there on a weekend, a lot of cars are parked in front of **Tony's Seafood** (415-663-1107), open noon to nine Friday through Sunday—oysters a specialty.

Bodega Bay

It is mainly a tourist town now, with commercial fishing way back in second place on the economic ladder. The newer, more expensive lodgings are on the south side of town; the first place you pass is the **Bodega Bay Lodge** (707-875-3525, 800-368-2468 x 5), its 80 rooms showing upper middle-class aspirations; it does have a good restaurant. Up CA 1 a mile, a tourist bureau/CoC on your right, open on weekends, has piles of folders on places to stay (800-905-9050). Down on the water at the Lucas Wharf is the **Lucas Restaurant** (707-875-3522), and a fish market, and just up the road is **The Tides Wharf & Restaurant** (707-875-3652), with oysters and eggs for breakfast. Cheaper digs can be found in town, notably at one of the older places, now with the upgraded name of **Bodega Harbor Inn,** which has 14 conventional motel rooms (707-875-3594), plus a number of house rentals available.

Do go to the harbor, the East Shore Road down to the waterfront being at the north part of town, and well-marked; as you get down to the bottom you will see the **Sandpiper Restaurant** (707-875-2278), the place for breakfast. There is a good deal of commercial fishing still done out of **Bodega Harbor,** thanks to the constant efforts of the U.S. Army Corps of Engineers to keep the place dredged. Take the West Shore Road out to **Bodega Head,** which skirts the shore and several marinas. Walk out on the head and ponder the fact that a nuclear power plant was almost built here back in the Sixties; construction had actually started when more rational people decided it was not such a good idea after all, as it sits right on the **San Andreas Fault.** You can look across the narrow channel to the slender **Doran Spit,** which protects the southern approach to the harbor.   ■

Lots of oysters for sale along Tomales Bay, and commercial oyster farming is big business. All this began over 100 years ago using oysters shipped in from Chesapeake Bay, and it now makes a number of oyster farmers quite wealthy.

After another three or four miles the road begins to angle away from the bay, going along **Keyes Creek,** past the remnants of the old bridge, then crossing over the creek.

51 Miles STAY LEFT on CA 1 as the Tomales-Petaluma Road goes off to the right. Arriving in the village of **Tomales,** with the **William Tell House**

Restaurant (707-878-2403) offering prime rib and steaks. And the **Tomales Bakery** with baked goods. North of Tomales it is ranching country.

56 Miles   STAY LEFT on CA 1 after crossing the **Americano Creek**, entering **Sonoma County**, with the Petaluma-Valley Ford Road going to the right.

57+ Miles   The Village of **Valley Ford**, made momentarily famous in 1976 when a fellow named Christo, an artist who thinks big, created a white cloth fence that ran for 22 miles across the Sonoma countryside, through Valley Ford, and on to the sea. And then he took it down, all 22 miles of it; transient art. **Dinucci's Restaurant** (707-876-3260) serves up pasta and all the Italian trimmings; must be a lot of Italian influence on the coast. If you like historical sleeping, stay at the **Valley Ford Hotel**, dating from the Civil War era, which has seven rooms (707-876-3600, 800-696-6679) and a Mexican-flavored restaurant.

61 Miles   The **Bodega Highway** goes off from CA 1 to the right, and the sign reads BODEGA 1.

Detour
To Bodega and Occidental

This is the inland **Bodega,** not to be confused with Bodega Bay, and is worth the detour, taking you to a pleasantly small collection of Victorian buildings, and places to eat, sleep, and spend your money.

Continue past Bodega on the Bodega Highway for four miles, crossing over **Salmon Creek,** until you see the turn to the left for the **Bohemian Highway** and Occidental. This continues up the Salmon Valley for three miles, and you come up a hill and into **Occidental,** a modestly guised old-world resort.

The town is basically four blocks, with a STOP sign in the middle. The 1879 **Union Hotel & Cafe** (707-874-3555) sits to the east side of the street, though it is a hotel in name only—no rooms. **Howard's Station Cafe** (707-874-2838) is in the next block, the place for breakfast. On the opposite side of the road is **Negri's Occidental Lodge** (707-874-3623) and Italian restaurant.

To get back to the coast, you definitely must take Coleman Valley Road, which starts at that aforementioned STOP sign, heading west. After a mile and a half the road turns LEFT, and then in a hundred feet goes RIGHT; if you go straight, that is Joy Road, which will run you back down to Bodega Highway. Take the right, where the sign reads: NARROW WINDING ROAD NEXT 8 MILES. It is a beaut, through ranching country, until suddenly the sea appears in the distance. Stunning sight. And then a steep descent to a STOP sign that meets with CA 1 about four miles north of Bodega Bay. Coleman Valley Road is one of the more scenic stretches of asphalt on this planet. ■

62 Miles   Back on CA 1, if the road is packed with Winnebagoes and the like, and you wish to avoid the hurly-burly and RVs of Bodega Bay, TURN RIGHT on Bay Hill Road, a small byway which bypasses BB entirely and puts you back on CA 1 just north of town. But if you have not seen Bodega Bay, stick to CA 1.

66 Miles   **Bodega Bay** in all its charm.

Leaving Bodega Bay, heading north, you ride past the northern end of Bay Hill Road, and now the road is going along the bluffs. It is a beautiful ride, which is why you see so many vacation houses on the inland side of the highway. And they all seem rather low and designed to hunker down when the winter storms come in. Practically the whole of this stretch of coast is part of the California State Park system, so it remains well-protected.

70 Miles   Pass Coleman Valley Road to your right. If you did not do the **Occidental** detour, it is worth your while to ride two miles up the road, turn around, and come back down, because the view is outstanding as you descend to the sea. Or ride up and have a view, then continue on Coleman all the way into Occidental, take a left onto the **Bohemian Highway,** seven miles downhill to Monte Rio and the bridge over the **Russian River,** then left on CA 116 and eight miles back to the coast.

Lots of options are available along the North Coast, and the idea is *not to rush.*

75 Miles   After passing the entrance to **Goat Rock Beach** the road curves right and drops down to **Bridge Haven** on the Russian River (with **Sizzling Tandoori Restaurant** (707-865-0625 and **Bridge Haven Campground**), then crosses over the river on the 1931 bridge to meet up with CA 116.

75+ Miles   STOP sign—TURN LEFT on CA 1, going toward Jenner.

Detour

VIA GUERNEVILLE, HEALDSBURG AND LAKE SONOMA—which is sort of a loop, as it brings you back to the coast 20 miles north of here.

TAKE THAT RIGHT onto CA 116 and head up along the north side of the Russian River for 12 miles, past **Duncan Mills, Monte Rio,** and into **Guerneville.** It is a hectic little community in the summer, sleepy in the spring and fall, and often flooded in the winter.

12 Miles STAY STRAIGHT at the second traffic light, staying on

River Road, as CA 116 goes right across the river.

17 Miles TURN LEFT after you enter **Hacienda,** angling onto the Westside Highway, headed for Healdsburg, while River Road crosses the river.

26 Miles TURN LEFT onto Kinley Road, just as you are approaching US 101.

28 Miles STOP sign—TURN LEFT **onto Dry Creek Road.**

39 Miles Come to the **Lake Sonoma Visitor Center,** below the dam; man-made **Lake Sonoma** is now a big recreation center and reservoir. Leaving the Visitor Center you are on Skaggs Creek Road.

41 Miles TURN LEFT as you ascend a grade, following a sign that reads: HWY 1 45 M./STEWARTS POINT SKAGGS SP RD (the sign is in error, as the distance is more like 36 miles). If you are accelerating madly as you go up the hill and miss the turn, going straight, a sign reading NOT A THROUGH ROAD will remind you you have gone wrong. The next dozen miles along Skaggs Springs Road are bliss-ful, as the **U.S. Army Corps of Engineers** have proved to the world that given an almost infinite amount of money they can indeed build a most marvelous road that doesn't have to handle much traffic.

54 Miles STAY STRAIGHT as the old Skaggs Springs Road dis-appears down to the right, and now the Corps of Engineers gives way to the **Sonoma Dept. of Highways,** who don't have nearly as much money to spend, and the asphalt is pretty beat up all the way to the coast. The going may be slow, but the road is a lovely one, running through thick woods.

72 Miles STAY STRAIGHT as a girder bridge spanning the **Gualala River** goes off to the right, headed for Annapolis. Now you start a climb.

75 Miles BEAR RIGHT staying on Stewarts Pt Skaggs Springs Road as you enter the small rag-tag community of **Point Stewart Indian Rancheria,** with Tin Barn Road dropping off to the left.

80 Miles STOP sign—arrive at **Stewarts Point** on CA 1.

■

76 Miles Jenner. Nice village. Tiny post office in a trailer, gas station with some rudimentary foodstuffs. A quarter mile up the road is **River's End,** a very nice place to spend the night (707-865-2484), and a lot of money on a tastily prepared dinner; it is a gourmet's retreat. You look over the mouth of

Fort Ross State Historical Park

Welcome to one of the furthest outposts of the Czarist empire. Russians involved in the fur trade came here in 1812, and their's was an uneasy relationship with the Spanish, and then the Mexican governments. Over the next 30 years the sea otter with its prime fur became an increasingly endangered species, and the Russians finally pulled out, leaving behind the name of the river, and a crumbling fort. Which was taken over by the state some 30 years ago, and has been fixed up and properly maintained. Great place! History the way I like it.   ■

Fort Ross is a friendly place, with few DO NOT ENTER signs to spoil your day.

the **Russian River** as it curves around a great sandspit and meets the Pacific Ocean; spectacular is a worthy description.

From Jenner the road winds along the coast, drops down into **Russian Gulch,** climbs up past a bluff and viewing area, and then . . . .

81 Miles   . . . CA 1 goes straight, Meyers Grade Road angles off to the right, threatening grades of 18 percent. In several places along the coast where it was difficult to construct a road, and where a road, even if constructed, might easily be washed out in a winter storm, the old-fashioned way was to build a road in the hills of the Coastal Range. It might have been more stressful for horses and passengers in the stagecoach, with steep ups and downs, but at least the mail got through. If you are tired of seeing the sea and surf, take this wooded run, and you can zip down to Fort Ross or Timber Cove.

CA 1 goes up along the **Jenner Cliffs,** running some 700 feet above the ocean, and here the road has often slipped into the sea, which is why the Meyers Grade Road is so well paved, as it has gotten frequent use as a detour. Now over **Jewel** and **Timber** and **Mill** gulches.

87 Miles   Oh Lord! Time warp! A stockaded fort appears on your left, and you half expect a sentry to hail you. That's the Fort Ross State Historical Park.

Past the Fort Ross Road going up into the hills, CA 1 rushes through the woods.

90 Miles   Over **Timber Cove Creek,** Timber Cove Road to your right, and there on the left is the **Timber Cove Inn,** with a very tall totem pole bringing peace to the world. It is a pleasant enough place to escape the hustle of San Francisco, and to stop along the road, but once you are there, you are there, and there is nothing much else nearby. The less expensive accommodations do not have an ocean view, while the better rooms can run up to $500 for a Saturday night (707-847-3231, 800-987-8319). It does have a good lobby and bar, but if I'm paying half a large for a room, I am not going to hang around the public places.

Back into the woods, with occasional glimpses of the ocean, the road curves and crests as it goes over creeks, past the **Ocean Cove Store** and on toward . . .

96 Miles   . . . Stewarts Point Store (1868) with general merchandise, and gas, on the left, Stewarts Point Skaggs Springs Road to the right, which is the end point for the previous detour. Next stretch of ten miles along CA 1 is all **Sea Ranch,** a tastefully planned development, begun in the 1960s, for the wealthy to have second homes on the Sonoma coast, and deny hoi polloi access to the beaches. Money does have its privileges.

99+ Miles   A sign for the **Annapolis Winery** points off to the right, along

Mendocino

Stories about the founding of Mendocino differ as to who the principles were but whatever the truth is, the town began life as a lumbering place in the early 1850s, cutting, milling, and shipping trees down to San Francisco. Going off to the Sierra Nevada with a pick and shovel was one way to seek your fortune, and it might or might not pan out, but selling lumber to the construction industry was a guaranteed way to get rich.

Mendocino had 50 good, booming years, and then **Fort Bragg,** up the coast a few miles, got a railroad line, and it was cheaper to move lumber by train rather than by ship. Mendocino went into a decline. After World War II it became an artists' colony (quaint expression), and then, inevitably, the tourists followed. Artists want/need to sell their works, and rather than schlep them down to The Big City the creative ones opened little galleries in town. And the word spread, and the art lovers came, and wanted to spend the night, and so it goes.

Today there are probably 50 places to stay within five miles of the old **Presbyterian Church** (dedicated in 1868). Right on Main is the **Mendocino Hotel,** dating from 1878, where you can get a small room with a shared bath, or an ocean-view suite (707-937-0511, 800-548-0513). For a B&B I recommend the **John Dougherty House** (circa 1870) on Ukiah Street, just two

blocks from the hotel (707-937-5266) which has a beautiful garden and superb views of the bay.

For large breakfasts, the upstairs **Bay View Cafe** (707-937-3200) on Main serves large portions. For more formal food I gravitate toward the **MacCallum House** (707-937-5763), built about 1882, on Albion Street; the raspberry cheesecake souffle with fudge sauce is to die for . . . and just might kill you. And the best place in town to loosen up is **Dick's Bar,** just two doors from the hotel, where the drinking is taken quite seriously.

The only trouble I have with Mendocino is that I sort of would like to move there myself. Except I know how long and wet the winters are. ∎

The Mendocino Hotel, established in 1878, still serves up good food and clean beds.

Annapolis Road, to the community of **Annapolis**. This road will loop back south to meet Stewarts Point Road. CA 1 continues along through grazing land, a mile or so in from the coast.

107 Miles Drop down to the **Gualala River,** cross into **Mendocino County,** and enter the town of **Gualala,** a useful collection of stores, restaurants, and motels.

At the very, very south end of town, just before you come to the first buildings, is the Old State Highway 501A, which goes up the hills to the right, becoming the Old Stage Road, returning to the coast some 16 miles later at **Point Arena.**

On the sea side of the highway is the **Gualala Country Inn** (707-884-4343), and the more upscale **Breakers Inn** (707-884-3200, 800-273-2537). On the other (inland) side of the highway is the **Gualala Hotel,** renting rooms since 1903 (707-884-3441) some with bath, and some sticking to the old-fashioned 1903 practice of having the bath down the hall; you may have to lug your bags upstairs, but it is a nice piece of history, with a good restaurant and bar. At the north end of town is the **Sandpiper Restaurant** (707-884-3398), open working-man's hours, 6 a.m. to 3 p.m., with honest, good, solid food.

Leaving Gualala along CA 1 the road runs straightish, wooded, a remarkable structure called **St. Orres Inn** on the right, looking a bit like a Russian fairytale by way of Disneyland; it has 20 rooms and cottages on 50 acres (707-884-3303). Continue past **Anchor Bay,** several small paved roads going to the east to climb up to the Old Stage Road. Remember, all those bridges you pass over so blithely, crossing gulches and creeks, were not around a hundred years ago.

121 Miles Arrive in **Point Arena,** which was a major town on the coast a hundred years ago. Farming was the main business, but having wheat and beef and whatnot did not do much good unless you could get it to market. And since the roads were pretty rudimentary, and wagons did not move very fast, most everything went out of **Arena Cove** on ships. And now it is out of the mainstream of the tourist industry. But there is a movie theater on Main Street, and **Carlini's Cafe,** and down the road the **Sea Shell Motel** (707-882-2000). Down on the wharf the **Arena Cove Bar & Grill** (707-882-2100) is recommended.

Up at the north end of town, just before CA 1 cuts left 90 degrees, is Riverside Drive going to the right, the northern terminus of the Old Stage Road that began in Gualala.

123 Miles Off to the left goes Lighthouse Road, at **Rollerville Junction,** and the two-mile stretch of bumpy asphalt that leads to the **Point Arena**

Fort Bragg

The American presence was started in the 1850s when a small detachment of troops set up camp to oversee a nearby Indian reservation, and the post was named for a company commander, one **Captain Bragg.** Apparently it was a delightful place, situated on a heavily wooded bluff.

Then with the Indians pacified, the lumbering interests moved in, and Fort Bragg was incorporated in 1889. **Charles Johnson** was founder of the **Union Lumber Company,** and the original mill was a few miles north of town, moving into Fort Bragg in 1885. In 1911 the railroad arrived from Willits, and this was the boom period for the town. And soon not a tree was to be seen.

Union Lumber was merged into **Boise Cascade** in 1969, and then acquired by **Georgia Pacific** in 1973. And now the company is closing down the mill, which essentially takes up over a mile of seashore on the south end of town.

So Ft. Bragg is going into the tourist business. The CoC is at 332 North Main St./CA 1, and a call (707-961-6300) will get you a passel of information. For entertainment the place is most famous for the **California-Western RR's Skunk Train** (800-777-5865), which takes the passengers on a 40-mile trip up along **Pudding Creek** and Noyo River and then drops down to **Willet;** they have both steam and diesel locomotives. My only concern with the train is that it is usually packed with children, who will be enjoying themselves immensely and noisily as you are trying to soak up the grandeur of the redwoods.

The town has several museums, best of all being the **Guest House Museum** by the railroad station, which inform and entertain. And what promises to become a Big Time affair are the **Paul Bunyan Days,** usually the first week in September, which shows the logging industry the way it never was.

For sleeping, I tend to the south end of town. As you cross the Noyo River, high up; take the first right turn after crossing the bridge. Right at that corner is the conventional **Harbor Lite Lodge,** with "view" rooms—got to have a view (707-964-0221). For a more unconventional setting, follow the road down to **Noyo Harbor,** and check in at the **Wharf-Anchor Lodge.** The Wharf is a restaurant, with five rooms (18 to 22) below that are right on the water, with the fishing boats chuffing by a few feet away (707-964-4283). I love it, though my wife has made some comment about the bark of the seals that live in the harbor; she's a light sleeper. The **Anchor Lodge** is behind the restaurant, and quieter, mainly for fisherfolk, not nearly as much fun.

My own choice is often the **Seabird Lodge** (707-964-4731, 800-345-0022), a half-block off Main and a couple of blocks north of the bridge. Large, convenient, and quiet.

For food beyond The Wharf, the **Tradewinds Restaurant** (707-954-4761) on Main feeds a lot of lumbering types. While the **Cliff House** (707-961-0255), south of the bridge, has "dramatic" ocean views. And **North Coast Brewing,** at 444 North Main (707-964-3400), has some excellent brew (sample the Old Rasputin stout) and a good grill. ∎

Light Station. The lighthouse stands 156 feet tall and was built after the 1906 earthquake destroyed the previous structure. The old lighthouse keepers' cottages are for rent, if you are of a mind to stay (707-882-2809).

On CA 1 the road drops down to the wetlands of the **Garcia River,** and try to imagine getting a wagon laden with produce across this stretch in the rainy winter of a hundred years back.

125 Miles A tall windbreak of eucalyptus trees is ahead; CA 1 keeps to the left, Mountain View Road to the left. To get to the town of **Elk** it is 15 miles up CA 1, or 51 miles via the **Anderson Valley.**

Detour
To Boonville and Back to Elk—another little loop

You will see a lot of interesting scenery if you head due east on Mountain View Road. The windbreak ends after a short stretch and the road, with new pavement, is winding into the Coastal Range, and winding is the operative word; it is a twisty one. Up and down, up and down, over the **Mendocino Ridges,** drop down to cross **Rancheria Creek,** and as you start up the road narrows. Then it is through some redwoods, and emerge in **Anderson Valley,** near the town of Boonville on CA 128. The tripmeter is reading 25 miles.

25 Miles STOP sign—and you are in Boonville—to your right are a couple of stores, two gas stations, several cafes, and the Boonville Hotel, a pleasantly old place. However, the problem is that the best rooms in this hotel, airy and spacious, are in front, subjected to the noise of the passing traffic on the highway . . . though trucks and RVs tend not to travel at night (707-895-2210—I ask for a quiet room at the back). Breakfast is included, and the restaurant serves lunch and dinner. In the morning the Redwood Drive-In is the happening place.

Head west on CA 128, and you will find wineries to the right of you, vineyards to the left of you. Anderson Valley is working hard to develop its reputation among the oenophiles, and at least ten vineyards and tasting rooms are in evidence. Pass through **Philo,** and a mile beyond . . .

33 Miles . . . TURN LEFT on the Philo-Greenwood Road on the left and the sign for Elk. Then it is back to a little ridge-hopping and valley-following.

51 Miles STOP sign—and you return to the sea at **Elk.**

∎

126 Miles Staying on CA 1 you come to the small village of **Manchester,** with some unexpected topiary (shaped trees) work on your right. You can go down to **Manchester State Park** and a five-mile stretch of shoreline which is famous for its beachcombing, as it is on the north side of **Point Arena,** and the wind and currents bring lots of flotsam and jetsam to rest here.

The original Point Arena Lighthouse was destroyed in the 1906 earthquake; this is its replacement.

CA 1 continues along through ranching land (just waiting to be gobbled up in the 21st Century by city-folk looking for country homes) to . . .

140 Miles . . . the little town of **Elk.** It was a milltown, until the mill closed 50 years ago, and now it has a relatively unspoiled air, with several cafes, B&Bs, the **Elk Cove Inn,** with 14 rooms (707-877-3321), and the **Greenwood Pier Inn & Cafe,** with a dozen rooms and cottages (707-877-9997). The place could be compared to Mendocino 30 years ago, but on a much smaller scale. On weekends the beds are usually booked far in advance, as the San Francisco contingent that has come to love this place keeps on coming back. Good food, like bangers and mashed (pork sausages and mashed potatoes, a staple of the British isles), is found at **Bridget Dolan's Pub** (707-877-1820).

The road hangs onto the edge of land on this stretch, and sometimes gets washed away in the winter. CalTrans is very active along here.

146 Miles Swoop around a long curve and find yourself looking down on the **Navarro River** and a long bridge. The original one was put across in 1917, as the automotive age came to the Mendocino coastline.

STOP sign—TURN LEFT on CA 1 on the north side of the river where CA 128 ends; if you take a right onto 128 you'll be in Boonville in 28 miles, back on US 101 in 47 miles. You are less than three (boring) hours from San Francisco at this point, which explains why the Mendocino coast is so populated in the summer. But you don't want to head back to the Golden Gate, so you go left, toward Fort Bragg, along the B&B Highway.

This is all tourism, but a tasteful tourism; you want tasteless, go to Orange County in Southern California and visit Disneyland and Laguna Beach. On a sunny summer day, this stretch of coast is unbeatable. Which is why a lot of people from the south try to figure out how to make a living up here.

The road swoops around **Navarro Point,** up past the village of **Albion,** over the high bridge above the **Albion River,** through **Dark Gulch,** then along to the village of **Little River** where the Little River Airport Road goes off to the right and then the Van Damme State Park. Cross over the river and slip around the inside of the bluff and down toward **Big River.**

156 Miles The Comptche-Ukiah Road goes off to the right, with the **Big River Lodge** on the corner; if you want a rural, untrafficked, motorcycle-friendly way back to US 101, this is it. It is 14 miles to the hill community of **Comptche,** and another nine to a small intersection with Orr Springs Road going straight, Low Gap Road off to the right; STAY STRAIGHT on Orr. Another three miles and the road runs through **Montgomery Woods State Preserve,** then past **Orr's Hot Springs** and on to Ukiah.

On CA 1, the road crosses Big River, with **Mendocino Bay** a beautiful sight to the left, and the road widens as you climb to the bluff that is the site of Mendocino. Big River was where the mill was a long time ago, and where the ships would load the lumber.

157 Miles Mendocino: TAKE THE FIRST TURNING TO THE LEFT, Main Street. The town is hopelessly hyped in the tourist and travel industry, but it is almost as good as promised.

161 Miles Cross **Caspar Creek** and TAKE A LEFT into **Caspar,** with the funky old **Caspar Inn** on the first corner. If you are a blues lover, you can eat and sleep at the inn, and listen to music on the weekends.

163 Miles On the sea-side of CA 1 are the **Mendocino Coast Botanical Gardens,** 47 acres of floral and arboreal splendor. Six bucks will get an adult in, and those who appreciate flowers and ferns and foliage will spend a good few hours walking about. A cafe offers sustenance after all that physical exertion.

164 Miles CA 1 meets up with CA 20; if you take a right on CA 20 you will be in Willits, on CA 101, in 34 miles. Nice road, but it is the major truck route for getting in and out of Fort Bragg.

164+ Miles Cross over the bridge high above the **Noyo River,** and look down to your right into **Noyo Harbor.**

180 Miles The village of **Westport,** a thriving lumber town a hundred years ago, now a somnolent place with a general store and gas pump. A mile beyond Westport a paved road, the Branscomb Road, heads off to the east, going to Laytonville on US 101, 20 miles away; however, there is about a five-mile stretch in the middle which is not paved. Just so you know.

CA 1 is running close to the coast, along **Westport-Union Landing State Beach,** crosses **Juan Creek,** and then wiggles inland. Kiss the coast goodbye. Climb over a low ridge, down to the non-existent town of **Rockport,** and several small grassy valleys.

193 Miles You have just come through an open grassy area of a dozen acres or so, with several abandoned buildings, and as the road curves to the right, crossing over the **Cottoneva Creek,** you see a dirt road going to the left, County Road 431, the Usal Road.

Detour
The Lost Coast/Dual-Purpose Section

This stretch of Pacific seashore gets a lot of comment, but very few visitors. Which is a good thing.

The Usal Road does get a minimum of maintenance, and the dirt surface climbs steeply to a ridge overlooking the ocean, and then disappears into the woods. After six miles the road comes to **Usal Bay,** and it is a splendid ride—for a dual-purpose bike, a bit arduous on a street machine.

After crossing **Usal Creek** the road tends not to be maintained at all, as it runs through the **Sinkyone Wilderness State Park.** It can be a tough road, especially after a tough winter, but this is where you would expect to see a stagecoach and four horses tearing around the corner in front of you.

This is all part of the **Lost Coast,** a hundred-mile stretch going from Usal Creek to the **Eel River** in the north. It is one of the most dramatic stretches of California coastal land left, and is definitely worth several days. A paved road does run about 35 miles from **Garberville** on US 101 to **Shelter Cove,** the only community on this stretch of coast. Usal Road connects after some 35 miles with Shelter Cove Road, and you can continue north on Kings Peak Road, in the **Kings Range National Conservation Area,** which goes on to **Honeydew.** I deal with Honeydew in Chapter 8, Trip #14. ■

If you take the Usal Road turn-off, just beyond Rockport, be prepared for 20 miles of very bad road. Sorry, the sign saying USE AT YOUR OWN RISK is partially hidden.

Ah yes, artistry abounds in Mendocino.

Staying on CA 1, the road zigs and zags upward through the forest, with logging trucks appearing.

207 Miles   End of CA 1. TAKE A RIGHT into Leggett, where food and gas awaits, and the **Chandelier Drive-Thru Tree** is the main attraction. For a $2 entrance fee to this pleasant tourist trap you can get a picture of yourself driving through the hole cut in this large redwood.

Connector

A TURN SOUTH onto US 101 will put you in San Francisco in less than four hours, while north will have you in **Eureka** (Chapter 8) in less than two hours. Anyone going north should definitely get off the 101 right after **Garberville**, and follow the well-marked 31-mile **Avenue of the Giants** through the **Humboldt Redwoods State Park.** And if you want to cut into a Eureka loop-trip, look for the HONEYDEW sign just past Weott, and head over to the Lost Coast; you'll do the best part of the loop in Trip 13, albeit in reverse from my description.

We can all count backward, can't we?   ∎

That's the Noyo River at the south end of Fort Bragg; commercial fishermen use this as a harbor.

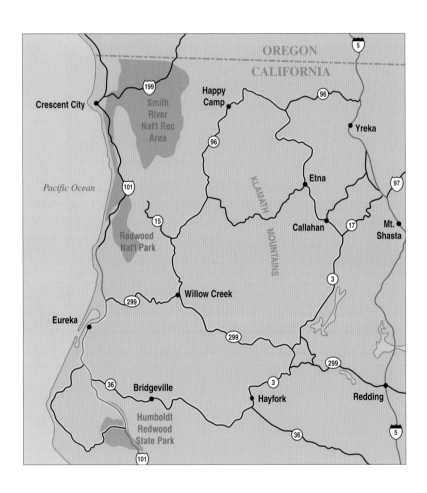

Far Northwest

Headquarters *Eureka*
Chamber of Commerce/Visitors Center *707-442-3738, 800-356-6381*
Getting There *Either take US 101 from north or south, or CA 299 going west from Redding, or sail into Humboldt Bay on your 45-foot ketch with the bikes lashed to the mast.*
Ground Zero *Starting point will be at the intersection of CA 255 and US 101 in Eureka—which is not to be confused with 255 and 101 in Arcata, seven miles to the north, as 255 does a long 180-degree curve to the north around Arcata Bay and rejoins 101. Don't worry, it's not all that difficult to figure out.*

Timber baron William Carson built this mansion in the 1880s, not as an ego thing, but to keep his employees working during a slump in the lumber business.

Although this area has some of California's "bestest" riding, it is the least visited. You might not want to be up here in the rainy season/winter, but for most of the year the place is motorcycling nirvana.

This section has I-5 to the east, the Pacific Ocean to the west, Oregon border to the north, CA 36 to the south, and covers roughly 10,000 square miles, including the **Six Rivers, Shasta-Trinity,** and **Klamath National Forests.** The riding is through mountains and along rivers, where good roads are never straight for long. The place is sparsely populated, but each little community has at least one cafe, and since they get by on local traffic more than tourists, the food is usually good. Lots of families depend on CalTrans wages to keep the larder stocked, so the roads tend to be in reasonable condition.

This chapter will have three Trips—but the last one will offer several options. Read on, you will find out all about it.

You are going to bed down in **Eureka,** way up on the California coast, further north than most tourists go. It's a seaside city, but a mite chilly for bathing suits, and made its money from fishing and lumbering. Small scale fishing is pretty iffy these days, and the wood business has its ups and downs, depending on how many trees are left to cut. However, tourism is becoming a more important source of revenue, and the city seems to thrive on the edge of **Humboldt Bay.**

A **Captain Winship,** working for the **Russian-American Fur Company,** sailed through the well-concealed entrance and into the bay in 1806 and recorded its presence as the best place to put in a ship between Puget Sound and San Francisco Bay. After the gold rush began, and searching miners poured into the mountains east of the bay, a town was started in 1850, incorporated 25 years later. Apparently all the highly educated miners spoke ancient Greek and liked to holler "Eureka!" ("I found it!") when they hit on a vein, so the name of this city also happens to be the state's motto. However, the supply of gold petered out, but what gave Eureka its boost was timber; there were a lot of trees to be cut down, to build buildings and shore up mines in other parts of the state.

There is an old part of town, which is where I like to go; the buildings are Victoriana at its best. At the north end of 2nd Street is a large, tall house with enough gingerbread trimming to keep a housepainter or two busy year round. It was built by an early lumber baron, **William Carson,** in 1885, when the lumber industry was in a slump and he wanted to keep his boys employed. It has now become a private club, called the **Ingomar;** obviously no one person, except perhaps Bill Gates, can afford to keep the place up.

US 101 goes right through the heart of Eureka, and nearly everything can be found within a couple of blocks of the highway. The place to stay is the **Eureka Inn,** a gorgeously large pseudo-Tudor hotel that takes up the entire block at 7th and F streets. It was completed in 1922, when the city was having its financial heyday, and the lobby is a suitably grand place, a real fire burning in the huge fireplace even in summer, as the fog tends to keep the place cool. The hotel changed ownership in 2006 and was closed; apparently it is going to have some refurbishment and open again in 2007. The CoC can tell you more.

Down at the other end of the pricing structure are a string of motels along US 101, some of which tend to be on the noisy side, as traffic motors through town constantly, but that is the price of saving a buck. My preferred choice is the **Best Western Humboldt Bay Inn,** at 5th Street in the south end of town, where US 101 splits, with one street going north, the other south, the motel being in between (707-443-2234); it is reasonably quiet.

For the food, you can cheerfully stay at the Eureka Inn and eat at the restaurant, with a rare sirloin and an '83 cab from the Wild Horse vineyard. Or walk a few blocks to the Old Town, where the **Sea Grill** (707-443-7187) can be found at 316 E Street, and have some splendid bass with garlic and shallots. If you want coffee and croissant in the morning, sit on the sidewalk at **Humboldt Bay Coffee Company** (707-444-3969), 2nd and F. With a harbor view, there is the **Cafe Waterfront** (707-443-9190) at 1st and F.

On the other hand, you cannot go to Eureka and not go to the **Samoa Cookhouse** (707-442-1659). Take CA 255 (a/k/a R Street) over the Samoa Bridge to the peninsula at the far side of the bay, turn left at the T-bone at Samoa Road, and immediately left again, and you are at the area's most famous restaurant, which began life as a cookhouse for the lumbermen 100 years ago. You sit at long tables (family style), with the secondary dishes on the table with you, and the waitresses bring you the meats of the day— steak, fried chicken, baked ham, grilled salmon, everything your doctor advised you against. All you can eat for $10 at breakfast, $11 at lunch, $14 at dinner.

If you want a slightly unusual place to stay, continue south on Samoa Road for three miles beyond the Cookhouse and you will come to the old **U.S. Navy blimp base,** now a general-aviation airport. The World War II officers' quarters have been turned into the **Samoa Airport B&B** (707-445-0765); very nice, and if you fly in, the management provides you with a car at no extra charge; sorry, no motorcycle available.

The city of Eureka offers museums, shopping (especially antiques, which you can't carry many of on the bike), and general hanging out.

Trip 13 Lost Coast

Distance *130 miles*

Highlights *If you do not like tight and twisty roads, stay away from this little stint—but it is a righteous ride, one that you will dine out on often. This run along the north section of the Lost Coast run is a beaut, and then you get the redwoods. Too much fun.*

0 Miles Take US 101 south.

15 Miles EXIT RIGHT at FERNDALE/FERNBRIDGE/CA 211, GOING STRAIGHT.

15+ Miles TURN RIGHT as the sign for FERNDALE comes up and cross the bridge over the **Eel River.** On the far side you cross several miles of flat estuarial land.

20 Miles Enter the charming town of **Ferndale**, with Main Street decorated by turn of the century Victoriana. The town was founded in 1852, on flat fertile land between the Eel River and **Bear River Ridge,** and was noted for its dairy herds.

This bridge carries US 101 traffic across the Eel River in the Humboldt Redwoods State Park.

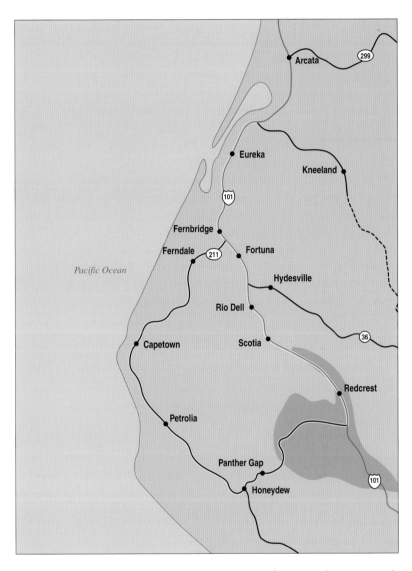

20+ Miles TURN RIGHT at the intersection of Main with Ocean, with the **Victorian Inn** (707-786-4949, 888-589-1808) being to your upper left, and a NO THROUGH ROAD sign in front of you. The Inn has a dozen individualistic rooms, and a good restaurant by the name of **Curley's.** Another upscale place to stay is the **Gingerbread Mansion,** a B&B just off Main at 400 Berding Street, with 11 very nice rooms (707-786-4000), and a great breakfast including eggs Benedict. On Ocean is the rather small, clean, rather ordinary **Fern Motel** (707-786-5000).

21 Miles TURN LEFT as you arrive at the Mattole Road junction; a tall sign stands to your left, two poles with the words CAPETOWN PETROLIA at the top. Unfortunately the arrow fell down long ago, but it was supposed to point left and direct you onto Mattole Road, beginning a steep climb up to the top of Bear River Ridge.

27 Miles You are on **Bear River Ridge,** and Upper Bear River Ridge Road goes off to the left (east), all the way back to Rio Dell on US 101. You STAY STRAIGHT, dropping down into **Bear River Valley,** and a lone ranch sitting by the river; this area was once known as **Capetown,** hence the sign back in Ferndale. You climb out of the valley onto **Cape Ridge,** the western end being Cape Mendocino, and you are atop **The Wall.** It is a helluva steep descent down to the beach, with pitches of better than 20 degrees.

39 Miles As the road comes off The Wall and flattens out by the sea, a regular sort of house sits off to your left; if you like the lonely life, or to occasionally hear vehicles that lose their brakes on The Wall come crashing down, this is the place to live. Now there is a miraculous flat six miles of uninhabited, pristine beachfront; quite a sight on the California coast. Look back after a mile, and get a proper appreciation for The Wall. You pass one ranch tucked back a ways into the **Branstatter Ridge.** This area was originally developed as a cattle-growing area to feed the lumberjacks, and a few head are still to be seen. But I imagine that transporting the hamburgers on the hoof out of this area would eat up whatever profit might be made.

45 Miles Start the climb inland, away from the sea.

51 Miles Enter the community of **Petrolia,** with a historical marker at the first left turn; the plaque commemorates the fact that near here was the site of the first drilled oil (as opposed to natural seepage) in California. In 1865 a ship at the pier near **Mattole Point** was loaded with barrels of crude that were taken down to San Francisco for refining. That little tidbit will win you a barroom bet. Not much in Petrolia, except a general store and a post office, and **St. Anthony's Church,** a lone bastion of Catholicism that has services on the first Saturday of every month. The only other church in town, insofar as I could see, was Seventh Day Adventist. The eating place in town is the **Yellow Rose Restaurant** (707-629-3476) serving lunch and dinners six days a week, breakfast and lunch on Sunday. It does not accept credit cards, and has a bar which usually stays open until the last client is gone.

52+ Miles You are approaching a bridge over the **Mattole River** (Mattole, by the way, was the name of a local Indian tribe), and down on the left is **The Hideaway,** with food and drink and good burgers; it was going through some financial troubles in the summer of '06, but the word was that it would be open again.

The Emerald Triangle

Around these parts farming is a mainstay of the local economy. But the farmers are not raising rutabagas or squash, they are concentrating on a far more profitable crop, marijuana. Since transportation is always expensive, and an ounce of *cannabis sattiva* can fetch more than a ton of potatoes, one can understand why so many people are cultivating Mary Jane.

The Emerald Triangle consists of three adjoining counties, Humboldt, Mendocino, and Trinity, where the land is good for growing this illegal product, and there is much wilderness—which is useful for hiding the small plots that the farmers use. If you happen to be motoring along happily in this pristine part of the world, and suddenly a helicopter swoops in low over your head, fear not, this is merely the local authorities out to destroy the evil weed before it is taken down to San Francisco and eventually destroys our entire civilization. ■

63 Miles If you really want to get away from it all, from the hustle and bustle of regular life, spend the night at the **Mattole River Organic Farm & Country Cabins,** a collection of six cottages under shady trees, kitchens included (707-629-3445). If you didn't bring your own grub to cook, you can go back to the Yellow Rose.

65 Miles KEEP LEFT at the fork as you enter the booming (?) hub of downtown **Honeydew,** which has one store, combined with post office, and two free-standing phone booths. The store is open seven days a week and does have gas, should you be on a Sportster with a peanut tank. Usually a collection of congenial folk will be sitting on the porch, sipping sodas, and discussing the important news of the day. Hemp farming is a mainstay of the local economy.

In front of the store the road forks, the right (southerly) turn, past the phone booths, being Wilder Ridge Road that heads toward Garberville after connecting with the Briceland Road, or Shelter Cove (that one is gravel, usually in good shape).

However, you want the left fork (straight, really), with Mattole Road crossing the Mattole River (once again, this being the fifth and final time) on a long single-lane girder bridge. Now you head uphill, and up, and up, gaining half a mile in altitude. You are going up a mountain, around Catheys Peak, and into the Humboldt Redwoods State Park.

US 101 up around the Humboldt Redwoods State Park has lots of tourist traps.

80 Miles Panther Gap, at 2,744 feet, with no markings. Then the road comes down off the mountain and into a small open valley along **Bull Creek.**

83 Miles The road goes into redwood-shaded dappled darkness, great stuff, like the "Star Wars" movie in which little rocket ships were darting amongst the trees. Do not forget, a big redwood tree is not forgiving if a mere motorcycle happens to crash into it. This is the main portion of the state park, and goes on for delightful miles.

88 Miles TURN LEFT onto the **Avenue of the Giants.**

All of a sudden you are out of the redwoods and beneath US 101. Do not go up the ramp, but GO STRAIGHT a hundred feet and you run into the middle of the Avenue of the Giants, 30 glorious miles of huge, tall redwood trees running along the **Eel River.** Not to be missed.

93 Miles   At **Redcrest,** a bit of private property in the midst of the state park, with the **Redcrest Resort & Cabins** (707-772-4206) offering hospitality on one side of the road, the post office and the **Eternal Tree House Cafe** (707-772-4262) on the other; that **Tree House** was hollowed out in 1910. Cheap way to build a home.

94 Miles   The **Immortal Tree,** which seems to be a marketing gambit more than anything.

99 Miles   Avenue of the Giants melds with US 101, and it is north to Eureka, past the lumber-mills at **Scotia** and **Rio Dell,** and the sign for CA 36 at Alton. Scotia is an old company town, owned by Pacific Lumber lock, stock, and barrel, but in recent time the company has been trying to extricate itself, and sell houses to the residents.

115 Miles   Fernbridge exit.

130 Miles   Arrive back to Ground Zero.

Avenue of the Giants

If you have come from the south on US 101, you might well have already ridden along the Avenue of the Giants, a/k/a CA 254. The southern end of the avenue begins at the well-marked exit off US 101 about six miles north of **Garberville,** and you soon enter a delightfully gloomy tunnel of trees, running along the east side of the **Eel River.** After 12 miles you, and the river, go under US 101 and start ambling down the west side of the big road. Another four miles and you came to **Humboldt Redwoods State Park** headquarters and information center, and four miles beyond that, having once again moved to the east side of US 101, you are at the Honeydew turn-off.

If you haven't ridden this stretch already, zip back south on US 101 18 miles and do it.

While doing this Lost Coast loop, head north on the Avenue of the Giants, with stunning, lovely, tall, tall trees lining the road, the Eel River just off to your right, and many places to pull off. However, as soon as you kill your motor the noise of the nearby 101 tends to intrude. Logging trucks share the narrow two-lane avenue with you, and hardly a dotted line in sight.   ∎

Trip 14 Trinity Return

Distance *244 miles*

Highlights *Ah, wilderness! This is just a joyful ride along rivers, through valleys, over mountain ridges, with lots of trees and very little traffic, mostly along CA routes 36 and 3 and 299.*

0 Miles HEAD SOUTH on 101, past the Ferndale exit, past **Fortuna**, to where the highway is no longer a freeway, and the sign for the village of **Alton** comes up.

20 Miles TURN LEFT where a small green and white sign indicates CA 36 going off to the east; go thataway. This is a little-trafficked road which connects 101 and I-5, and it begins by cutting across the flatlands.

That's Mount Shasta, second tallest mountain in the Lower 48 at 14,162 feet, only 332 feet less than Mt. Whitney.

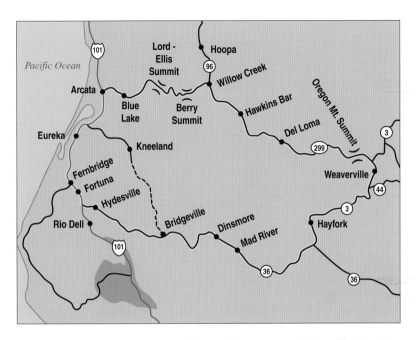

23+ Miles TURN RIGHT as the two-laner enters **Hydesville**, keeping
you going toward Bridgeville. A sign reads: NO TRAILERS ADVISED PAST
BRIDGEVILLE; motorcycles are just fine. The road runs along the **Van
Duzen River**; the pavement is not really in great shape, but perfectly sound.
45 Miles **Bridgeville** comes up with a defunct concrete bridge over the
river, built in 1925, celebrating its name. The new highway 36 bypasses the
tiny town, but if you TURN LEFT and go 200 yards you will see several
houses, a defunct store, and a sign for KNEELAND, to the north. You want
east, so you backtrack to CA 36, and start climbing up the south side of
McClellan Mountain; the river goes around to the north. Drop down toward **Dinsmore**, with a gas station and a small airstrip, and rejoin the Van
Duzen in a narrow valley. In a couple of miles you enter **Trinity County,**
and the road gets better. Leave the Van Duzen River behind as you cross
over a low ridge and come down to the Mad River.
68 Miles The community of **Mad River** has a small general store and two
pumps out front, one selling diesel, the other low octane. The sign over the
store door reads: DON'T BLINK OR YOU'LL MISS US; the post office is next
door, and the only other business in town, the **Mad River Burger Bar**, appears to be open when the burgermeister chooses (707-574-6646). Just a
100 yards east from the store there is a sign along the road: NEXT SERVICES
39 MILES.

Weaverville

This is a town of about 3,000, struggling to stay solvent as a tourist place, and it has its own rustic charm. Miners found gold up here in 1850, and as the story goes, there were three of them, and they drew straws to see who would get immortalized. Mr. Weaver did.

Downtown is rather attractive, with a number of two-story buildings lining the tree-shaded thoroughfare, several with outside curved staircases going to a second floor porch, which was often the access to the shop owners home. This is a very nice architectural touch.

In the 1870s, after most miners had left because the original easy-to-get-at wealth was gone, a large number of Chinese miners showed up, willing to work harder for less money. The 1874 Joss House is a historic relic of that time.

For those looking for a pillow, old-time ambience is to be found at the **Weaverville Hotel** on Main Street, with seven rooms (530-623-2222). The **Red Hill Motel & Cabins** (530-623-4331) is a rustic place just on the west side of town. Should you be imitating the miners of yore and imbibe too much at the watering holes on Main Street, the **49er Gold Country Inn** is just a couple of hundred yards away (530-623-4937).

Food in Weaverville is plentiful, with some two dozen places catering mainly to the tourist. But in the eight non-tourist months they have to please the locals, so the chop is okay. My personal favorite is the **LaGrange Restaurant** on Main Street (530-623-5325), which has a fine selection of edibles. The breakfast lot crowds into the **Nugget Restaurant** (530-623-6749), an old-fashioned Mom & Pop sort of place. ■

The road starts a climb, and a beautiful climb it is. The Trinity County engineer had to have had some appreciation for motorcycling, as the curves are banked precisely right. This climbs up to **South Fork Mountain Summit,** 4,077 feet (on the "longest continuous ridge in the North American Continent"), and then plummets beckoningly down the east side. This is 20 miles of such perfect riding you will be tempted to go back and do it again.

98 Miles   TURN LEFT at an unmistakable intersection in the middle of the woods, following CA 3 to the north, while CA 36 goes straight, headed for Red Bluff.

Connector
To Red Bluff

Red Bluff is on Interstate 5, a mere 56 miles to the east along CA 36, and a nice ride it is. But there is some grand riding north of here, so you really don't want to take this road unless you are in a goldanged hurry. Also, remember that Red Bluff lies at a 300-foot altitude in the upper **Sacramento Valley,** which means it gets powerful hot in the summer, real cold in the winter. ■

110 Miles Roll into **Hayfork,** in a lovely valley watered by the **Hayfork Creek,** and about 2,000 people. Gold was mined and dredged in the area for nearly 100 years, but after World War II it was farming and timbering. Recently they've fallen on hard times, though, since the lumber mill closed down. Due to "environmentalists," I was told.

Leaving Hayfork the road is flat for several miles before beginning the climb to **Hayfork Summit** (3,654 feet). And from the top you can see the top of **Mt. Shasta,** which at 14,162 feet is two miles higher than you are, in the far distance, some 75 miles to the northnortheast.

Some very decorative construction fronts Main Street in Weaverville.

A little band of touring riders stops on Lord-Ellis Summit to admire the view, along CA 229.

133 Miles TURN LEFT where CA 3 meets up with CA 299 at a bridge over the **Trinity River.** Hanging that left onto CA 3/299 will take you toward Weaverville. A right goes to Redding.

140 Miles Enter downtown **Weaverville.**

Leaving town you stay on CA 299, heading over **Oregon Mountain Summit** (2,897 feet), and then refinding the Trinity River at **Junction City** (1,460 feet, just to give you an idea of altitudes). CA 299, blessed by our government with the name of **Trinity National Scenic Byway,** is another east-west crossover, but it has 15 cars for every one that was on CA 36. Which still is not a lot, as there are very few cars on 36. It is a great river ride.

169 Miles Enter **Del Loma,** and the Del Loma Resort has sumptuous cabins, swimming pool, etc. (800-839-0194).

184 Miles **Hawkins Bar,** with a permanent population of 20-some, and a cheerful general store where the village action takes place.

195 Miles Enter **Willow Creek,** major metropolis, with several motels and two gas stations.

But we are headed back for Eureka, and the road continues alongside Willow Creek for a few miles, climbs up and crosses over **Berry Summit** (2,859 feet), drops down to cross **Redwood Creek,** back up over **Lord-Ellis Summit** (2,262 feet), and makes a long, long descent to **Blue Lake** and the coastal plain. As you climb over the last ridge you can see the clear-cutting that had been down on the far side of the valley. Seriously ugly, but so isn't a lot of life. We hope it grows back.

Willow Creek

This community supports about 1,500 souls, and has two motels, a hamburger joint, pizza place, and **Cinnebar Sam's** (530-629-3437). Cinnebar is the old-fashioned name for mercuric sulfide, which I can only presume was mined around here. Considering the nature of the town, Sam's place is a tad on the pretentious side, but it does have a verandah, which unfortunately overlooks a down-at-the-heels parking area and some trailers, with the river not really visible in the near distance. I tried the Toad-In-The-Hole, and it was, in a word, interesting; should I eat there again, I would probably order something more identifiable, like a steak or fried chicken. A number of local micro brews are available in bottles.

If you wish to stay here, in anticipation of heading north and east of CA 96 to Yreka (see Trip #3), the motel of choice is the eponymously named **Willow Creek Motel,** which has taken over the old stage stop and hotel that was built in 1890. The motel is not on The Strip, but a half mile north of town on CA 96, just after you cross over **Willow Creek** on the bridge. Very quiet, very pleasant, very old-fashioned— with a coffee maker in the room. (800-724-1762, 530-629-2115).■

229 Miles   Enter **Blue Lake,** where CA 299 turns into a divided highway.
235 Miles   MERGE LEFT, taking the southerly side of US 101, heading toward Eureka.
244 Miles   Arrive back in Eureka.

Trip 15 Klamath River Run

Distance *399 miles*

Highlights *I have done this as a long loop, but I imagine that most readers will use this trip as a connector that will lead to either Oregon or Mt. Shasta, the last being the most scenic way to Lassen Volcanic National Park.*

If you are doing a full loop of California and do not want to return to Eureka, you should follow the Connector that will lead you to Mt. Shasta. I am also going to run a connector via Redding, just to give another option. If you do the full 399-mile loop you will repeat the Weaverville-to-Eureka section that is described in Trip #2, but you might well have not done that trip. And if you do repeat those excellent 100 miles, you will just get to enjoy them a second time.

0 Mile   Ground Zero, CA 255 and US 101, head north on US 101.

9 Miles   EXIT RIGHT, taking the well-marked exit for CA 299, Blue Lake and Redding; the first six miles of 299 are divided freeway. Leaving the flat lands and climbing into the mountains it becomes the **Trinity Highway** going up over **Lord-Ellis** (2,262 feet) and **Berry** (2,859 feet) summits.

49 Miles   TURN LEFT after entering **Willow Creek** . . . I had more to say on that little community at the end of the Trip #2 description. In the

These Harley riders have just had lunch at the Frontier Cafe in Happy Camp, along CA 96.

center, so to speak, of town, is the well-marked left turn onto CA 96; 150 miles of unwedded bliss are ahead of you. Leaving Willow Creek CA 96 runs alongside the **Trinity River.**

57 Miles   An official **Vista Point** is on your right, looking over the Trinity River and the **Tish Tang A Tong Creek** (don't ask; I do not know). You are about to enter the **Hoopa Indian Reservation,** where the football team is called the Warriors, and nobody has raised a fuss about the name.

61 Miles   The village of **Hoopa** has a motel, the **Tsewenaldin Inn** (530-625-4294) and a casino, though the latter is very small-time, with nickel, dime, and dollar poker.

71 Miles   TURN RIGHT after you cross the bridge at **Weitchpec,** where the **Trinity** and **Klamath** combine, going upstream along the Klamath; going left follows the Klamath downstream and runs you into the reservation panhandle.

83 Miles   Cedar Camp Road to your left, and the **Klamath River Lodge** down to your right. This is a rustic fisherman's paradise, with few amenities, and you bring your own food and drink, and do it up in your cabin.

87 Miles Enter **Orleans,** population 630 at last count; on the left is the **Orleans Mining Co.** Cafe (530-627-3213) with lots of skillets hanging on the walls and a skilled cook in the kitchen. The road is good, fast, and should be treated with respect; it would be a hassle getting a med-evac helicopter in along these parts.

103 Miles STAY LEFT on CA 96, after crossing another bridge, going into Siskyou county, a confluence of the Salmon and Klamath rivers, and highways, as a road runs off to the right to the Forks of Salmon.

Alternate Route
Via Forks of Salmon

And a highly recommended one if you are headed to **Mt. Shasta** . . . as long as you do not suffer from vertigo (I mean that seriously) and do want to take one of the most scenic roads in the state. At that little intersection right after the bridge take the RIGHT turn to Forks of Salmon. Superb! The narrow Salmon River Road runs through the woods, and then emerges right on the edge, and 40 feet above, the **Salmon River.** A hundred or so years ago some enterprising folk blasted a narrow path along the cliff that went straight up from the river for a hundred feet; some say it was for a narrow-gauge railway, and narrow it is. No guard-rail between you and the long drop to the river. And if two cars meet, one will have to back up a long way.

After clearing the cliff the road gets to the community of **Forks of Salmon** (17 miles) which has a post office and a general store and gas pumps. Right after the village the road forks, and I recommend going right, which takes you along Cecilville Road beside the **South Fork Salmon River.** In **Cecilville** (35 Miles) is **Doyle's Camp,** aiming to please fishermen, hunters, and motorcyclists, with a restaurant, whose hours depend on the time of year, and a few beds for the weary (530-462-4685), and gas.

The road from Cecilville to Callahan is one of those mysteries, a perfectly surfaced road that must average 30 cars and trucks a day at most. Somebody went to a lot of time and effort to do this, and I am grateful. It goes up over the **Pacific Crest Trail,** with a couple of major switchbacks, and then down into the valley of the **South Fork Scott River.** You enter **Callahan** at 65 Miles, TURNING RIGHT at the STOP sign onto CA 3.

■

Back on CA 96: after **Somes Bar,** a huddle of houses just beyond the Forks of Salmon turn, the next 30 miles of CA 96 are deliriously fast, mostly flat, up along the **Klamath.**

137 Miles As you enter **Happy Camp** (Pop. 1,110), slow down. One sees the sheriff and his crew a lot, and I think ticket revenues are used for funding the annual Xmas party. Where Second Street runs into 96, there is the **Frontier Cafe** on your left (530-493-2242). Good eats, six days a week 6 to 8, on Sunday 7 to 7. If you want to spend the night, the **Forest Lodge Motel** is up the road a half-mile, at 63712 Hwy 96 to be exact (530-493-5424, $45-plus). Right opposite the motel is the turn for Indian Creek Road, which runs up into Oregon, meeting with US 199 at O'Brien. It you are Oregon-bound, it is a good route to take.

CA 96 is labeled, according to my AAA map, the **State of Jefferson National Scenic Byway,** which commemorates a short-lived secessionist movement back in 1941. **Seiad Valley** goes past, then **Hamburg** (with the **Rainbow General Store** selling cold juice), and then another decision to make after you cross over a bridge at the confluence of the Scott and Klamath rivers.

167 Miles TURN RIGHT at the intersection of CA 96 and Scott River Road, just after you cross over **Scott River.** To your right a private campground sits in mild desolation, a sign indicating some connection with the **Lost Dutchman Mining Association.**

Connector

If you want to head off east and pick up I-5, go straight on CA 96; no worries, you won't get lost. However, after 32 miles you will be at the intersection with CA 263. If you are going north and up to Oregon, stay to the left and you will meet up with the Interstate in two miles; if south, take the turn to the right onto CA 263, headed for Yreka, and in nine miles you will be at an I-5 interchange, and in **Yreka.**   ∎

But the original plan is to follow Scott River Road. The pavement is a bit on the narrow side as it goes along to **Scott Bar,** a very small community, and then rises up higher on the hillside as it follows **Scott River** upstream.

186 Miles Jones Beach, not quite like the one on Long Island, but a spit of sand out in the cold, cold river. The Scott is an official **Wild & Scenic River,** and here it is slithering between the **Marble Mountains** and the **Scott Bar Mountains.**

192 Miles The Quartz Valley Road goes off to the right, you stay straight.

193 Miles This is the beginning of **Scott Valley**, and the **Scott Valley Winery** is off to the left; there soon won't be a town without its own wine label in all of California.

198 Miles TURN RIGHT at the T-bone junction with CA 3 at Fort Jones, you go right. This stage of CA 3 as it goes south through Scott Valley is pretty mundane, with a reasonable amount of traffic on the two-laner.

210 Miles Etna, an old town with a main street and late 19th Century brick buildings, but it has a long, long ways to go before it can consider itself gentrified. If you are here, we can presume you did not take the Forks of Salmon Alternative described earlier on, but here is another chance to see and ride some great back country.

Detour
It is 13 dullish miles down to Callahan on CA 3, 89 brilliant miles if you go on Sawyers Bar Road to **Forks of Salmon,** and then cut back on Cecilville Road. This can be a two-hour (really fast) or four-hour (leisurely) detour. Go down Etna's main street, which becomes Sawyers Bar Road, and in ten miles you are at **Salmon Mountain Summit** (5,958 feet), between the **Marble Mountain Wilderness** to the north, **Russian Wilderness** to the south. A steep downhill, and soon you are riding along the north side of the **North Fork Salmon River,** past Snowden and Sawyers Bar, to Forks of Salmon (41 miles).

Hang a very sharp left over the bridge onto Cecilville Road, and it is a splendid ride of 48 miles back to CA 3 at **Callahan.** ■

Assuming no detour, you go south from Etna.

223 Miles Callahan isn't even really trying to succeed, just a couple of ramshackle old buildings on each side of the road, selling groceries and whatnot.

224 Miles A big sign just before the bridge over the **East Fork Scott River** indicates that CA 3 goes off to the right: to the left, or, more accurately, straight ahead, is the Gazelle Callahan Road, a sign reading GAZELLE 25.

Connector
To Mt. Shasta & Lassen National Park
Head out on the Gazelle Callahan Road, going up a valley, past the turn to **Kangaroo Lake** (kangaroo and gazelle in California?) over **Gazelle Mountain Summit** at 4,921 feet, and down into the broad valley of the **Shasta River.** The road goes through lush grazing

land, and as you go by the entrance to the **Double RR Ranch,** you suddenly see a giant snow-capped mountain.

That is **Mt. Shasta,** for many years thought to be the highest mountain in the Lower 48, at 14,162 feet, and it wasn't until the 1860s that the little needle-nosed peak in the middle of the southern Sierra Nevadas, **Mt. Whitney,** was measured and found to be 332 feet higher. Shasta is much more impressive, a huge, great cone sitting out in the middle of nowhere. A sight to behold.

After 25 miles Gazelle Callahan Road ends at Old Highway 99; take a right, going south toward **Weed** (town of, named not for vegetation but timber magnate Abner Weed, who prospered in the area around 1900; the **Weed Lumber Mill** is now part of the **International Paper Company**) and to **Mt. Shasta,** town of, and hook onto CA 89, which will get you to the national park in two hours. Or you might just want to have a closer look at Mt. Shasta itself. The closest you can get to the top on a motorcycle is **Panther Meadow,** at about 7,000 feet, taking the **Everett Memorial Highway** which runs out of downtown Mt. Shasta. The run up the mountain is absolutely spectacular, with a wide, smooth road and many, many turns.

This sculpture of a prospector sits at the entrance to the little town of Etna, on CA 3.

If you have a d-p bike, you can circle around the east side of Shasta on the old Military Pass Road, which cuts off US 97 about 14 miles northeast of Weed, and then connects with Forest Road 31 after another dozen miles, which in turn runs back to Mt. Shasta (town of).

If you want to stay in Mt. Shasta, nice digs are the **Strawberry Valley Inn,** which is an old-fashioned motel (i.e. one story) turned into an inexpensive B&B, on the south end of the main drag in town, Mt. Shasta Boulevard. **Susie Ryan** is the innkeeper, and gives her clients a glass of wine or bottle of beer in the evening, and a "continental" breakfast in the morning (1142 South Mt. Shasta Blvd., 530-926-2052). Breakfast of a more serious nature can be found seven days a week at **Lily's** (530-926-3372), just up from the Inn at 1013 S. Mt. Shasta. Dinner at the **Piemont Restaurant** is recommended (530-926-2402), or ask Susie for her recommendation.

Picking up CA 89 for the run to Lassen, this road runs through the high-country pine forest of the **Cascade Range,** mostly straight shots of two-lane highway. Not very exciting, but quite picturesque. It is 80 miles along CA 89 to reach **Old Station,** just north of Lassen, and Chapter 9 deals with that.   ∎

These rafters are enjoying the cool waters of the Klamath River on a 95-degree day.

Way back at that intersection with the Gazelle Callahan Road, if you headed south on CA 3, you would go up over . . .

229 Miles . . . **Scott Mountain Summit** at 5,401 feet, with big signs indicating that this road is not cleared of snow at night. If you are traveling this road at night in the winter on a motorcycle, you might want to check in with your psychiatrist.

A historical plaque up at the summit tells you this was the old California-Oregon stage road, opened in 1860, and kept running all winter with the help of sleighs. This avenue of commerce and communication fell into decline after the railroad came up the Sacramento River Canyon in 1887. But if you can imagine sledding over this mountain 120 years ago . . . where is my electric vest?

236 Miles The mountain road comes around a curve and starts to flatten, with a big pile of road-work gravel to the left, and the start of Forest Road 17. Ahead is the bridge over the **Tangle Blue River,** and to your left is the west end of Forest Road 17.

Detour

If you want to have a good time, and are adept at riding a lot of dirt road, TURN LEFT onto Forest Road 17/a/k/a Parks Creek Road, and head up alongside the **Little Trinity River.** The road was paved recently, and even more recently washed out, so there are a lot of bumpy stretches, but since the state is determined to have this as part of the **Trinity Heritage Scenic Parkway,** it should be in good condition by 2007.

After ten miles the road leaves the river behind and begins a serious climb into the **Scott Mountains.** The asphalt is intact along here, and the road crests after 16 miles. Now begins the descent to the eastern side, along **Parks Creek,** and at 20 miles you cross a wooden bridge, with the medieval-looking gate of the **Stewart Springs** resort to the right, a straight shot down to Old 99 Highway to the left. Twenty-five miles after leaving CA 3 you are at Old 99, with Weed just four miles to the south.

Now go anywhere you want.

■

---

260 Miles Back on CA 3: at **Coffee Creek** the U.S. Forest Service has a ranger station, with information about hiking trails and such, for the athletically inclined. I got so hungry reading about the 19-mile Grizzly Lake hike I went across the road to the **Forest Cafe** and had a piece of pie.

263 Miles Trinity Lake shines in front, third largest lake in California, covering some 16,000 acres, though there are a lot of logs and other debris floating in many of the coves, which reduces its aesthetic qualities. The Trinity Dam was completed in 1961, and the water has submerged much of the mining history of the area. Mostly the road, CA 3, stays a distance away from the lake, and all you see are pine trees.

269 Miles TURN OFF at Trinity Center, and a general store has gas and food.

288 Miles A left turn is marked RUSH CREEK ROAD and LEWISTON; if you wish to spend the night in these parts, Weaverville, straight on CA 3, is a more romantic bet (see Trip #15).

Detour

If you are in a hurry to get to **Redding,** and you might well be the first person in the world to be that (sorry, Reddingites, I do apologize), take the Rush Creek Road. After 10 miles you reach **Lewiston,** an old mining town, pretty ramshackly, with the old girder bridge across the **Trinity River** closed. Take a left up the hill and there is the **Lewiston Valley Motel** (530-778-3942) right next to the **Mountain Valley Grill** (530-778-3177), open from 6 to 9 every day. Not a bad place to spend the night.

In the morning, continue on the road toward Redding, taking Trinity Dam Boulevard to the right, and in four miles you will find yourself on CA 299, where you turn left.   ■

Back on CA 3, you follow the Trinity River south.

295 Miles A STOP sign puts you in Weaverville, with sustenance and sleep dealt with in the preceding Loop #2. If you want to go back to Eureka TURN RIGHT on CA 299 and follow Trip #2 routing back to the coast.

399 Miles Arrive back at Ground Zero in Eureka.

Connector
From Weaverville to Redding

If you want to go to Redding, which will lead toward **Lassen Volcanic National Park,** TURN LEFT on CA 3/299. After seven miles KEEP LEFT after the Trinity River bridge, CA 3 going right, CA 299 more or less straight toward Redding.

After 19 miles Trinity Dam Blvd comes in from the left, and CA 299 goes steeply up to **Buckhorn Summit** (3,215 feet), with lots of RVs in the way. This now goes down steeply for a few miles, then flattens out as it passes **Whiskeytown Lake.**

At 44 Miles you come into the remains of the town of **Shasta** (not to be confused with Mt. Shasta 60 miles to the north), now a state historical park. Shasta was the county seat from 1851 to 1888, and during the gold-rush days life was hectic. As many as a hundred wagons could come through in a single day, making merchants very happy; imagine a hundred semis a day stopping in some small town. Now all that is left are the ruins of brick buildings, and the restored courthouse. But it is all very trim and neat.

Fifty miles after leaving Weaverville you arrive in **Redding,** named for one Major B. B. Redding, a land agent for the **Central Pacific Railroad** back in the 1870s. It is a big place, now the Shasta county seat, and a major crossroads in the **North Sacramento Valley.** It has a lousy climate—very hot in summer, very cold in winter. The last time I was there (July) the temperature was 111 degrees. But it has motels, restaurants, and all the necessaries. The visitors' bureau number is 800-874-7562.

Cheap digs can be found at the **Redding Lodge** (1135 Market St, 530-243-5141); as a matter of fact, all of Market Street, which is part of CA 273, the old main drag, is littered with the detritus of motels of eras past. Out at the Interstate's Hilltop Drive exit are the newer chains, from **La Quinta** to **Motel 6**. For the slightly different, try the **River Inn** down at 835 Park Marina Drive (530-241-9500) on the **Sacramento River;** ask for a river-view room. Restaurants are everywhere.

North-south through Redding is I-5, east-west CA 299 leads you to I-5, at which point CA 299 heads north while CA 44 goes to Lassen Volcanic National Park. ∎

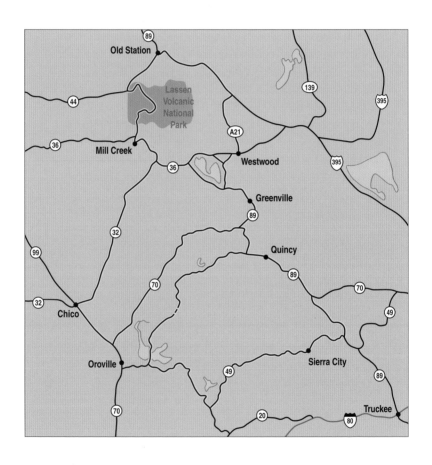

Northern Sierra Nevadas

Headquarters *Quincy*
Plumas County (Quincy) Visitors Bureau *800-326-2247*
Best Time to Visit *May through September, though the road through Volcanic National Park can be closed until July.*
Getting There *On a north/south run, Quincy lies on CA 89; on an east/ west route, look for CA 70; the two state highways run together for some 30 miles, and headquarters is along that stretch.*
Ground Zero *Will be right in front of the courthouse, where CA 70/89 takes a right turn.*

Here we see Lassen Peak in the month of July; the snow can stay a long time at these latitudes and heights.

This is a tootle through **Volcanic National Park** and the northern third of the Sierra Nevada mountain range: This is high country you are in for the most part, on the ridge of the **Sierra Nevadas** which runs about 4,500 feet above sea level. Though two of the loops take you down some 4,000 feet into the **Sacramento River Valley,** where the land is low-lying, and distinctly warm in the summertime.

    Quincy, the seat of **Plumas County,** gets five feet of snow and four feet of rain every year, mostly in the winter months, and is best known (among motorcyclists) as the site of the annual **49er Rally** put on by the BMW 49er Club at the **Plumas-Sierra County Fairgrounds.** The county itself covers some 2,600 square miles, well over half of which is national forest, and has less than ten bodies per square mile.

Along the narrow Feather River Canyon, the highway and railroad compete for space; here, the road has the high crossing, on a bridge built in 1932.

Although these visitors from Germany have great mountain riding in the Alps, riding through Volcanic National Park is unlike anything in Europe.

Downtown Quincy has two parallel one-way streets (Main going east, Lawrence, west), so a brief jaunt and U-turn gives you the whole place. This is a working town, not a resort place, but has half a dozen places to sleep, like the **Gold Pan Motel** on the north side of town (200 Crescent Street, 530-283-2265) with 56 rooms, or the older, single-story **Spanish Creek Motel** right across Highway 70 (233 Crescent Street, 530-283-1200) with 25 rooms.

The town has more than a dozen places to eat; the best establishment for breakfast or lunch is the celebrated **Morning Thunder** (530-283-1310, 557 Lawrence Street). For dinner try **Moon's** (530-283-0765, 497 Lawrence Street), with a rather good wine list to accentuate your taste in fish, fowl, or dead cow, or **Sweet Lorraine's** (530-283-5300, 384 West Main Street) which offers excellent food and the most sociable bar in town—and some jazz.

If you want a nice place to pick up an Associate of Arts degree, try the **Feather River College**. For the historians among us the **Plumas Museum**, right behind the four-story courthouse (built in 1921, and you cannot miss the Greco-Roman structure), has lots on local Indians, mining, and railroads.

Trip 16 Via Lassen Volcanic National Park

Distance *214 miles*

Highlights *This is an easy loop, easy roads, but the 30 miles you spend inside the park will probably slow you down, as there is much to see and do. Especially if you are a volcanologist.*

0 Miles Head north on CA 70/89, past the airfield. Climb over a small ridge and the road wiggles along through the woods.

11 Miles TURN RIGHT where CA 70 and 89 split, taking 89 north to **Greenville** and Lassen. The road takes you along the **Indian River** into **Indian Valley**, the almost defunct mining and lumbering community of **Crescent Mills**, then on through Greenville to **Canyon Dam**, a village with several stores and a gas station.

32 Miles TURN RIGHT just after Canyon Dam, onto CA 47, which will go up the east side of **Lake Almanor.**

39 Miles TURN LEFT onto A13, angling northwest toward the town of Chester.

43 Miles STOP sign—TURN LEFT onto CA 36. Cross over the northernmost arm of Lake Almanor.

That is 10,457-foot Lassen Peak behind me, in Lassen Volcanic National Park, and snowless in late August.

44 Miles Official **Vista Point,** so you can stop and admire Lake Almanor. This is a big lake that was created in 1915 after damming the **North Fork Feather River,** and has over 50 miles of shoreline. This all used to be called **Big Meadows,** a good place to raise cattle in the late 19th Century, and the area became the summer home for wealthy types from the Sacramento Valley.

49 Miles Crossing over the **Feather River** and entering **Chester.**

51 Miles GO STRAIGHT as CA 36 meets CA 89, going west together.

59 Miles The **Black Forest Lodge** is on your left, an unremarkable building with remarkably good German food, from sauerbraten to bratwurst, washed down with good beer. (530-258-2939).

62 Miles CA 32 goes off to the left, heading down to Chico. (Keep this in mind for the next loop.)

69 Miles **Childs Meadow Resort** on your right, with 20 motel rooms, several chalets/cabins, and a cafe running from 8 to 6 (530-595-3383).

71 Miles A road marked CA 172 goes off to the left, while CA 36/89 goes up over **Morgan Summit** (5,155 feet).

Chester

This is a slightly run-down, but pleasant, touristy town, pop. 2,200, elevation 4,550 feet. One main street, a half dozen motels, a dozen places to eat, and a major tourist season of about three months, minorly touristed the rest of the year. Make the bulk of your money in the summer, and play out the profit through the other nine months.

I'm not much on B&Bs, for good reason. Show up on a rainy day and you can see the lace curtains fall back into place and the owners saying, "Oh no, are those the people that have the reservations; they'll muddy everything up."

But the best B&B in Chester, the **Bidwell House,** is extremely scrumptious, with 14 rooms, and present managers, Kim and Ian James, think that motorcyclists are rather nice people. Though I could imagine some bikers they might not think highly of. John Bidwell built the house in 1901, and it is a lovely sprawling place under large trees. Along with excellent breakfasts, a superb kitchen, orchestrated by Ian, turns out dinner three nights a week. (530-258-3338, 1 Main Street, at the very east end of town).

If you are into a very rustic setting, 17 miles north of Chester at the end of Warner Valley Road (partially dirt) is the **Drakesbad Guest Ranch** (530-529-1512), with a stunning setting just within the **Lassen National Park** boundaries. Reservations are essential, and I would say a two-night stay is the minimum to get a proper appreciation for the place. ■

Alternate Route

CA 172 is an entertaining roundabout way of getting to Lassen, taking 14 miles to cover what the direct route covers in three miles. I suggest you take the detour.

The road runs along **Mill Creek** into a summer community called, curiously enough, Mill Creek, then climbs up to **Mineral Summit** (5,266 feet), and drops down to intersect with the cross-roads community of **Mineral** at the junction with CA 36 (9 miles). **Lassen Mineral Lodge** is at the intersection, with rooms and food (530-595-4422). And gas across the road. Take a right on CA 36 and head back up the mountain, and at 14 miles you intersect with 89 as it heads north into the national park. ■

74 Miles TURN RIGHT at the fork, staying on CA 89 and heading north, while CA 36 goes west toward Mill Creek and Red Bluff.

79 Miles Enter **Lassen Volcanic National Park** and pay $5 (per motorcycle) for the privilege; definitely worth it.

79+ Miles To the right is **Lassen Chalet,** with souvenirs and some basic food. No grand hotel here in this park, nothing with gorgeous vistas and a fine restaurant; the Chalet is as good as it gets. The fact that the snow closes the park down from November to June might have something to do with that. It is a great 29-mile trip through the park, with the maximum allowable being 35 mph. Sort of. The road climbs quickly at the beginning, past the stinky **Sulphur Works,** around **Diamond Peak,** and past **Lake Helen.**

85 Miles If you want to take a three-mile hike, park at the **Bumpass Hell** lot and head down into this ten-acre Hades. Apparently a fellow named Ken Bumpass (this was back when names were names, and nobody laughed) used to take tourists down into this hellish scene, full of bubbling pits where the water is actually boiling from thermal heat. Nowadays there are boardwalks to stay on, but poor old Bumpass had the misfortune to step on some fragile crust and stuck a leg in; parboiled it was, and had to be amputated.

Lassen Volcanic National Park

We might tend to forget we are standing on a volcano, with bubbly bits perking out all over, even though the last major eruption was nearly 70 years ago. It blew its stack over 300 times in the seven years between 1914 and 1921. Mess not with Mother Nature. In the midst of this chaos, it was declared a national park in 1916, thanks to the efforts of Representative John Raker; hence **Raker Peak** in the north of the park.

The road runs around **Reading Peak,** to **Summit Lake** (7,000 feet), through the **Dersch Meadows** and the **Devastated Area** (so named for the lava flow that occurred in 1915), and over **Emigrant Pass;** if you can imagine taking a wagon train through here 150 years ago, think about one Peter Lassen, who did just that. And hence got a small portion of immortality. The **Lassen Emigrant Trail** was active from 1848 to 1851, and as befits a frontiersman, old Pete died in 1859 while prospecting, attacked by Indians who objected to all this white-man's possessiveness. ∎

A father and son are doing a little bonding while riding through the Sierras; they have just spent the night at the Timber House in Chester.

87 Miles The pavement is up to 8,512 feet, right south of **Lassen Peak,** highest point the road gets to in the park. If you wish to leave the bike in the parking area and climb the rest of the way to the 10,457 foot peak, be my guest; that's about a five mile round trip, and if your math is any good you appreciate that you are going up 2,000 feet, and then coming down.

The road goes down through the **Dwarf Forest** to **Manzanita Lake.**
107 Miles The **Loomis Museum** (B. F. Loomis documented the whole cycle of eruptions back in the late teens, and was instrumental in having the park established) sits at the lake, and will tell you all you wish to know about the park, and volcanoes.

108 Miles STOP sign—TURN RIGHT after exiting park and meeting CA 44. CA 44 goes off to the west to Redding, and CA 44/89 goes northeast.

109 Miles Somebody with a sense of humor named **Eskimo Hill Summit,** at 5,933 feet.

118 Miles Cross over **Hat Creek,** with a store and cafe beside the road.

121 Miles You arrive in **Old Station,** once a stop for the **California Stage Company,** also a military post in the late 1850s, now offering a few tourist services.

121+ Miles TURN RIGHT with CA 44, letting CA 89 go up to Mt. Shasta; a Forest Service information station is at this intersection.

122 Miles Last view of **Mt. Shasta** as the road ascends to the Pacific Crest; this is officially the **Feather Lake Highway.** Now it is high country, flat and sparsely grassed, as you pass the turn to the right for Butte Lake, the turn to the left for Pittville. A railroad runs just to the north of the road. Long fency lines parallel the road, the important highly stressed corner sections being shored up with rocks.

145 Miles The **Bogard Rest Stop** is on your right.

150 Miles TURN RIGHT at the sign reading WESTWOOD 18, with an arrow pointing to the right on County Road A21. Take it. If you turn left, a gravel Forest Road will lead you to **Feather Lake** in a mile. County Road A21 consists of 18 fast miles on a very well-paved, very lightly trafficked cut-off.

166 Miles Cross railroad tracks just passing through the forest.

168 Miles TURN RIGHT as A21 ends at CA 36.

171 Miles TURN LEFT onto CA 147; you are going to start retracing your steps in a couple of miles.

182 Miles STOP sign—TURN LEFT onto CA 89 here at **Canyon Dam.**

203 Miles STOP sign—TURN LEFT on CA 70/89, toward Quincy.

214 Miles End of ride, downtown **Quincy.**

Trip 17 Deer Creek & Feather River Canyon

Distance *185 miles*

Highlights *I could say a lot about this loop, but the important fact is that the Feather River Canyon is one of the most delicious rides imaginable—a definite must. I will run you up CA 89, down Deer Creek (CA 32) across CA 99, and back up Feather River CA 70. Easy as eating apple pie.*

0 Miles Leave Quincy going north on CA 70/89 (this is partially a repeat of Loop 1.)

11 Miles TURN RIGHT at **Greenville Wye**, keeping on CA 89 toward Greenville, Canyon Dam, and southwest shore of Lake Almanor.

46 Miles STOP sign—TURN LEFT, keeping on CA 89.

47 Miles TURN LEFT at well-marked turn to CA 30, and sign reading CHICO 52—and just follow your front wheel for the next 52 miles. Can't go wrong.

That 1912 girder bridge crossing the Feather River gives one access to the Belden Resort, a very fine place to spend a night or two.

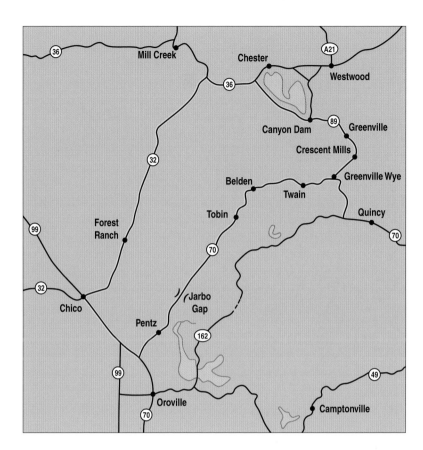

The road (Deer Creek Highway) begins through a meadow with a split rail fence, then into heavy woods, following along **Deer Creek,** curving lots; it is a good road, although not particularly inspiring, but a very pleasant ride with a moderate amount of traffic. About 14 miles along the road leaves the forest, and the creek, and after about 25 miles the road flattens out a tad, just a long, long descent alongside **Little Chico Creek Canyon** (redundant, as the Spanish *chico* means little) into the valley of the **Sacramento River.** Past **Forest Ranch,** past the TRAFFIC LIGHT at Bruce Road, all the way to CA 99.

99 Miles   TURN LEFT after going under CA 99 freeway, following signs for CA 99 South, and get on the freeway, which goes through flat grassland; no sign of a city anywhere, as it all lies just to the west of the freeway.

112 Miles   EXIT RIGHT at the BUTTE COLLEGE/DURHAM exit, and TURN LEFT at the STOP sign, on Durham-Pentz Road. And through the fields, crossing over CA 191 and continuing on into the foothills.

121 Miles   GO RIGHT where Durham-Pentz ends at Pentz Road, where a sign indicates that CA 70 is to the right.

122 Miles   STOP sign—TURN LEFT onto CA 70. In a mile or so CA 70 becomes a stretch of freeway for the next seven miles. You cross over an arm of **Lake Oroville,** little figuring that this is a product of the **Feather River,** which is running way off to your right, unseen behind the hills.

130 Miles   At Jarbo Gap (2,250 feet) the road starts a descent, and you realize that a monstrous river is roiling along well below you; do not go over the edge. You can see the **Union Pacific** railroad tracks running well below the level of the road, on the far side of the canyon. Dramatic.

136 Miles   The 1932 high bridge, carrying the road, crosses high above the Union Pacific bridge. The road is a sight, with huge sheets of granite curving down on both sides. Several tunnels add to the pleasure, especially if you are wearing darkly shaded glasses on a very bright day. No room for error here. Most of the highway bridges, you will note, date from the 1930s, when FDR had the **Works Project Admininstration** in full force, and fixing bad roads was a major user of manpower. The Feather River Highway was opened in 1935.

150 Miles   At the **Tobin** crossing, where rails and road have changed position, the railroad now higher than the pavement, the "historic" **Tobin Resort** (530-283-2225) has been recently refurbished, and offers all amenities.

159 Miles   A few miles up the road the **Belden Resort** is also in full swing. What a place! Cross the old (1912) girder bridge, and you are in another world. A dozen cabins can each sleep from two to seven people (more, if you are very friendly), crowded camping, and there is a restaurant and saloon

Chico

You might wish to go into Chico (Alt. 200 feet); this fabled city is home to many events and institutions, including **Chico State College,** which for several years held the dubious honor of being ranked **#1 party school** in the nation.

The town began life as the **Chico Ranch** in Spanish land-grant days, and became a cattle-raising center, and had access to markets via the boats chuffing up the **Sacramento River.** Now it is noted for being very hot in the summertime.   ∎

With the EPA requirements for expensive new gas holding tanks at service stations, many places, like this one in Greenville, have gone out of business. (Don't worry, there's another station in town.)

and even a gas pump (530-283-2906). Every July the place hosts a motor-cycle extravaganza (by invitation only) and upward of a thousand people show up. How they all fit in this relatively small place is still unexplained.

Back on CA 70, past the Caribou turn-off, **Rich Bar, Virgilia, Twain,** with the abandoned lumber operation, and **Paxton.**

174 Miles STAY STRAIGHT as CA 70 meets up with CA 89 at what is called locally the **Greenville Wye,** staying on CA 70/89. For the railroad buffs, the **Keddie "Y,"** which refers to the railroad tracks splitting and going in two directions, is just a couple of miles further on.

185 Miles Arrive back in **Quincy.**

Trip 18 Bucks Lake & Yuba Pass

Distance *184 miles*

Highlights *This loop involves two more crossings over the Sierra Nevadas, including the northern end of CA 49, which is a doozer as it goes up along the Yuba River and over Yuba Pass, the northernmost pass of note in the Sierra Nevada range.*

Love these signs: north and south in the same direction.

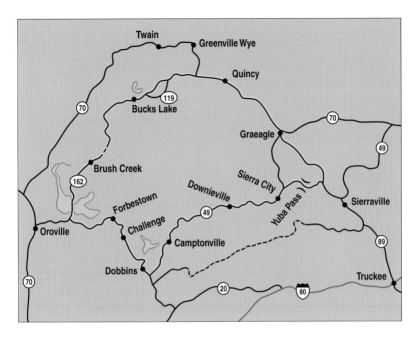

0 Miles Head west out of town on Forest Road 119, aiming for Bucks Lake.

2 Miles A plaque off on the right side of the road describes the mining operations that existed along **Spanish Creek** from 1851 to 1905. It is of most interest to note that Gopher Hill, the biggest hydraulic mining operation in **Plumas County**, is now the site of the county dump.

9 Miles STAY RIGHT at the fork in the woods, with the RV's taking the low road, Big Creek Road, to the left, the motorcyclists taking the high Butte County Road to the right. Climb up and over **Bucks Summit** (5,531 feet), then drop down to **Bucks Lake**, at 5,153 feet.

17 Miles **Bucks Lakeshore Resort** on your right, with 11 cabins going for $70 a day on up. The management likes a minimum of a two-day stay, but if you are passing by and they have an empty one, negotiations can be successful. (530-283-6900). Down the road is the **Bucks Lake Lodge,** with a dozen rentals (530-283-2662).

18 Miles STOP sign—TURN RIGHT onto Big Creek Road, which is now the Oroville-Quincy Highway, the low road you did not take. Lovely new stretch of road, FR 119, paved by the U.S. Forest Service, winding along a ridge, generally open to great vistas.

28 Miles The road enters the woods, and it's now the old, patched pavement.

Hydraulic Mining

What's that? That was an efficient, and environmentally disruptive, way of separating gold from the rest of the earth. In the early 1850s miners hoped to find a nugget lying on top of the earth, or get a pan and scoop up a bit of gravel from a placer (sort of like a gravel bar, instead of a sand bar), swirl it around with some water, and pick out the gold bits.

After the easy stuff got taken, miners, and big mining companies, could either do tunnel (hard-rock) mining or hydraulic mining. The latter ran water by gravity feed into great huge nozzles which would blast away at the earth and carry everything off downstream, where sluice boxes would separate the gold from the dirt. Some of these hydraulic digs moved thousands of tons of earth, and eventually downstream ranchers complained, and the lawyers got involved, and off to court everybody went. The California Supreme Court ruled in 1884 that hydraulic mining had to stop. Score one for the Greens. ■

31 Miles The summer community of **Brush Creek** is scattered through the woods, and the road gets quite steep and twisty. Then the woods open up, and somewhere along that stretch FR 119 becomes CA 162.

44 Miles Lake Oroville (Alt. 601 feet) can be seen, all done by damming up the **Feather River.**

49 Miles Cross over a miniature Golden Gate Bridge over an arm of **Lake Oroville.**

52 Miles TURN LEFT, where a sign pointing to the left indicates FORBESTOWN ROAD, a/k/a Forest Road 174.

58 Miles STAY RIGHT as road forks; left goes to **Feather Falls,** while you stay right (straight, really) on to **Forbestown.**

59 Miles STAY RIGHT at fork, staying on FR 174, a/k/a Challenge Cut-Off Road, after passing through the town named after Mr. Forbes. With a general store, open daily, and a museum, open on weekends; this **Yuba Feather Museum** is best known for the thousands of photographs from the last half of the 19th Century, recording the history of the era.

68 Miles STOP sign—TURN LEFT toward **Challenge** on County Road E21/FR 174.

71 Miles TURN RIGHT a hundred yards after the **Forest Service Information Station,** which sits on the right, with a white wooden church on the left, at DOBBINS 16 sign, staying on FR 174.

82 Miles   STOP sign—TURN LEFT, directions pointing to BULLARDS BAR DAM 2; this is County Road E20.

85 Miles   Big damn dam damming **Bullards Bar Reservoir,** and you ride along the top.

91 Miles   STOP sign—TURN LEFT onto CA 49 at this junction.

93 Miles   A sign proclaiming "historic" **Camptonville** points off to the right, but if you turn you will find most of the history is lost in the detritus of modern civilization, including a lot of abandoned cars. For the d-p types, you can search out the west end of Henness Pass Road, and have an interesting time crossing the Sierras on a long stretch of dirt.

Now it is up along the rushing **Yuba River,** very nice. Pass **Goodyears Bar.**

111 Miles   **Cannon Point,** with a real 12-pounder on a pedestal, and you can look down on **Downieville.**

112 Miles   Sign for the **Sierra Shangri-La,** with a turn to the right, over a bridge, and up along the river for a quarter mile; they offer both cottages and B&B (530-289-3455).

121 Miles   In **Sierra City,** the **Mountain Creek Restaurant & Buckhorn Tavern** (530-862-1171) does excellent meals.

Downieville

Named for a Major William Downie in 1850, the town had more than 5,000 inhabitants in that decade. A good many more than today, where a 350 number is voiced about. Nice place to spend the night. Try the **Riverside Inn** first, a wonderfully antiquated building right on the river, with all the 10 rooms above the water ($60-plus 530-289-1000); the place is often reserved a year in advance on the weekends, but mid-week is more accessible. More conventional is the **Downieville Inn,** with 11 rooms ($45-plus, 530-289-3243, 117 Main St.). Food at the **Downieville Diner** (530-289-3616) or the **Downieville Bakery & Cafe** (530-289-0108)—which turns out an excellent Cornish pastie, a traditional miners' meal.

Do go across the river to **Durgan Flat** and the courthouse, and admire the refurbished gallows, which were last used to hang someone in 1888. And Galloway Road (dirt) running uphill from the gallows, with a big sign saying it is very, very steep. You can clamber up and meet the Henness Pass Road at the top, but it is a bear; best done on a dual-purpose machine.   ■

That's the old Downieville gallows behind me, which has done its duty in executing cattle rustlers, murderers, and the occasional motorcycle speeder.

Alternate Route

At the 128-mile mark there is Bassett's General Store and a short-cut, cutting off about 17 miles on the loop back to Quincy. TURN LEFT onto Gold Lake Road, a/k/a Forest Road 24, and go north 15 miles over **Snag Lake Summit** (6,700 feet) to meet up with CA 89 near **Graeagle**.

■

137 Miles   Yuba Pass at 6,701 feet; Forest Road 12, on the right, will take you south on a dirt road to **Henness Pass,** if you so desire.

Now a steep descent begins, going down into **Sierra Valley.**

142 Miles   STOP sign—TURN LEFT onto CA 89 to get back to Quincy.

Connector
To Lake Tahoe

If you TURN RIGHT at the STOP and follow CA 49/89, in five miles you come to **Sierraville,** where CA 49 goes straight and you TURN RIGHT by the old general store, keeping on CA 89.

Nine more miles and you come over a rise in the woods, and to the right, the west, is Henness Pass Road, which can take you all the way back to **Camptonville** in about 45 miles, the first third of which are paved; the drop on the dirt section is about 4,000 feet. Easy for a d-p bike.

In 30 miles you arrive at Interstate 80. It is 14 miles to **Lake Tahoe,** 33 to **Reno,** and about 100 miles to **Sacramento;** you're on your own.   ∎

158 Miles   Coming into **Graeagle,** with Gold Lake Road off to the left. Just ahead is the bridge crossing over the **Middle Fork Feather River.**

160 Miles   STOP sign—TURN LEFT at Intersection with CA 70, going toward Quincy, a long, straightish road through the woods.

184 Miles   Enter downtown **Quincy.**

This couple rode out for a look at New Bullards Bar Reservoir, which dams North Canyon Creek.

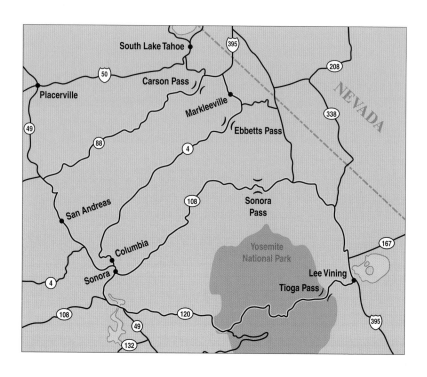

High Sierra Passes

Headquarters *Sonora*

Tourist Information *532-4212, 800-446-1333*

Best Time to Visit *May through November, though check in the spring to make sure the passes are open, and in the fall to make sure they haven't already been closed.*

Getting There *No big interstates or freeways near Sonora, which is all to the good, but getting there is easy. From the east or west is best done via CA 108, from north or south, CA 49.*

Ground Zero *Start at the TRAFFIC LIGHT at Washington and Stockton, right by the Sonora Days Inn.*

For those of us who love mountain riding, the rides do not get much better than this. In a short linear north/south distance, 70 eagle-flying miles, lie four of the great passes across the **Sierra Nevada** (Snowy Mountain) range,

Ebbetts Pass, at 8,730 feet, is, for my motorcycle money, the most entertaining pass in the Sierras to ride.

This is a reproduction of an 1850s store in Coloma, near where gold was discovered in 1848.

Tioga (9,945 feet), **Sonora** (9,624 feet), **Ebbetts** (8,730 feet), and **Carson** (8,573 feet). However, in order to connect all those passes, it is more like 500 road miles, enough to keep any sporting motorcyclist deliriously happy for a day or two.

Traffic is generally light, except on Tioga in the summer, so the rider can take full advantage of the pleasures of the road. It is best to take these passes two per day, though I have met riders who have gotten up early on a June morning and nabbed them all in a day. That is a bit more work, and competition, than I am interested in.

Each pass has an east-west road some 60 to 90 miles long, and then the north-south roads that connect them at the east or west ends. The landscape goes from the hot **San Joaquin Valley** on the west side, with vineyards and cattle and oak trees, through thick fir forests at the midway point, breaking out into rock and lake and isolated evergreen as the road goes over 8,000 feet. Where the views are superb.

The asphalt is usually in good condition, but services are not frequent. Since all these passes are closed in the winter, there is not much call for gas stations and garages at the top.

Sonora is a likeable town, the seat of **Tuolumne County,** steeped in history, and with steep roads to the west going up into the mountains. What a miserably poor play on words!

The town sits in the **Sierra Nevada** foothills at about 1,800 feet elevation, with a reasonable year-around climate. It can get hot in July and August, But right behind is the high ridge of the Sierra Nevada, and the temperature drops as you climb. Which also means that when winter comes, these passes will be closed by snow.

Sonora is a tourist destination, more for the Mother Lode and 49er families than the pass-seeking motorcyclists, which means that food and beds are plentiful. It's a smallish place, only 5,000 or so year-round inhabitants, and walkable.

Smack in the middle of town, at the corner of Washington and Stockton streets, is the old **Sonora Inn,** dating from 1896 but extensively redone in 1931; in 1998 it was incorporated into the **Day's Inn** chain, which seems to have done it no real harm. The Sonora Days Inn has 30 rooms, while the two-story motel unit (circa 1960) behind has another 34 (160 South Washington St., 209-532-2400, or 800-329-7466). Outdoor parking is in front of the motel units, but Sonora is a pretty safe place. Up Washington Street a quarter mile is the **Sonora Inn of California,** which used to be the **Sonora Townhouse Motel,** a rather bleak, three-storied, asphalted presence with 112 rooms (350 South Washington St., 209-532-3633, 800-251-1538). Back to the old motel concept is the **Sonora Gold Lodge,** on Stockton about half a mile west of the Sonora Inn, with 42 ground-level units (480 Stockton St., 209-532-3952, 800-363-2154).

Food is where you find it. **The Miner's Shack** (157 S. Washington, 209-532-5252) has a goodly array of omelettes in the morning. **Banny's Cafe** (209-553-4709), a block off the main street at 83 South Steward Street, is good, as is the **Diamondback Grill** (209-532-6661), at 110 South Washington. The most elegant fare is, so I've heard, at the **Seven Sisters Restaurant** (209-928-9363) in the **Black Oak Casino,** a few miles out of town.

Trip 19 Ebbetts & Carson Passes

Distance *223 miles*

Highlights *Ebbetts happens to be my favorite pass of the four, because it involves some seriously twisty roads, meaning that very few other people use it. You can always tell when there is a vehicle ahead of you on the downhill sections from the toasted-brake smell.*

0 Miles Head north on CA 49, right through the center of old Sonora.

2+ Miles BEAR RIGHT onto Parrotts Ferry Road.

3+ Miles **Columbia Gem Motel** is a rustic place alongside the road, recently refurbished, with genuine cabins (209-532-4508).

4 Miles Enter **Columbia.**

8 Miles Cross bridge over **New Melones Lake.**

Big trees grow in Sequoia National Park.

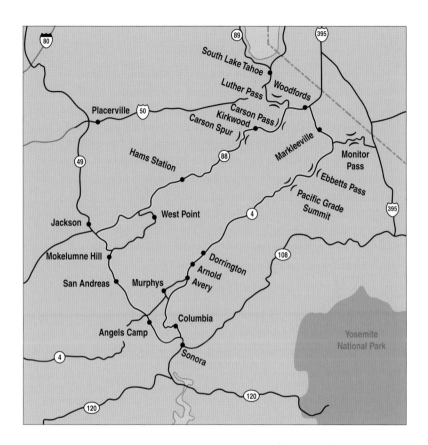

Columbia State Historic Park

This place is very much worth a stop, even an overnight stay. The brick town flourished in the 1850s, continued on for a good many years, and then fell into disrepair. The state salvaged the place, from jail to livery to saloon, and it now offers a pleasant, although somewhat commercialized, view of the Gold Rush past. If you stay at the **City Hotel,** or the nearby **Fallon Hotel,** you get a better appreciation of the past; I must recommend the top-of-the-line balcony rooms in the **City** (209-532-1479, 800-532-1479). And dinner at the **City Hotel Restaurant,** staffed by hotel-school trainees from the nearby **Columbia College,** is to be commended. Less formal food is served at the **Columbia House Restaurant** (209-532-5134). ■

Into Murphys

If you take a left on Main Street and go downtown, you will be rewarded by a visit to the **Murphys Hotel,** first opened in 1856. A lot of well-known 19th Century personalities have stayed there, from Mark Twain to Ulysses S. Grant. The current owners bought the place in 1963, after the local sheriff came in one night and closed the place down because he felt the crowd was too rowdy. The alleged rowdies were a group of **University of the Pacific** students, and being outraged at the insolence of this public servant, purchased the hotel and proceeded to drink at will. "Historic" hotel rooms and much newer (and quieter) motel-type rooms available (209-728-3244, 800-532-7684). **Galvin's Family Restaurant** (209-728-3964), on CA 4, is where all the pick-up trucks are parked early in the morning.   ∎

14+ Miles   STOP sign—TURN RIGHT onto CA 4.
17 Miles   Murphys turn-off.

Alternate Route

A very nice alternative to the next 11 miles of CA 4 is to take Sheep Ranch Road, which goes off Main Street just beyond the Murphys Hotel; a big MERCER CAVERNS 1 MILE sign points the way. Follow that, past **Mercer Caverns** (I'm claustrophobic, so spelunking is not high on my agenda), and after six miles the road forks, **Sheep Ranch** to the left, and Fullen Road to the right, marked: CAUTION NARROW ROAD; go right, and there is a beautiful four-mile stretch over the tops of the hills, with great views; highly recommended. Fullen Road merges with Avery Sheep Ranch Road and heads on into **Avery,** where you TURN LEFT onto CA 4.   ∎

24 Miles   Avery, with the back way to Murphys, Sheep Ranch Road, going off to your left.
28 Miles   Enter **Arnold,** which is not dedicated to the body-building politician Mr. Schwarzenegger, but is a working town, strung out over three miles.
29 Miles   Meadowmont (what dullard thinks up shopping-center names?) **Shopping Center** on your left, and the **Snowshoe Brewing Company** is just beyond. If you are in the sidecar, stop and have a pint of

their Snowweizen; the driver can have a soda.

32 Miles **Calavaras Big Trees State Park** is on your right, and worth a visit. Back in the 1850s this grove of giant sequoias was considered one of the wonders of the world, and people would come from San Francisco to view them. We've become too jaded in this present age, and tend to say, "Is that all? We came all this way just to see that?" before returning to our video games.

36 Miles **Dorrington,** and the **Dorrington Hotel** (209-795-5800), built circa 1860. This was on the Big Trees—Carson Valley Toll Road, charging a stiff fee for users from 1862 to 1910. Now it is a long, easy, sometimes four-lane, uphill run through the woods.

59 Miles Enter **Bear Valley,** a ski resort with beds, food, and gas (209-753-2301).

61 Miles CA 207 goes off to the left to the ski area. CA 4 narrows as it continues eastward, and it is closed in the winter.

63 Miles Drop down to **Alpine Lake,** loitering in the sunlight at 7,400 feet. The **Lake Alpine Lodge** has all amenities during the June to September season, or whenever the road is opened and whenever it is closed. The landscape at this altitude is rock, sparse fir trees, lakes, and distance.

71 Miles A mildly ferocious climb and we are at **Mosquito Lake,** on the **Pacific Grade Summit** (8,050 feet). Why water comes out of mountaintops rather than emerging in the valleys has always been, for me, one of those inexplicable bits of geology; makes not a bit sense to me.

A seriously twisted descent takes us down into **Hermit Valley** (7,060 feet); I don't know if a hermit ever lived there, but it certainly must have been remote before the age of the motorcycle and motorcar. And now more of a torturous climb to the actual pass.

76 Miles **Ebbetts Pass,** at 8,780 feet. And another entertaining descent that has been known to knock the brakes out of many a motorhome. Thankfully we have only half a ton or less to slow with three disc brakes to do the job.

87 Miles CONTINUE STRAIGHT as CA 4 vanishes after merging with CA 89 going north (CA 89 south, the turn to the right, goes over Monitor Pass, which you don't want). Our road will go straight north along the **East Fork Carson River,** usually with a lot of hopefuls casting their lines. Past the **East Fork Resort,** where fishermen are being photographed with their catch.

92 Miles Enter **Markleeville,** seat of **Alpine County,** named for one Jacob Marklee who built a bridge there across what is now known as **Markleeville Creek** and collected tolls back in the early 1860s. Who needs investment bankers and stock brokers when you can build a small wooden bridge and make good? However, Jacob was shot dead during an argument in 1863, and it might just have been someone disputing the toll charges. The **Wolf Creek Restaurant** (530-694-2158) serves great meals, though opening hours depend on the time of year; the place was originally called the **Hot Springs Hotel,** and if you want to soak your tired bones, go west of town four miles to **Grovers Hot Springs State Park** (open 2 p.m. to 9 p.m. Monday through Friday, 9 a.m. to 9 p.m. on the weekends). If you want to stay in town, the **J. Marklee Toll Station Motel** (530-694-2507) will gladly put you up.

99 Miles   STOP sign and   TURN LEFT   (west) on CA 89/88 at the Woodfords junction.

105 Miles   GO STRAIGHT on CA 88 at **Picketts Junction,** as CA 89 goes off to the right at the junction and north to Lake Tahoe. CA 88 is now doubling as US 50 Alternate, should something happen at **Echo Summit** (7,382 feet) on US 50, which parallels CA 88 some ten miles to the north.

114 Miles

   Carson Pass (8,573 feet) after going through the valley, past **Red Lake,** and up the hill; Kit Carson crossed over the Sierras here in 1843, while scouting for John Fremont's **U.S. Army Topographical Corps.** I wonder when the army dismantled that useful corps? It is probably all done by satellite now.

   Then it is down to **Caples Lake** and past **Kirkwood,** where the **Kirkwood Inn** (209-758-7350) has been feeding passers-by since the 1860s.

122 Miles   Carson Spur (7,900 feet). Great views over the wilderness to the north. Past **Silver Lake** and **Tragedy Springs**—could be a good story behind that name.

To Lake Tahoe

If you are of a mind, you can go up over **Luther Pass** (7,740 feet) to **Tahoe Valley** and do a 72-mile loop of **Lake Tahoe.** I would recommend a clock-wise loop, as that way you stay on the side of the road nearest to the water. Traffic gets to be a bit much, as tourists flock here in the thousands, as do golfers who play the ten courses adjacent to the lake, so the riding is not very good. **Emerald Bay State Park** is one of the nicer places, but crowded. Loop around to **Crystal Bay** and you cross into Nevada, and then into **Incline Village,** a ski resort, and down to connect with US 50 at **Glenbrook,** and then to the hellish gambling paradise of **South Lake Tahoe.** And back into California, and back down to **Picketts Junction.**   ■

132 Miles STAY STRAIGHT as US 50A goes off to the northwest on Mormon Emigrant Road, to rejoin US 50 at **Pollock Pines.**

148 Miles There is **Ham's Station** (209-295-4810), offering sustenance; hours can be erratic. Roads with names like Cat Crossing and Panther Creek indicate there was, or is, a fair amount of wildlife.

152 Miles Shake Ridge Road goes off to the right, which can take you to Fiddletown and then to Plymouth on CA 49, or turn at Lockwood Junction to Daffodil Hill and Volcano, and then back to CA 88; great rides, no matter which way you go. Volcano has an impressive B&B, and weekend restaurant, called the **St. George Hotel** (209-296-4458).

162 Miles Entering **Pioneer,** a sign points off to the right: DEFENDER GRADE RD, WEST POINT.

Alternate Route

Going via **West Point** provides a very countrified alternative to the hurly-burly of Jackson and CA 49. If you take this route, it is less than two miles to meet up with CA 26, where you take a left, and that takes you on to the lazy town of West Point, and then on another 16 miles to **Mokelumne Hill,** on CA 49.   ∎

165 Miles CA 26 goes off to the left, toward West Point, while, Pioneer Road to the right, leading to Volcano.

177 Miles TURN LEFT on CA 49, after CA 88 meets this road at **Jackson;** this is a thriving town, named after one Colonel Alden Jackson, once fallen on hard times, now making its way back by the dint of hard labor.

Leaving town, go south on CA 49.

185 Miles Arrive at **Moke Hill,** more easily pronounced than Mokelumne Hill. CA 49 just skims the town, but do TURN LEFT and go in and take a look. Fanciest place is the **Hotel Leger,** on top of the hill, a white, two-storied affair, claiming to be "in continuous operation since 1852." There are a dozen rooms done up in 19th Century Martha Stewart, some with private baths; and a restaurant and a saloon (209-286-1401). Half a block along is the **Adams & Co. Saloon,** in the old IOOF (Independent Order of Odd Fellows) building, an interesting place to knock back half a dozen whiskeys . . . as long as you are staying at the Leger.

191 Miles A sign says the Old Road is off to the left; I recommend taking it to San Andreas, where it rejoins new CA 49.

192 Miles **San Andreas,** with a small old section, and the **Black Bart Saloon** serving up sarsaparilla and whiskey, though not mixed.

205 Miles Enter **Altaville,** which is sort of a suburb of **Angels Camp.** At

Jackson

Turn right, following the sign for "Old Town," and you are in a sinister neighborhood—or so it was a mere 45 years ago.

During the early gold-rush days Jackson was the scene of placer mining, but that washed out, and by the late 1860s hardrock mining was the word, with deep tunnels going down into the center of the earth. A lot of viewable relics of that era are very much visible, especially the **Kennedy Mine** apparatus. That lasted well into the 20th Century, but during World War II the mines were closed to aid the war effort, the miners going to fight, and the chemicals used in extracting the gold from the ore being used elsewhere.

After WWII, the price of gold was frozen at $35 an ounce, and the cost of production was well above that. To support itself Jackson turned to sin, and became a well known gambling and red-light center. So well known that in the later 1950s the state had to crack down. So phase three on the town's economic development has become the tourist industry.

Down at the south end of Main Street is the **National Hotel,** dating from 1862; it has 30 rooms, (cheaper ones without bath, 209-223-0500) but my preferred accomodation is the **Bordello Suite** . . . a deal. More conventional lodging can be found at the **Best Western Amador Inn** on CA 49, with 118 rooms (223-0211, 800-543-0221)

Food is everywhere. For breakfast I go out to **Mel & Faye's Diner** on the highway (209-223-0853), where Mel & Faye have been feeding locals for over 50 years. For a snack try **Fat Freddy's** (209-223-2525) on Main, kitty-corner to the National Hotel; Fred turns out a fine hot hound for a reasonable price. A lot of Italians must have moved here, as **Teresa's Place** (209-223-1786) and **Buscaglia's Ristorante** (209-223-9992) on Jackson Gate Road provide lunch and dinner.   ∎

the TRAFFIC LIGHT a left turn puts you on Murphys Grade Road, the back way to Murphys.

206 Miles Enter **Angels Camp,** named after one George Angel in 1849; so much for the ethereal ones. The place was made famous by Mark Twain's story, "The Jumping Frog of Calaveras County," and a frog-jumping competition is held every summer, which is the high-point of the year. Otherwise, not much there, really. If you want to stay, the **Gold Country Inn Motel** has 40 rooms (209-736-4611), and is right next to **Rodz Grill**

(209-736-0170), and opposite the **Angels Camp Museum.** Downtown, a quarter-mile south, is **Sue's Angel Creek Cafe** (209-736-2941), serving from 5 a.m. to 2 p.m., and for dinner you can go down the sidewalk to **Crusco's** (209-736-1440).

Pass the intersection with CA 4 going east to Ebbetts as CA 49 crosses **Angels Creek,** and we go straight toward Sonora. The road goes through **Frogtown** (not much there), winds down past a large quarry, and down to the bridge over **New Melones Lake,** and up the other side.

214 Miles   A sign tells you that the **Mark Twain cabin** is off to the left, a very, very sharp left, about 300 degrees. Go for a mile up the little road and you find a replica of the cabin that Mark Twain is said to have stayed at in 1864 and 1865. It is behind a black, wrought-iron fence, and was definitely in great need of repair when last I saw it. But the Twain buffs will love it.

217 Miles   A sharp corner to the left, and Rawhide Road, a shortcut to Jamestown, goes off to the right; it is a good way to avoid the Sonora traffic if you are headed south or west.

220 Miles   Parrotts Ferry Road goes off to the left; you are now back-tracking.

223 Miles   Arrive at the **Sonora Inn.** Back again.

The best bed in Jackson's National Hotel is in the Bordello Suite; definitely worth the price.

Trip 20   Sonora & Tioga Passes

Distance *244 miles*

Highlights *This is pass-bagging at its best, two gorgeous High Sierra runs that will take you all darn day. Get an early start.*

0 Miles Go east on Stockton Street, CA 108 Business, going east toward Twain Harte.

0+ Miles TURN LEFT at traffic light, big sign saying RESTANO WAY. And immediately, after 100 feet, TURN RIGHT on Mono Way, following CA 108 Business.

1+ Miles TURN LEFT at traffic light, where 108 B joins CA 108, and heads east over Sonora Pass to meet US 395. The clutter of expanding business boxes in the four-lane road, but that is the price of progress.

9 Miles The four-laner continues, but the sign points to the left for a detour along the old road through **Twain Harte.**

Yosemite National Park at its best—the view from Glacier Point to Half Dome.

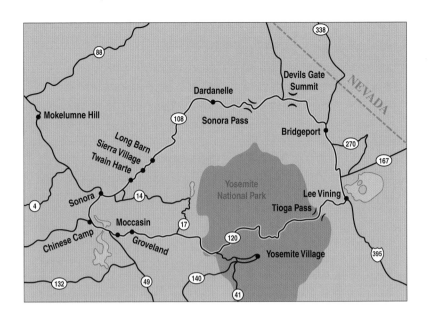

Detour

Into Twain Harte, named for the 19th Century writers Mark Twain and Bret Harte, who passed this way. The old Route 108, now Twain Harte Drive, curves into town. On the outskirts is the **Gables Cedar Creek Inn,** quite old-fashioned, backing on to a nine-hole golf course, with a number of cabins to rent (209-586-3008). The town announces itself as Twain Harte with a gloriously unattractive framework over the entrance to **Joaquin Gully,** where old 108/ Twain Harte Drive veers off to the right. On Joaquin Gully Road is the **Sportsman's Coffeeshop** on the left (209-586-5448), and the **Little Cottage Cafe** on the right (209-586-1402); different menus for different palates. Twain Harte Drive meets CA 108 about a mile further on. ∎

16 Miles Come into **Sierra Village,** where all the pickup trucks are parked outside **Wens Donuts & Stuff;** Breakfast & Lunch.

19 Miles The village of **Long Barn** is down off to your right, and you can go through by paralleling the new 108 for a couple of miles. Having a big four-laner bypass your town is great for the lives of cats, dogs, and children, but less good for business.

25 Miles The four-laner ends, and you are going back to the narrow road; much more fun.

Bridgeport

The town consists of one wide street which is awash with motorcycles during the annual "unofficial" motorcycle jamboree every summer. Don't even think of getting a room in town that weekend, as everything is booked solid as soon as the previous one is over. The **Bridgeport Inn,** established in 1877, will welcome you, and they have motel units out behind, while the hotel rooms offer genuine 19th Century hospitality (i.e. no phone, tv, or bathroom—that being down the hall); the trick is to get the Mark Twain Suite, which does have a bathroom (760-932-7380). Along Main Street a hundred yards is the more conventional **Best Western Ruby Inn** with 30 rooms (760-932-7241).

Food is found at the **Bridgeport Inn,** the **Hays Street Cafe** (760-932-7141), **Rhino's Bar & Grill** (760-932-7345), or any number of other places. Justice is still meted out in the 1880 courthouse. ■

Bridgeport is the seat of Mono county, and the courthouse has been dispensing justice for well over a hundred years.

29 Miles Summit Ranger Station, should you have any enquiries.

31 Miles Cross over the **Stanislaus River** and the **Strawberry Inn** is on your left, wining, dining, and lodging travelers since 1939 ($75-plus, 965-3662, 800-985-3662).

38 Miles The sign reads: NOT PLOWED; for you Sunbelt folk that means the road is not open in the winter. It can shut and reopen a couple of times in late fall, but once the first big snow comes, that is it for wheeled traffic. Though not for snowmobiles.

46 Miles The **Donnell Vista** looks down on **Donnell Reservoir,** and northeast to **Dardenelles Cone.**

49 Miles The Clark Fork Road heads northeast to a dead end.

51 Miles Dardanelle (Pop. 2). With gas, store, and cabins. The Dardanelle Resort, at 5,700 feet, is the place to stay on this road, in my mind, but bring your own food and be prepared to cook it. Joann Cheney is half of the population, and a permanent resident. A number of summer people have little houses in the area, but none live there. In the winter, when the road is closed, snowmobilers come in. Joann has eight cabins to rent and four motel units (209-965-4355).

Now the road, leaving the valley, starts some serious climbing. Way back in the early 1860s some enterprising types were building a toll road between Mono Lake and Sonora. Now try to imagine going over this in a stagecoach. **67 Miles** Sonora Pass, at 8,624 feet. And it is even more precipitous on the east side.

Down, down, down into **Pichel Meadows,** where that large resort-looking structure on the far mountain turns out to be the headquarters for the **U.S. Marine Corps Mountain Warfare Training Center.**
82 Miles STOP sign—TURN RIGHT at junction with US 395; the elevation here is 6,950 feet.

This old lumber-mill on CA 49 is part of the Marshall Gold Discovery State Historic Park, where gold was found in 1848.

Over **Devil's Gate Summit** (7,510 feet) on 395, and down into the valley of **Bridgeport Lake.**

99 Miles Bridgeport, seat of **Mono County,** greets you.

106 Miles The turn to **Bodie,** probably the most interesting ghost town left, since it has been preserved as a California State Park.

113 Miles Staying on US 395 you come up to **Conway Summit** (8,138 feet), and after that a great elongated S-curve takes you down to the valley, and **Mono Lake** is spread out in all its geologic grandeur in front of you.

118 Miles CA 167 goes off to the east to Hawthorne, Nevada.

To Bodie

You really should make this trip. Who knows how many more times you will pass this way and have this opportunity. Take it, and you will have a proper appreciation for what a ghost town really is. The road out to Bodie is ten miles of pavement, three of graded dirt, maybe a touch washboardy but easy to traverse.

Come up on the rise of a hill, and before you is the remains of Bodie. It looks big, but remember that only five percent of the original town remains. Ghost towns, before they became ghostly, were often quite large, until the precious metals gave out, and then people walked, rode, drove off, leaving the buildings behind. Then scavengers would come along and tear down structures to use the wood else-where, or fire would burn everything up, and few ghost towns remain.

Bodie is a State Historic Park and has been left to preserve itself, weathering away at a natural rate. Two bucks will get you past the gate guard. Bodie boomed in the 1870s, with some 10,000 people liv-ing here by 1880. Summer temperatures, here at 8,300 feet, were well over 100 degrees, and the winter temps went to 20 below zero. It was a rough place to live, so the boys drank a bit, and shot each other when provoked, and generally carried on. Not your average God-fear-ing community, although a number of churches tried to remedy that.

The town folded up when the Depression hit, the buildings happily crumbled away, and 30 years later (1962) the state stepped in to pre-vent the "souvenir hunters" from destroying the place. It's a beaut. Take it in.

When you leave, you can either retrace the entry road, or angle off from the toll-booth on Cottonwood Canyon Road, which runs for 11 mildly rough miles down to Mono Lake and CA 167. ■

126 Miles   Lee Vining, a small town that operates off of the tourist trade, and much of that is dependent on whether or not **Tioga Pass** is open. Half a dozen motels cater to the passers-by. The best is the **Yosemite Gateway Motel** (760-647-6467, 800-282-3929), in the middle of town on the lake side of main street—nice balconies overlooking the lake. At the north end of town is **Murphey's Motel,** with 44 units (760-647-6316, 800-334-6316). At the south end is the **Best Western Lake View Lodge** (760-647-6543) with 46 units.

There are several obvious places to eat, but since they cater to the transient crowd the food is pretty so-so. The best joint is the **Whoa Nelly Deli** (760-647-1088), which is in the Mobil gas station just as you turn west toward Tioga Pass; I kid you not.

126+ Miles   TURN RIGHT onto CA 120, heading for Tioga Pass and Yosemite National Park. A positively grand ride up, climbing 3,000 feet in 11 miles along the walls of the **Lee Vining River,** through the **Inyo National Forest.** Not that there are a lot of trees along the road, as a forest can encompass many different landscapes.

Connector
To Death Valley

If you've had enough of these mountains, and want some wide open spaces, keep on heading south on US 395 for another 122 miles. You go through **Bishop, Big Pine, Independence,** and **Lone Pine,** and at the south end of Lone Pine you TURN LEFT onto CA 136, clearly marked: DEATH VALLEY. Now turn to Chapter 13 for the rest. ■

136 Miles   **Tioga Pass Resort** (209-372-4471) on your right, the last genuinely free enterprise for the next 60 miles, with gas, food, lodging, and a small store. **Tioga Lake** and **Ansel Adams Wilderness** to your left.

138 Miles   The top of **Tioga Pass** (9,945 feet), and a motorcycle rider pays $10 to get into the park; the pass is good for seven days.

The Tioga saddle is a longish one, traveling across the top of the world, and then down a little to **Tuolumne Meadows,** from where many backpackers go hiking off to confront Mother Nature on the terms established by REI and North Face (two of the major purveyors of camping goods).

The scenery is dramatic, with clean granite bluffs all over the horizon. To quote **Charles Frazier,** author of *Cold Mountain,* "Earth has not anything to show more fair. Dull would be the soul who could pass by the sight so touching in its majesty."

The southern entrance to Sequoia National Park, looking up at Moro Rock.

And **Tenaya Lake,** also ringed with granite. Now the road gets into heavy fir, and the vistas become tunnels. And down and down and down, past **Porcupine Flat,** all the way to **Crane Flat** (6,200 feet), where gas is available, and a small store with very limited foods.

184 Miles   STOP sign—and TURN RIGHT at Crane Flat, following CA 120. If you go left, you are on Big Oak Flat Road going into **Yosemite Valley.**

Connector
To Kings Canyon, etc.
To get down to **Kings Canyon** and **Sequoia National Parks** (Chapter 11), take CA 41 93 miles south to Fresno, and then take the VAN NESS, CIVIC CENTER, CA 180 exit and head east.   ■

192 Miles   Hodgdon Meadow, and the **West Gate of Yosemite.** Show that you have paid your money. And then head west on the North Yosemite Highway/CA 120.

201 Miles   On your right is the turn for Cherry Lake, just before crossing the bridge over the **Tuolomne River.**

To Yosemite Valley

You've paid your $10 to get in, might as well see the rest of it. And it is worth it. I first rode over Tioga in 1965, coming from Massachusetts on my Velocette Venom, and when I got to the valley I was so taken by the beauty that I got a job and stayed for a month. Unfortunately, it is a lot more crowded now.

You descend toward the valley, through two tunnels, with glimpses of **Half Dome** in the distance. Stop at the vista points. Down on the valley floor CA 140 cuts back to go to Mariposa, but you stay with the road going upstream along the **Merced River.** When it crosses over, it becomes one-way going east, passes the CA 41 turn that goes south to Wawona and Oakhurst, and goes all the way into the valley, and is one-way west on the north side of the river . . . a result of much too much traffic.

The valley is a gorgeous, stunning, beautiful, incredible place, if you just lift your eyes above the crowd. Yosemite Valley is full of commercial activity. If you want to stay in the valley, and money is flush, do go to the **Ahwahnee Hotel** (209-252-4848). That phone number will also get you reservations at the **Yosemite Lodge** and **Camp Curry,** which are considerably cheaper. But not nearly as nice.

For food, the Ahwahnee dining room (209-372-1489) will be happy to accomodate you, but the Pavillion Buffet (209-372-8303) is a good deal less expensive. ■

Although it's a hazy day, Half Dome, at the east end of Yosemite Valley, is visible over my front wheel.

Alternate Route

This is officially U.S. Forest Service Primary Route 17, and provides a great ride, if a trifle bumpy and twisty. At **Cherry Lake,** about 13 miles along, you TURN LEFT onto USFS 14 (Cottonwood Road), going west to **Tuolomne,** which is a superb, and completely unused road, built for the convenience of the workers at the **Cherry Valley Dam.** From Tuolomne a run down County Road E17 takes you back to **Sonora.**   ■

The small town of Jamestown attracts a fair number of morbidly inclined tourists who like to see an effigy hanging from the gibbet on Main Street.

217 Miles Enter Groveland. The **Groveland Motel & Indian Village** will allow you to sleep in a cabin or mobile home, a three-bedroom Victorian house, or a pseudo-teepee with communal bathroom (209-962-7865). I prefer going along half a mile to the **Groveland Hotel**, circa 1849, with a dozen elegant rooms and an excellent restaurant (209-962-4000, 800-273-3314). Just up the street is the **Iron Door Saloon**, dating from 1852, and the **Iron Door Grill** (209-962-6244). Breakfast has got to be taken at **P.J.'s Cafe** (209-962-8638), at the east end of town; the "A.M. Sourdough Sandwich," with sausage, cheese, and egg, is truly tasteful.

223 Miles At the top of the hill, called **Priest Grade**, the road splits three ways, and there is the **Priest Station Motel**. It is a pleasantly ramshackle place, with 16 very different rooms/cabins, but it is a great place to sleep. Just to sit on the deck with a Tecate beer in hand and look down on **Don Pedro Reservoir** is a charm, and you can rent one of the three cabins on stilts that look as though they are about to slide down the hill. But they won't . . . or at least haven't so far. The management is well-accustomed to motorcyclists, especially foreign ones, as this place seems to be on a number of European websites. All three of the roads that go down the hill from there are great riding. (209-962-4181, 800-300-4181).

226 Miles As you cross the bridge at **Moccasin**, CA 49 comes in from the left, and 120/49 continue together alongside **Don Pedro Reservoir.**

235 Miles STAY RIGHT on CA 49 at **Chinese Camp**, while CA 120 goes off to the left. Not much in Chinese Camp except for a few shabby houses and a couple of brick buildings from the Gold Rush days.

238 Miles STAY RIGHT as CA 49 merges with CA 108, heading east into Sonora.

241 Miles Enter **Jamestown**, with CA 49 skirting the town, past the Harley-Davidson dealership; if you want a genuine Harley experience, stay at their "motel," a nice studio behind and separate from the shop (209-984-4888). When entering Jamestown, if you take the well-marked turn to the Business District, you will find an interesting street about a half mile long, with lots of food and trinkets available. And the restored **National Hotel** to eat and sleep at (209-984-3446). Also in Jamestown is the **Railtown State Historical Park,** with old steamers chuffing about on a six-mile run.

243 Miles EXIT RIGHT of the CA 108 road that bypasses Sonora, taking CA 49 into Sonora.

244 Miles Arrive back in downtown **Sonora.**

Trip 21 A Linear Route Through Two National Parks

Headquarters *Being a 222-mile linear trip, there isn't one, but I list a number of watering spots and rentable mattresses along the way.*

Information *Since the focus of this chapter is on two national parks, I will give the park info number (559-565-3341).*

Best Time to Visit *April through November, though check to make sure that the road through Sequoia National Park will be open, and call Ponderosa Lodge (559-542-2579) to check the condition of the Western Divide Highway.*

Getting There *The logical place to start is in Fresno (the Spanish word for "ash tree"), which is a big city on the east side of the San Joaquin Valley. The place gets a bad rap these days for urban problems, but it has its positive place in history. In 1910 it became the site of the first state college in California, and that year as well the Industrial Workers of the World made the first effort to organize the unskilled farm labor. You want to find CA 180, which goes east/west through the city, and head to the east.*

Dropping steeply down to Kings Canyon from Grant Grove Village, the road affords some spectacular views.

This is a high country delight, taking in two national parks (Kings Canyon and Sequoia), some magnificent foothill riding, and then a trip along the western crest of the Sierra Nevadas.

To simplify map-orientation, we will start in Fresno, end in Kernville, which covers 222 miles—except with side trips, like down into Kings Canyon, that will add a good deal more mileage to the route.

0 Miles Ground Zero, such that it is, to be used only once, will be in Fresno at Kings Canyon Road and Cedar Street, heading east on CA 180. Unfortunately, Fresno signage is not the best in the world, but all you need to do is find that CA 180; in central Fresno it is known as Ventura Street, which turns into Kings Canyon Road. My own personal theory is that Fresno does not like its unofficial status as the **Gateway to Kings Canyon,** and wants to get tourists lost in town so they will stay the night and spend money.

Leaving Fresno (Alt. 294 feet) the road is straight, boring, a way to get out of the valley. Go through **Centerville** and across the **Kings River;** life starts to improve as you get into the Sierra Nevada foothills.

Kings Canyon

Do, and this is good advice, do go down into **Kings Canyon;** lots of people give it a miss because they don't want to do a 35-mile trip, and then have to turn around and come back. Those folk are not bright. First, how many times in your life will you have the opportunity to visit Kings Canyon, which is truly an awe-inspiring spectacle? Second, it's a hell of a good ride. So go.

A little over a mile down the road on the right is **Grant Grove Village** (6,555 feet), with a store, rustic cabins to rent (559-335-5500), and information; that one phone number secures reservations at four places in the Kings Canyon/Sequoia national parks. Lodging is open here the year around, but elsewhere is usually closed from November through April. At Grants Grove's Visitor Center you should buy your $10 ticket admitting you to both national parks; it is good for a week.

On the left as you leave the village is the turn to go see the **General Grant Tree,** a seriously big hunk of lumber, and a little larger than the **General Lee Tree;** as you might guess, this place became popular right after the Civil War, and in 1890 Congress declared this the General Grant National Park—which was incorporated into Kings Canyon when that was declared a national park 50 years later, in 1940.

Seven miles further on, after going through **Cherry Gap** at 6,897 feet, is the turn to the left for **Hume Lake;** keep it in mind, as that's the way I'll take you back to get to Sequoia NP. Straight north of you is **Spanish Peak,** running just over 10,000 feet.

Continue on, and soon you get a huge view of the canyon below, where the **Middle Fork** and **South Fork of the Kings River** meet. You are going down there, over 2,000 feet down.

Down toward the bottom you cross over **Ten Mile Creek** and there is the privately owned **Kings Canyon Lodge,** a nicely funky place where you can get drinks, food, and lodging in eight cabins (559-335-2405). You can also get expensive gas out of old circa 1938 gravity-feed pumps, probably the last active pair in the nation—until the EPA-crats find out about them.

From there it is another 22 magnificent miles up along the **Kings River** to the end of the road, which runs along the bottom of a canyon that is 3,500 feet deep; quite impressive. About four miles before the end of the road is **Cedar Grove,** with food, lodging in a small 18-room lodge, but no gas.

Now head back 27 miles to the Hume Lake turn-off, and turn left. After a little over four miles you come to the lake, with store and gas, and then it is another five and a half miles up to the **Generals Highway** (Civil War again) that leads into **Sequoia National Park.** ■

30 Miles   Pass through **Squaw Valley** (1,700 feet) you will come to . . .

34 Miles   **Clingans Junction,** which is not much more than a gas pump and store—but the place is important, as it may be the last gas station you will see for quite some time. Sometimes a sign is up announcing LAST GAS. Now the road starts a serious climb of several thousand feet, entering the Sequoia National Forest.

50 Miles   CA 245 goes off to the left. If **Sequoia National Park** happens to be closed for any reason, like a sudden snowstorm blocking the highway, this provides an alternate route south.

Alternate Route

Go down on CA 245 11 miles to **Badger,** and you will see a road to the left saying: HARTLAND 10; do not take it. Go on another mile, where CA 245 makes a major curve to the right, in front of the **Mountain House Bar & General Store,** and another road goes to the right, also marked: HARTLAND 10. Take that, officially known as County Road J21, locally called Dry Creek Drive. A mile along, if you are looking for a place to stay, **Sierra Lakes Campground & Cabins** is the game in town (559-337-2520), off on Stagecoach Road. Eighteen miles later J21 ends at CA 216, alongside the **Kaweah River,** turn left, over the river, and half a mile further on 216 ends when it meets CA 198, at a Texaco station in **Lemoncove.** ■

Staying on 180, keep going east.

54 Miles   STOP & THINK at the three-way intersection in the middle of the woods. Straight goes to Sequoia NP, and eventually becomes CA 198, left on CA 180 goes to Kings Canyon NP.

Back at that three-way intersection, if you mistakenly choose not to go down into Kings Canyon, continue east . . .

57 Miles You are at the turn to **Hume Lake.** You're officially out of Kings Canyon National Park and back in the Sequoia National Forest. There are two lodges in the next ten miles, but nothing to rave about.

61 Miles Enter **Sequoia National Park,** created in 1890 and dedicated to the Big Trees, the Giant Sequoias, or *Sequoia gigantea* in the proper Latin. This is the bigger cousin to the coast redwoods *(Sequoia sempervirens)* that one finds near the coast of California. The giant sequoia can grow to over 300 feet tall, have a diameter at the base of 40 feet, and last 3,000 years; definitely worthy of a national park. For the botanically inclined, there are another 1,400 plant species in these two contiguous parks.

There is not much point to my going into detailed descriptions of the park; you have to go and see it yourself. The road goes over 7,335 feet, so you are high up.

78 Miles **Lodgepole** has a visitor center, and commercial enterprises such as a store and laundry, and cafe, and the comfortable John Muir Lodge. Lodgepole, by the way, refers to the lodgepole pine, a very tall, slender tree.

80 Miles The **General Sherman Tree** is off to your left, where all the tourists are; it is said to be the biggest, by bulk, tree in the world. Or put another way, the biggest living thing in the world.

82 Miles On top of the hill is the **Giant Forest** complex, with the **Giant Forest Museum** and lots of parking. You are at over 6,600 feet here, and for a little dead-end side trip, take Morro Rock Road to the left. It goes past **Hanging Rock,** which is a worthy, if tiring climb, with about 2,000 steps to the top. And then continues on to the Tunnel Log—70 years ago a tree, with a 21-foot diameter, fell across the road, and the fix-it boys figured out the best way to cope with it was to hack a tunnel through. The road ends out at **Crescent Meadow,** and you return to the main road. Now the descent to the south starts, which has a drop of over a mile.

84 Miles The turn to **Crystal Cave,** a steep six-mile road descending some 2,000 feet. If you like hiking and caves and a 48-degree temperature (very nice on a hot day), try this one, but remember you must get your ticket at either the Lodgepole or Foothills (to the south) visitor centers.

98 Miles After a very exhilarating descent down to the **Kaweah River,** you come to the **Foothills Visitor Center** and the park headquarters, at 1,300 feet. You exit the park at **Ash Mountain** . . . and pick up CA 198. For whatever legal and territorial reasoning, the state highway number does not go into the national park; I think that may have to do more with whose responsibility it is to pay for highway repairs than anything else.

99 Miles Several small lodges and a restaurant appear, just before the **Pumpkin Hollow Bridge** (1,922) that crosses over the Kaweah River. As a

Mineral King

If you like serious twists and turns and climbing, this is the road for you. A sharp turn to the left, and after a hundred yards a sign says that it takes 90 minutes to go 25 miles. Ha, you say; ha, ha, I say, it will take you a while. The road climbs from about 1,000 to over 7,000 feet in those 25 miles, and while a Gold Wing towing a trailer could do it with ease, the rider had better be good. Halfway up a park ranger greets you, as you are re-entering **Sequoia National Park.**

There are a couple of short dirt stretches near the top, several government campgrounds, and a small commercial enterprise at **Silver City** which has a little store, cafe, and a dozen rustic (i.e. communal showers) cabins to rent (559-561-2223).

At the end of the road is **Mineral King Valley,** a beautiful place that the Disney Corporation tried to buy and turn into a ski resort; the **National Park Service** got a hold of it instead, for which I am quite grateful.

But I remain bemused at the thought of the men who came up here in the 1870s looking for silver—the trip up would have taken a lot more than 90 minutes. More like 90 hours.   ■

The store up on top of Mineral King, in the tiny community of Silver City, sells canned tomatoes and excellent hamburgers, but no gas. (Photo by Jeff Haynes)

place to stay I do recommend both the **Buckeye Tree Lodge** (559-561-5900), and the next-door **Gateway Restaurant & Lodge** (559-561-4133); the restaurant opens at 11 a.m., 8 on Sundays.

101 Miles   A sign indicates that a forest-service fire station is coming up, and a green sign, pointing to the left, says: MINERAL KING 25.

103 Miles   The **White Horse Inn** (559-561-4185), a steak joint which toasts the meat properly, is on your right.

104 Miles   Enter the community of **Three Rivers**; the **Wee Three Bakery & Restaurant** (559-561-4761) is on your left, open for hearty breakfasts and lunches.

105 Miles   A Chevron gas station is on the right, the first since **Clingans Junction**.

107 Miles   If you are in need of a room, watch out for the **Best Western Holiday Lodge** on your right, easy to miss the entrance if you are going fast. This is a conventional place, close to the river, with 54 rooms and you want a "riverview," which costs more (559-561-3427).

Now the road, CA 198, whisks around the southern side of man-made **Lake Kaweah**.

116 Miles   STAY STRAIGHT at intersection with CA 216 going off to the right, as mentioned in the Badger Alternative at the beginning of this chapter; pass the Texaco station on the corner.

Now you are entering **Lemoncove**, where lemon trees are grown, and several small stores still stay open.

122 Miles   TURN LEFT. You are passing a large grove of trees on your right, which the owner has conveniently signed: OLIVES. He was probably tired of having city-folk stop and ask what sort of trees they were. A green sign pointing left says BALCH PARK 42, the road, Yokohl Drive, cutting off just before you get to the **Yokohl River** bridge.

125 Miles   TURN LEFT. A sign pointing left reads: BALCH PARK 41 (even though you've come three miles), and you turn left, continuing on Yokohl Drive. This is a nice, somewhat beat-up, little-used country road along the Yokohl Valley, with a ranch or two, the Milo forest-service fire station, then you zig-zag over a low rise and drop into the **Tule River Valley**.

145 Miles   STOP sign—TURN RIGHT following County Road J37 (Balch Park Road); if you take the left you will have an extra, very pleasant, 30-mile trip through **Balch Park** itself and **Mountain Home State Forest**, as the Balch Park loop comes right back to J37.

152 Miles   STOP sign—TURN LEFT, by big red barn, J37 intersecting with CA 190. If you go right, in less than a mile you will be in downtown **Springville**, with gas, food, stores, and the ten-room **Springville Inn** (559-

A lot of labor went into building the road up to Mineral King, which included the construction of a lot of bridges. Photo by Craig Erion

539-7501). Leaving Springville the road (CA 190) goes east along the **Middle Fork Tule River**, into the **Sequoia National Forest**, and begins to climb and twist a whole lot as it hauls itself up over 3,500 feet.

166 Miles Come into **Pierpont Springs**, at 4,500 feet, which means a lot cooler than Springville in the summer, with the business center of town taken up by the combined market, post office, restaurant, bar, and four-room motel called the **Pierpont Springs Resort** (559-542-2423). The larger adjoining community, just off the main road and more often found on the map, is **Camp Nelson.**

Leaving town a sign reads: QUAKING ASPEN; that is not a town but a national forest campground ten miles along. And those ten are gnarly miles indeed, the road getting even tighter and twistier, and great fun for a motorcyclist who likes that sort of thing. If you are a Freeway Rider, you might not be so enchanted.

176 Miles Now you are on the **Western Divide Highway,** which means the **Kern River** has divided the Sierra Nevada mountains here, running down the middle, and you are on the west side, running along the divide that sends creeks either east into the Kern, or west into the **Tule River.**

Mysteries of California Highway Numerology

Technically the numerical designation CA 190 disappears soon after you leave **Pierpont Springs,** vanishing completely in the national forest, to reappear miraculously 35 crow-flying miles later on the east side of the Sierra Nevada Mountains, in **Olancha,** on US 395. It is almost as though in some long-gone day an engineer sitting at a desk in some sterile office penned a line that would go from Pierpont Springs to Olancha—without bothering to check the feasibility, or practicability, of building such a road.

CalTrans does mystifying things with its enumerations, as though some autistic child prodigy is responsible. Don't fret yourself about this, as CA 190 does become that **Western Divide Highway.** ∎

At the Ponderosa Lodge, on the Western Divide Highway, trout and scrambled eggs are a breakfast specialty; Craig "Fireball" Stein prepares to dig in, as Craig Erion looks on.

178 Miles The **Ponderosa Lodge** is on your left, at 7,250 feet, with gas, food, a bar, and lodging (559-542-2579); if it is a weekend, and you don't like cheerful music, ask for a cabin away from the lodge, where you can stagger back to for a quiet sleep after a night of carousing. Try the grilled trout and scrambled eggs for breakfast.

Beyond the Ponderosa the road, the Western Divide Highway, is not cleared after the snow-season starts. But we motorcyclists are not going to be going up there in the winter. However, the Divide is a great ride in the other three seasons, a smooth road running south along that western ridge of the Sierras.

191 Miles STOP sign—TURN LEFT; the road is now weaving tightly, heading downhill. After a few miles you can see a small lake and a lot of RVs way down below to the right.

197 Miles CURVE RIGHT, with sign indicating: JOHNSONDALE 1, KERNVILLE 27. The left turn is a 20-mile dead end up along the Kern River.

198 Miles Sign for R-RANCH IN THE SEQUOIAS to the right. It used to be an old logging community, **Johnsondale**, until some slightly befogged, or shysterish, types figured they could sell time-shares in this denuded valley.

2022 Miles After more downhill and over the **Johnsondale Bridge** spanning the **Kern River**, and you see a road going off to the left, with a sign: SHERMAN PASS, BLACKROCK STATION—more on that in the Kernville chapter. You STAY STRAIGHT.

Now the road runs right along the Kern River, east side. Lots of RVs and 4x4s on the weekends. Past a small dam put up by **California Edison**, then **John McNally's Fairview Lodge**, a delightfully classic establishment, and a few miles further on the modern **Kern River Golden Trout Resort**—but we are headed into Kernville. Boogie on.

222 Miles **Kernville**, we have arrived. Now go on to the next chapter to see where to stay.

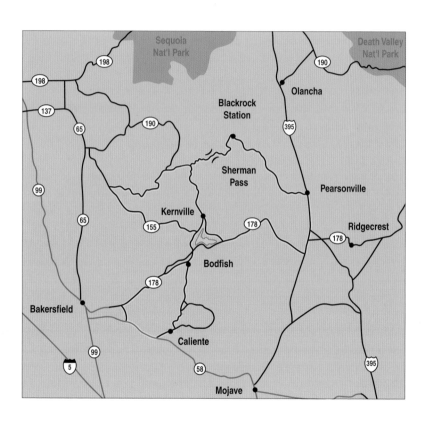

Southern Sierras

Headquarters *Kernville*
Chamber of Commerce/Tourist Bureau *800-350-7393*
Getting There *The easiest way is to take CA 178 east from Bakersfield, or west from CA 14 near Ridgecrest in the Mojave Desert, get to Isabella Lake, and go north a few miles.*
Ground Zero *Start in front of Circle Park, opposite Cheryl's Diner.*

This little trio of Trips takes place way down at the southern end of the **Sierra Nevadas,** that 430-mile long range of mountains that stretch from **Lassen Peak** to **Tehachapi Valley.** The roads we will be on go from 9,200 feet on **Sherman Pass** in the mountains down to 800 feet in the San Joaquin Valley. You can't complain about this place to stash your bags for a night or two or three. Unless it is on Labor Day weekend when half of the San Joaquin Valley is trying to escape the heat.

Sherman Pass stands 9,200 feet above the level of the far-off Pacific Ocean, 130 miles away. (Photo by Craig Erion)

I will say that the loops I have planned are not for the cruise-control set. The roads are 90 percent crooked, and the views are magnificent, the countryside superb.

Kernville sits astride the **Kern River,** at the north edge of Isabella Lake. For the historically impaired, Edward Kern was a topographer (early sort of mapmaker) who came to the area with John Fremont's expedition of 1846. **Isabella Lake** (which was very small at that time) was named by Spaniards who passed this way for that queen of Spain who sent Columbus across the ocean blue. The dam on the Kern River was completed in 1953, and the original Kernville got drowned, except for a few houses that were hauled up to the new location at the north end of the lake. The new site used to be called **Whiskey Flats** in the bad old days, and one small part still retains that moniker.

The Kern River area was reasonably quiet until gold was discovered in 1854, and then the usual rush took place. After the gold panned out, lumbering and ranching took over, and now the main source of revenue is the mysterious migratory animal, the tourist.

That $2.98 cooler holds a steak for supper, a pint of milk for breakfast coffee, and a six-pack of Sam Adams. (Photo by Craig Erion)

At the only general store in the area, Craig Erion awaits the return of those who have gone to purchase the fixings for supper and breakfast.

Places to stay: lots. Right down in the middle of town, which is quite small, opposite Whiskey Flats (or **Circle Park,** as maps refer to the place), is the **Kernville Inn,** with swimming pool and a two-minute walk to the river, and 26 units (760-376-2206). Next door is **Cheryl's Diner** (760-376-6131), for an outside breakfast. And across the road is the **Sportsman's Bar,** where the serious come to drink.

Upper-scale accomodations can be found at **Whispering Pines Lodge,** a B&B right on the east side of the Kern River just north of the main part of town, with 18 rooms (760-376-3733). Very good breakfast, and a nice swimming pool, in case you do not wish to immerse yourself in the cool mountain waters of the river.

A mile further up the river is the wide spot in the road calling itself **Riverkern,** and there is a delightful old motel, the **Sequoia Motor Lodge,** with some 20 units (760-376-2535); ask for #17, which overhangs the river. Right across the road is **Cheyenne's Stage Stop & Dining Hall,** which serves up dead cow the way it should be.

As well as eating and sleeping, Kernville has a good museum just up the street from Whiskey Flats, on Big Blue Road. And the ubiquitous antique stores. And fishing. Yes, fishing. There is a fish hatchery you can visit, and for the price of a fishing license you can throw a hook in the river and catch your own trout, put it in a skillet with some olive oil and tarragon, and have a superb meal.

Trip 22 Bodfish-Caliente Road & Kern Canyon

Distance *92 miles*

Highlights *This is a great half-day, which can be turned into a full day with the slightest inclination. The distance is short, but the time will be long. You won't even average 30 mph for most of the trip.*

0 Miles Cheryl's diner on your left as you head south on the west side of the **Kern River**, past the golf course, and the river turns into **Isabella Lake**.

4 Miles Enter the strung-out (physically, not emotionally) town of **Wofford Heights**, and pick up CA 155 going south; if you take 155 west—that's another loop (#3).

Several campgrounds and recreation areas are along the lakefront, and on the right is the turn to **Keyesville**, the site of the original gold mining claims. One has to ride a bit of dirt road to get there.

11 Miles CA 155 crosses over CA 178, a freeway at this point, and officially ends. But the road goes on for another 300 yards.

On top of Sherman Pass, 9,200 feet, with Mt. Whitney in the background.

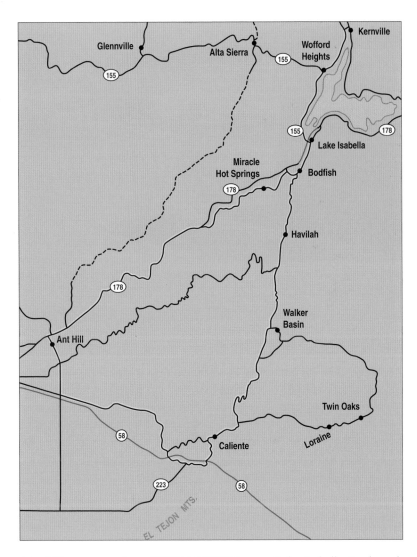

11+ Miles STOP sign—TURN RIGHT, onto Lake Isabella Boulevard; you have just entered the town of **Lake Isabella,** which trys to separate itself from Isabella Lake by transposing the words. The original town of Lake Isabella was also drowned in the mid-fifties, and this long strip of commercial enterprises is the result.

14 Miles Lake Isabella Blvd. has turned into the Bodfish-Caliente Road, and you will see the **Country Korner Market** on the right, and the turn onto Kern River Canyon Road. You GO STRAIGHT, but you'll be back at this corner in two to six hours, depending how you hustle.

Whiskey Flats, in Kernville, is not nearly as raucous as it was during the gold mining boom of 150 years past.

Now you start a hard charge up the hill, with two long switchbacks carrying you over the summit, and down into a small valley.

21 Miles   The community of **Havilah,** with the restored courthouse and schoolhouse. Gold was found here in 1864, and **Kern County** was organized in 1866, and this became the county seat. Hard to imagine now, because it is such a tiny place. Its bureaucratic glory only lasted to 1872, when the job went to Bakersfield, and the gold began petering out in the early 1880s. Some people still look for it in the hills, but nobody has made a real strike in the last 100 years.

24 Miles   The Breckenridge Road goes off to the right, with a steep climb out of the valley, and a long, long descent in the **San Joaquin Valley** east of **Bakersfield.** It meets up with Comanche Drive after 36 miles. It is a nice road, much of it through national forest, but the views while riding from west to east are better. So STAY STRAIGHT.

25 Miles   At the top of a rise and on your right is a **Trading Post,** more of a general store, where cold sodas are appreciated on a hot day.

Now you drop down into **Walker Basin.** Joe Walker was a busy man back in the 1830s, hiking over much of this territory. His name appears on any map of California a dozen times, from **Walker Pass** east of Isabella Lake to the town of **Walker** on US 395, just north of Yosemite. Those were days of true adventuring.

29 Miles   STOP sign—TURN RIGHT.

Detour
Via Twin Oaks

If you want to do a 28-mile loop, rather than the 12-mile run over **Lions Trail,** you could go left, zig and zag east and south for two miles, and catch onto Walker Basin Road. Keep on STRAIGHT, and after three more miles you find the **Cowboy Memorial,** an interesting little tribute to the life of the cowboy which ex-cowpoke Paul de Fonville and his wife Virginia have been working on for more than 20 years; "Just $500,000 and I'll have it all done and there won't be anything like it." Truth. Call 661-867-2410 for details.

Keep on Walker Basin Road, and after cutting through the **Piute Mountains** you come to the **Piute Mountain School,** and 13 miles from that STOP sign you arrive at the **Twin Oaks General Store** (661-867-2075), with hamburgers, sandwiches, and the like available. By this time the road has become Caliente Creek Road.

A little further on are the remnants of the old **Amelie Mill,** where gold and silver ore was processed for over 70 years, finally shutting down in the 1950s. Then the community of **Loraine,** and 12 more miles west along **Caliente Creek** and you arrive at the intersection with Lion Trail, a/k/a the Bodfish-Caliente Road.   ■

Presuming you TURN RIGHT at the STOP, you hustle down the west side of **Walker Basin Creek,** pass the west end of Walker Basin Road and the Rankin Ranch, where the dudes and dudettes come to stay, ride horses, and punch a few cows. Then you climb gently up on **Lions Trail,** as the locals refer to that stretch, come over the top, and down steeply to **Caliente Creek,** with four switchbacks. Good fun.

31 Miles BEAR RIGHT at the intersection with Caliente Creek Road, a natural turn. A sharp left will take you up to Lorraine and Twin Oaks.

34 Miles Enter the almost defunct community of **Caliente,** now reduced to a post office and lots of railroad track belonging to **Union Pacific.** Bounce over the track, past the post office, road curves right, and then heads under the railroad, the sign reading: BAKERSFIELD, HWY 58.

34+ Miles TURN RIGHT at the small intersection, continuing on Bodfish-Caliente Road, which winds up a delightful valley. If you go straight, a sign reading BAKERSFIELD HWY 58, you will be on Bealville Road, which goes up a hill, under a railroad bridge, and connects with CA 58 in about a mile.

39 Miles Take a right on Bena Road, which turns into **Edison Union**

It is hard to believe today, but the tiny town of Havilah was the seat of Kern county from 1866 to 1872.

Highway, which crosses Comanche Drive after 12 miles.

51 Miles TURN RIGHT onto Comanche Drive, going north. If you are in need of gas, food, or a bed, go forward another four miles to the intersection with the Weed Patch Highway/CA 184, where there is everything a motorcyclist could want, excepting a dealer—those are in Bakersfield.

53 Miles Comanche Drive crosses the aforementioned Breckenridge Road, if you care to head back to Havilah. This is the best direction to take Breckenridge Road, as the drop from **Breckenridge Mountain** down into **Havilah Canyon** is spectacular. Comanche continues through the aged **Ant Hill** oil field, with rather decrepit equipment peacefully pumping away.

56 Miles STOP sign—TURN RIGHT onto CA 178, the **Kern Canyon Highway.** The road is wide and straightish for the first several miles, and then as it gets into the canyon proper it gets appreciably narrower, and much more curvaceous. It is a great road if there is no traffic, merely a good road if you get caught behind a freight-train of ten cars and RVs. Ah well . . .

The **Kern River** is rushing along beside you to the left, and numerous signs advise against swimming; a goodly number of lives have been lost in that turbulent water.

65 Miles   BEAR RIGHT after the sign: KERN CANYON ROAD 1/4 M. The main road, CA 178, goes more or less straight, and turns into a four-laner after crossing the river; the old Kern Canyon Road is much more fun. It winds along on the south side of the river, high up and farther and farther away from the water.

Then it gets back closer to the river, and a sign on the left, just as you come on a bridge, directs you to **Miracle Hot Springs.** This is open from seven in the morning to ten at night, and a forest ranger may ask for a nominal parking fee. The springs are right down by the river, and on one side of a small wall the water will be 104 degrees, on the other, 54 degrees or less.

Continue on, past Borel Road.

78 Mile   STOP sign—TURN LEFT; Kern Canyon Road ends at the **Country Korner Market,** and you go back to Lake Isabella, retracing your steps.

81 Miles   TURN LEFT where the sign reads: KERNVILLE, heading up CA 155 to Wofford Heights, then straight on.

92 Miles   Back at Whiskey Flats. Have a beer or a sarsaparilla at the Sportsman's Inn.

A good use for lost hubcaps.

Trip 23   Sherman & Walker Passes

Distance *151 miles*

Highlights *These are the last two passes in the southern Sierras, and Sherman, though paved, is not often visited by street motorcyclists. Off-roader motorcyclists by the dozens congregate up on top of these mountains, as there are hundreds of miles of ORV trails to follow.*

0 Miles Cheryl's is now on your right, and you head over the bridge toward **Sierra Way.**

0+ Miles STOP sign—TURN LEFT, heading north on Sierra Way. Past the **Jame's Store** on your right, a full-service market, including gas. A dozen pillow-stops are on your left, **McCambridge Motel, Whispering Pines B&B,** etc.

3 Miles Riverkern, with **Cheyenne's** and a general store on the right, Sequoia Motor Lodge on the left.

Visible right above the motorcycle, Mt. Whitney, at 14,494 feet, is the highest peak in the contiguous United States; you can hike to the top, if you are so inclined.

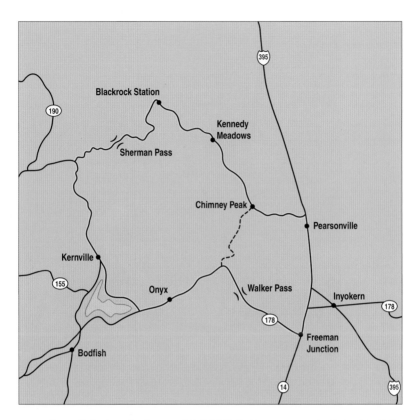

15 Miles Fairview Lodge and McNally's Restaurant (760-376-2430), "Home of the 40 oz. Steak." No thanks, I'm big enough.

Past the burned-out **Road's End Resort,** victim of a big forest fire in 2002, then the inlet for the **California Edison** turbine powerplant, and swoop around a very large, half-acre turn-off area, so people can put their toes in the water.

20 Miles VERY SHARP TURN TO THE RIGHT at a well concealed intersection, cutting back about 300 degrees; the sign reads: BLACKROCK STA 36, US 395 67. This is the road to **Sherman Pass.**

Make the turn, and climb, climb, climb. Do watch out for debris on the road for the next 67 miles; this is a forest service road, is not kept open in the winter, and is not swept in the summer. Which means that when some sand or dirt is washed onto the pavement, it stays there until the passage of vehicles, which are few, blows it off. I talked with a ranger who said that at least once a year some motorcyclist will go too fast, ride beyond his line of sight, hit a skiddy bit, and wrap himself around a tree. You have been warned, and my lawyers have a copy of this book.

Since the U.S. Forest Service hates for people to get lost, the signage is usually quite good, as it is here in the Sequoia National Forest.

The pavement is quite good, and there is nary a straight stretch on the way up. The last logging trucks came down in 1998, and the few vehicles you generally see will be 4x4s and the occasional RV.

26 Miles Turn to **Horse Meadows Campground,** with six miles of asphalt, four of dirt, having running water and pit toilets. I camp up there at least once a year because it is both accessible and remote.

36 Miles Up to the top, **Sherman Pass** at 9,200 feet. From the viewing area you can see **Mt. Whitney** (14,494 feet) some 40 miles to the nor'nor'east. As a personal note, the gent for whom the mountain is named, and who calculated its height, geologist Josiah Dwight Whitney, was raised in my hometown of Northampton, Massachusetts.

The next 20 miles are running along a ridge of the mountains, staying above 8,000 feet; very nice riding with clear forest and the occasional meadow.

53 Miles   TURN RIGHT at the intersection in the middle of the woods; **Blackrock Ranger Station** (8,150 feet), is straight ahead a hundred yards, with a ranger giving out information. You want to go to the right, on the clearly marked KENNEDY MEADOWS road.

After ten miles the road starts a descent toward **Kennedy Meadows** and the **South Fork Kern River,** with a scattering of houses in the far distance.

66 Miles   The **Kennedy Meadows General Store** (559-850-5647), with a pot-bellied stove inside and gasoline pumps outside, is on your left. The place has a little patio and serves lunch food during the warmer months. The road up to here, County J21, is kept open all year around. The area has about 35 permanent residents (and no telephone), and about 350 property owners who have vacation homes. A left turn will take you up a dead end at the **Kennedy Meadows Campground,** but you want to GO STRAIGHT southeast toward US 395.

68 Miles   Grumpy Bears Resort (559-850-BEAR) is on your right, which constitutes a restaurant that claims to open at 11 o'clock summer and winter. His three-egg sandwich is a serious brunch.

77 Miles   You come up to the **Chimney Peak fire station** and **Chimney Meadow;** if you have a d-p bike, or are adept on your K1200LT, you can take a 15-mile dirt road down south to join CA 178 eight miles west of **Walker Pass.**

Now you can see down to the **Mojave Desert** east of you, and the road starts a steepish descent through **Nine-Mile Canyon.** Keep your eyes on the road, please, and stop when you want to admire the view. There is no guardrail on your right, and it would be a hell of a bumpy ride to the bottom.

87 Miles   STOP sign—TURN RIGHT at the junction with US 395.

Connector
To Death Valley

If you want to head into **Death Valley** from here, take a left and head north on US 395, and in 32 miles you will be in **Olancha** at the intersection with CA 190—which you last saw east of **Pierpont Springs** in Chapter 11. And that leads into Death Valley.

■

Heading south on 395 you are cruising along the four-laner at 2,500 feet along the western edge of **Indian Wells Valley.** If you need gas there is a big Shell station three miles south on the east side of the highway at **Pearsonville,** right next to the **Pearson Speedway,** where stock cars run most weekends. And that is about all there is to Pearsonville.

97 Miles STAY STRAIGHT on CA 14 heading for Los Angeles, a well-marked Y in the road, as US 395 goes southeast toward Inyokern and San Bernardino.

99 Miles A big sign on the right reads: MOJAVE RED, INDIAN WELLS BREWING CO.; out there in the middle of roughly nowhere is a brewery, and the **Indian Wells Lodge,** where dinner is served. The brewery grew out of a bottled water company, as the old wells have served a lot of people over the years. This is part of the **Joseph Walker Trail,** as that mountain man traipsed along here around 1834, making use of this watering hole.

101 Miles CA 178 goes east toward Inyokern and Ridgecrest; ignore it.

104 Miles TURN RIGHT onto CA 178, heading for **Isabella Lake** and **Bakersfield;** if you read the historical plaque, you will find that this is called **Freeman Junction,** though who Freeman was, I have no idea.

The road, CA 178, ascends up **Freeman Canyon,** although it does not look like a canyon at all, being quite open on both sides of the road.

The Fountain Springs Saloon has been around since 1858—though maybe rebuilt a few times.

Thanks to the thoughtfulness of our government, the national forests have excellent campgrounds, such as this one at Horse Meadows, about 15 miles from Sherman Pass.

113 Miles   Arrive at **Walker Pass,** 5,250 feet; it's not a high pass, but that made it all the more useful in the days of horse- and oxen-drawn wagons. Back in the 1850s this was the communications route between those on the east side of the southern Sierras, and those on the west.

Now the road starts a nice curving descent to **Canebrake Creek.**

121 Miles   The dirt road down from **Chimney Peak** is on your right.

CA 178 weaves around a number of curves, and a valley of green trees appears in front as Canebrake Creek merges with the **South Fork Kern River.**

133 Miles   You have just passed downtown **Onyx,** with several stores and a gas station, and you want to stop at the original **Onyx Store.** There it is! A raggedy old building with a huge tree stump out front, run by Six-Shot Sharon, one-time mayor of Whiskey Flats (an honorary role). The store claims to have been around since 1851, but whether or not any of the original boards are still in use is moot.

138 Miles   TURN RIGHT where a sign points to Kernville; you are now headed northish on the **Sierra Highway.** The road goes north for a mile, crossing over the **South Fork Kern River,** then west for about seven miles, then north again, and it is all a good ride. You pass the little **Kern Valley Airport** after ten miles, and straight on into town.

151 Miles   Arrive back in Kernville.

Trip 24 California Hot Springs & Parker Pass

Distance *110 miles*

Highlights *Not much traffic, lots of twisties, and even the opportunity to soak in a warm swimming pool.*

0 Miles **Cheryl's** is on your left.

4 Miles TURN RIGHT in the middle of **Wofford Heights**, following CA 155 to the west, up the hill, toward Glennville and Delano. This stretch is officially called Evans Road, though I have never heard anybody refer to it as such.

11 Miles You are at **Greenhorn Summit** (6,102 feet), which is just west of the mountain resort community of **Alta Sierra**. At the summit roads go left and right.

The sign at Fountain Springs will tell you whether the road over Parker Pass is open or not.

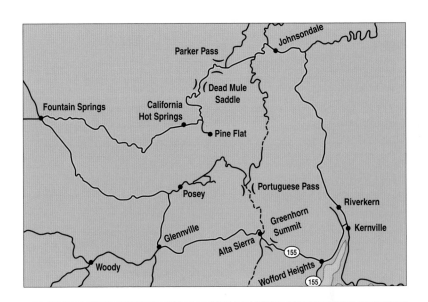

Dirty Options

To the left, Rancheria Road, begins with pavement, and degenerates to gnarly dirt as it goes for 35 miles south along the ridge of the **Greenhorn Mountains** and dropping down 5,000 feet to CA 178 near the Comanche Road intersection.

To the right the road is also called Rancheria Road, and this is seven dirt miles, usually in good condition, that goes to **Portuguese Pass** at 7,280 feet. From Portagee you can either go north on some seriously bad pavement to meet good pavement near **Johnsondale,** or go west down to **Posey**—where you'll get on my regular route.

■

24 Miles STAY STRAIGHT (a bit to the right, maybe) in Glennville, while CA 155 curves off to the left. As you entered **Glennville** (Pop. 130 or thereabouts, Alt. 3,150 feet) a fire station was on your right, followed by the **Crazy Horse Restaurant & Saloon** (661-536-8114, breakfast from seven on weekdays, eight on weekends) and then a green and white sign indicating that Delano is off to the left along CA 155, but you want the one pointing to PORTERVILLE and the POSO CK REC AREA, along White River Road.

25 Miles STOP sign—TURN RIGHT onto Jack Ranch Road, sign reading FOUNTAIN SPRINGS 18, winding pleasantly through ranch country until it T-bones into Old Stage Road.

In Glennville, on CA 155, the Crazy Horse is the only eating and drinking game in town.

30 Miles TURN LEFT onto Old Stage Road, which parallels **Arrastre Creek,** running past the **White River Cemetery,** a really nice twisty bit. If you went right, you'd get to Posey and Portuguese Pass.

47 Miles STOP sign—TURN RIGHT at **Fountain Springs** (Alt. 800 feet) onto M56, a/k/a Hot Springs Drive, a sign reading CA HOT SPRINGS 18. The intersection has only a fire station and the **Fountain Springs Saloon** (Since 1858); around 1858 Fountain Springs was a way-station for the **Butterfield Overland Stagecoach Company,** but whether that is the original building is somewhat doubtful. The barkeeper doubles as cook from 9 a.m. to closing. No gas here, and the next gas on the route is in **Kernville,** over 60 miles away; if you are in need, go west seven miles to **Ducor.** If you are riding late in the season, a sign at Fountain Springs will tell you if Parker Pass is CLOSED or not.

   The ride out to the **Hot Springs** is a delight, and you are hardly aware you are climbing (unless you are two-up on a 125 Vespa) until you come over a ridge and look down, way down, to the community of Hot Springs.

65 Miles **California Hot Springs** (3,040 feet) on your right, with food and drink and 9 to 5 hours daily. The big pool is about 90 degrees, but the two smaller, hotter tubs are an invigorating 100 and 105 degrees; inside the big building there is a large dance-floor (805-548-6582 for details).

68 Miles TURN LEFT when Hot Springs Drive ends by butting into another road; **Hot Springs Ranger Station** is a hundred yards up the hill. Should you go right you will be in **Pine Flat** in half a mile, where the **Rabbit Foot Trail Inn** has eight rooms and a bar and haphazard dining hours (805-548-6813). If you are headed back to Kernville, best way is over **Parker Pass,** with a nice nine-mile climb, over **Dead Mule Saddle** and **Cold Springs Saddle** to the pass itself (6,400 feet): now it is all downhill.

79 Miles STAY STRAIGHT at four-way intersection, with the Western Divide Highway going off to your left, a trailhead to your right.

82 Miles That road down from **Portuguese Pass** is on your right.

85 Miles BEND RIGHT at three-way intersection. The road left dead-ends after going up along the **Kern River** for some 20 miles.

Past **Johnsondale,** remains of a logging community, now better known by the large sign: R-RANCH IN THE SEQUOIAS.

110 Miles Arrive back at Ground Zero in Kernville.

The western slopes of the Sierras are ranching country, and this homestead is on Old Stage Road between Glennville and Fountain Springs.

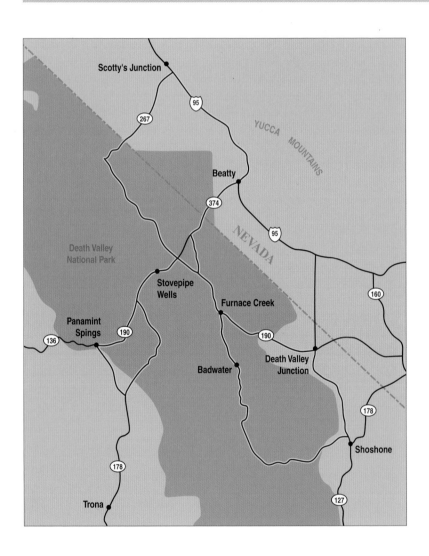

Death Valley

Headquarters *Furnace Creek Ranch*
Park Service Headquarters *760-786-3200*
Getting There *It's a snap. You can come north along US 395, which parallels Death Valley on the western side, and take CA 178 via Ridgecrest and Trona, or CA 190 from Olancha. Or, if coming south on 395, take CA 136 from Lone Pine. I-15 is to the south, and you can go up CA 127 from Baker to Shoshone, and meet with CA 178. On the east is US 95, running up from Las Vegas through Nevada, and you can cut off at Beatty, or if coming down from the north, at Scotty's Junction.*
Ground Zero *Pull out of Furnace Creek Ranch onto CA 178/190.*

This is one of my favorite places, except maybe in July and August. Smooth roads, lots of interesting things to see, both geological and historical, and superb night skies. **Death Valley National Park** covers some 5,300 square miles (bigger than the state of Connecticut), and altitudes go from 279.8 feet below sea level (Badwater) to 11,049 above (Telescope Peak)—though you can only ride a bike up to 8,133 feet, at **Mahogany Flat.**

Furnace Creek is roughly smack dab in the middle of the Valley of Death. That name is a misnomer really. More on that in a bit.

Stunning place, Death Valley. I first went there in 1967, attending the last official **Death Valley Motorcycle Rally** on a Triumph TR6R, and have been going back ever since. I love it, whether I'm on a pavement-pounder or dual-purpose motorcycle. Even after 40 or more trips I always find something new. I ran into snow on **Salsberry Pass** at eight o'clock in the morning in April . . . that was new.

Some soulless people come to the valley, go through, spend a night at **Furnace Creek**, see **Zabriskie Point** and **Badwater**, yawn, and move on. "Been there, done that, bye." But for anybody who has an appreciation for the desert and for desolation, the place is an endless variety show.

There are hundreds of miles of paved two-lane road within the park, often smooth and unblemished by the passage of heavy trucks. The biggest hazards are, of course, the recreational vehicles, huge, slow-moving tortoises with sightseers rather than drivers at the steering wheel.

I remember coming in with a small group of bikes, and as we rode from Stovepipe Wells to Furnace Creek there was a 30-footer trundling along at a

Abbreviated Valley History

Indians cheerfully lived in and around the valley for thousands of years, having the good sense to stay away during the summer; a number of reliable springs provided water for man and beast. In December of 1849 some California-bound emigrants tried to take a short-cut through the valley, and 27 wagons came down **Furnace Creek Wash,** with several families and a group of bachelors who called themselves **Jayhawkers.** Camp was made, a discussion was held, and they figured they were well and truly lost. The group began to split up, some going west, some south, and some just staying until help would come. Eventually everybody made it safely away from the valley, except for one Jayhawker who died while walking out.

According to undocumented lore, one of the emigrant women, as her group climbed up toward **Emigrant Pass,** turned and shook her fist at the innocuous landscape, shouting, "Goodbye, valley of death!" Maybe, maybe not.

One of the Jayhawkers picked up an odd rock, and much later he found that it was nearly pure silver. The gold and silver rush was on, and prospectors headed to the area; the miners were followed by saloons and prostitutes, and many mining towns appeared and vanished.

However, the real money was in **borax;** this unromantic mineral is used in everything from cleansing agents to making glass, and the image of 20-mule teams hauling wagonloads of borax off to the railhead at Mojave is seered in the minds of today's Boomer generation, thanks to a television show called "Death Valley Days," which featured a B-movie actor called **Ronald Reagan.**

The borax era lasted roughly from the mid-1870s to the 1920s, and then the **Harmony Borax Company** got rid of a lot of unwanted real estate by making a gift of Death Valley to the **National Park Service.** Now the main business is tourism, and lots of them come, all year around. It is amazing what air-conditioning can do to counteract an outside temperature of 120 degrees. **Furnace Creek** has always been considered the epicenter of the valley, as it has a constant and prodigious supply of water.   ∎

stately 35 mph, with a "Cruise America" sign on the back indicating it was a rental. As we went by a small dog was frantically trying to bash its brains out on the windshield, with the red-faced man-at-the-wheel fighting hard to keep from leaving the road and driving across the desert (a definite no-no by park rules) and down into Salt Creek. As we were gassing up at Furnace Creek he pulled in, got out, and started imprecating against us, calling us dangerous, irresponsible, and some rather less choice words. We calmed him down by pointing out that with his obviously limited skills at steering his mobile bathtub, it was he who was the more hazardous.

Other than that, and the sheriff and the CHP officer who live in Death Valley, there is not much risk to the motorcyclist. Except if one is a little too throttle happy.

Death Valley is a national park, and a haphazard system of collecting an entry fee might set you back $5. If they don't catch you at the entrance just south of Scotty's Castle, you are supposed to present yourself at the museum at Furnace Creek and pay up. Do it; that may be the most worthwhile $5 you will spend.

These are the 20-mule-team wagons that made history, hauling borax from Death Valley to the refining plant at Mojave; that last wagon was a water tanker, to keep the men and mules from dying of thirst along the way.

A nice view from Mt. Laguna over the Anza-Borrego Desert.

National parks lease out the concession rights to various organizations, and the one at Furnace Creek is called Xanterra Parks & Resorts. **Furnace Creek Ranch,** some 200 feet below sea level, used to be a real ranch, raising cattle to feed the miners; that's all gone. Now there is a big hotel/motel called the **Ranch Resort,** along with a store, cafeteria, restaurant, saloon, tennis courts, golf course, airstrip, date palms, horses to rent, et cetera.

At the Ranch (760-786-2345) most rooms are in the large, dull, two-story buildings which house the bus-loads of tourists that come to this place; it is worth it to spend a little more money on one of the reconditioned parkside bungalows (my own preference). Or you can go a mile away to the **Furnace Creek Inn** (same phone), where a "luxury" view will cost you a good deal more. There is a "dress code" at the Inn, but only for dinner, and that merely requires a jacket; a good Langlitz leather jacket will do fine against the next table's Brooks Bros. blazer.

The Ranch is far more rowdy than the Inn, and preferable to my tastes. The saloon used to be a delightfully dark and gloomy place, very Old West, but a couple of years back some dolt decided that light and airy would be the new design; I'm surprised he didn't use ferns to enhance the decor. Too bad, but the beer is still cold. The Ranch has great grassy swards to stroll across, palm trees to walk under, and a swimming pool to dive into.

The paved roads in the park are very definitely entertaining riding, from the high-speed sweepers coming down from **Scotty's Castle** to the twisty stuff between **Wildrose Canyon** and **Emigrant Pass.** Plus there are miles and miles of dirt roads for the dual-purpose riders.

Motorcycle Notes: Not much in the way of dealers in Death Valley. An excellent Honda/Yamaha shop, **Desert Sport Center,** is in **Ridgecrest** (760-375-2540), 125 miles west of Furnace Creek Ranch. To the east about the same distance is Las Vegas, which has got every dealer possible.

These editors from a German motorcycle magazine have come to see Death Valley up close and personal.

Trip 25 Badwater, Shoshone, Death Valley Junction

Distance *127 miles*

Highlights *If you want to get on the throttle, you can do this in under two hours; most people who have never been here before will take all day.*

0 Miles TURN RIGHT coming out of **Furnace Creek Ranch,** heading east on CA 190/178.

0+ Miles TURN RIGHT as you come on a rise, with the **Furnace Creek Inn** up on your left, a well-marked, BADWATER, road, CA 178, cuts sharply to the right; that is the one you want. CA 190 goes straight ahead to Death Valley Junction.

Twenty Mule Team Canyon is five miles of good dirt road that any bike can deal with—presuming the rider is competent.

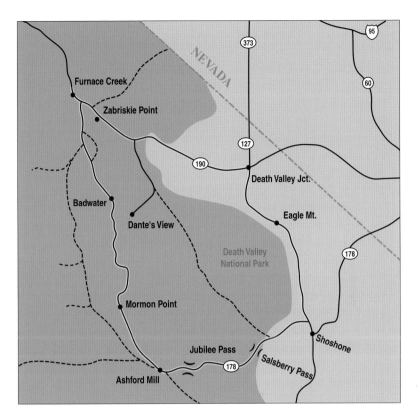

3+ Miles Entrance to **Mosaic Canyon,** with a left turn up a short dirt road to a parking area, where you start a hike. Very pretty, very geological, which will get you up to **Zabriskie Point.** My recommendation, being a lazy cuss, is to go up to Zabriskie and walk downhill. It is one of the more popular hikettes in the park, and you will pass lots of people.
5 Miles On the left, the north end of a one-way road to Artists Palette; this is the end not to enter.
7 Miles On your right, the northern entrance to the **West Side Road,** 35+ miles of sometimes good, sometimes bad (depending on the past winter and the amount of repairs being done) dirt road. If it has been raining, forget it, unless you have a d-p and you are willing to get dirty. If dry, a Gold Wing can go through.
10 Miles The south entrance to Artist Drive, which is a very pleasant one-lane (paved), one-way jaunt for nine miles through the foothills of the **Black Mountains,** one of the many smaller groups that make up the **Amargosa Range.** Lots of attractive geology to see out there, especially in the afternoon when the western sun is striking these rocks.

West Side Road

If you take the **West Side Road,** there are a couple of smaller roads shooting off to the west, which are good for dual-purpose bikes. After five-plus miles Trail Canyon Road used to climb up to **Aguereberry Point**—but not for the last 30 years or more, as a big slide took out a big chunk of the road, leaving nothing but a steep mountainside. Another five miles, and **Hanaupah Canyon** dead-ends after a few miles. Another 10 miles, passing the grave of Shorty Harris and the remains of the **Eagle Borax** works, and **Johnson Canyon** goes off to a dead end, becoming impassable long before you get to the ruins of **Hungry Bill's** ranch. Another five miles, by some old tanks, **Galena Canyon** goes east a short way to an old talc mine. Seven more miles, and there is a cut back to the east, Warm Spring Canyon Road; this one, if you follow it for about 33 miles, will take you right out of Death Valley and into **Panamint Valley.** At the turn clock 0 on your tripmeter; you will beat up a long, rocky wash and come into **Striped Butte Valley;** at 15+ miles keep to your left; another five-plus, also keep left. The only possible problem is climbing that little cliff right at **Mengel Pass** (4,326 ft); it's not for the faint of heart, but lots of people do it. That leads you into **Goler Wash,** which runs out to Panamint Valley and Wingate Road, going north to **Ballarat.** Good d-p exercise. If you are staying on the Westside Highway, just three miles will bring you back to pavement on CA 178.   ■

12 Miles   To the right is the turn to the **Devil's Golf Course,** down a mile of good dirt road. Wind and rain and a couple of million years have left neatly formed stacks of salt and gravel scattered all along the old lake bottom, and if you are needing salt for your picnic, just take a pinch of the white stuff.

14 Miles   To the left is a turn up a two-mile dirt road to the parking area for the **Natural Bridge.** A short quarter-mile hike brings you beneath the arch, which is about 50 feet above your head.

The road develops a few twists and turns along about now, as it hunkers in under the steep cliffs to the left (east), avoiding the potentially marshy bits of the **Salt Creek Basin.**

17 Miles   Badwater; where you park the bike you are about 270 feet below sea level, and a white sign up on the cliffs behind you reminds you of where you would be if somebody dug a 200-mile trench from the **Pacific Ocean** to Death Valley—put some turbines along there and you could generate some real electricity as the ocean rushed in. If you want to get the full impact, you can walk out onto the saline flats about three miles and get down to -279.8 feet.

South of Badwater the quality of the road deteriorates a bit, as it is not heavily used and the USNPS has only limited funds. But it is still a good road, although with a lot of patches, and it swoops around the edges of the slag that has come off the hills, great honking curves of a mile or more, where the last guy can see the first in a chain of 20 fast-moving sportbikes.

Come around **Mormon Point** and the road begins a gentle, barely perceptible climb.

43 Miles The southern junction of the West Side Road.

45 Miles **Ashford Mill,** or better put, the small remains of the old borax mill; not the sort of place to take a vacation in. I have slept on the picnic tables there, much against park regulations, and the place has a pleasantly eery aura about it.

47 Miles Highway 178 makes a sharp left here, to the east, to take you up over **Jubilee Mountain,** while Henry Wade Road goes straight.

51 Miles The road gets right twisty as you come up on **Jubilee Pass** at a modest 1,290 feet, cut deep through the mountain. The road slips down into a valley and immediately starts to climb again.

56 Miles You are up at **Salsberry Pass,** at a somewhat more lofty 3,315 feet. Then you drop down into **Greenwater Valley** (I'll let you figure where that name came from) and leave the National Park.

Mr. Wade's Road

You can go straight on Henry Wade Road, a dirt and sand track that will tie into CA 127 after 33 miles; the sign recommends high clearance and four-wheel drive. I recommend dual-purpose, although I watched a friend run a Sportster over it years ago. The road runs along the **Amargosa River,** which is flowing (!?) north into Death Valley; the river is usually dry unless very heavy rains have fallen, but at one point the road crosses the river and there is a stretch of soft sand. No real problem for a d-p bike or a well-ridden naked motorcycle. A Gold Wing or a GSX-R1000 might find it a bit much. ■

62 Miles Off to your left are the beginnings of a small collection of dirt roads heading north into Greenwater Valley. They all more or less congeal after a mile or so into one 28-mile dirt road that goes up the valley and connects with the road to **Dante's View.** More on that from the other end.
72 Miles STOP sign—TURN LEFT, as CA 178 connects with CA 127. Our route goes left, but a short trip to the right, to Shoshone, is good.

Connector To Palm Springs

If you are interested in heading south to **Palm Springs,** you can take CA 127 south to Baker, then CONTINUE STRAIGHT across I-15 onto Kelbaker Road, going through **Kelso** and on to **Amboy** on old US 66. Then the Amboy Road goes south to 29 Palms, and you can turn to Chapter 14 to figure out what to do next.

∎

Cruising north on CA 127 you are riding beside the **Amargosa River,** which flows (when flowing, which is very, very, very rarely) south past Shoshone to the **Dumont Dunes.** The 25 mile stretch from Shoshone to **Death Valley Junction** is best known for its flatness and fast curves. Ahead of you is **Eagle Mountain,** a great hunk of stone sticking up some 2,500 feet from the desert floor, out in the middle of nowhere. In the distance you see a cluster of buildings; it will take a few minutes to get there, although you think they are just a mile away.

Shoshone

Go right one mile if you are interested in gas, food, or a place to sleep. Or information. That is the tiny town of Shoshone, which flourished briefly as a mining center, and now has become a small stop on the back way into Death Valley. You can get a room at the **Shoshone Inn,** an old-fashioned motel with 16 units (760-852-4335). Next door is the **Charles Brown General Store;** Mr. Brown was a local politician who basically owned the town, until he died and passed the whole thing along to his grand-daughter Susan. Across the road is the **Crowbar Cafe** (760-852-4123); serving good, filling food seven days a week from seven in the morning to 9:30 at night. Don't miss the **Shoshone Museum,** which has a bit of everything that has withstood the ravages of a hundred years of use and exposure to the elements. ∎

Badwater is more than 270 feet below sea level. If I could just dig a ditch from the Pacific Ocean to Death Valley and stick in a couple of water turbines to generate electricity, I could let gravity make me rich. (Photo by Craig Erion)

97 Miles   Death Valley Junction, you have arrived.
90+ Miles   Just north of the Opera House CA 190 turns to the left, back to Death Valley.

Alternate Route Via Beatty

If you want to skirt the east edge of the national park, you can go north on CA 127 to the Nevada state line, and continue on to Beatty, Nevada.

Seven miles along, at the state line, where CA 127 morphs into NV 373, you will find **Longstreet's Inn & Casino,** with a restaurant and 60 rooms (775-372-1777), and some ordinary gambling. Across the road is the old **Stateline Saloon & Gambling Hall,** right next to **Mom's Place,** offering beer, gas, and packaged food.

Continue north, you come into **Amargosa Valley,** with Mecca Road going off to the west. Curious place, this valley, with good and plentiful well water right here in the middle of the **Amargosa Desert,** and there is a turf farm and a 5,000-cow dairy not far away.

After 23 miles NV 373 ends where it butts into US 95 at **Lathrop Wells,** where a really ugly and cheap fake-front joint called the **Amargosa Saloon & Casino** will, if open, try to liberate your money. Take a left, and you are headed toward Beatty, Nevada. The road is quite open and straight, going through the Amargosa Desert, and other than the **Yucca Mountains** to your right, the **Funeral Mountains** to your left, and lots of dirt roads disappearing into the mountains, there is not much. A monstrous sand dune sits off to the left.

After 52 miles you arrive in **Beatty.** More on that metropolis in Trip #27.   ∎

Back at **Death Valley Junction,** head west on CA 190 as the long straight road climbs slightly.

107 Miles   You cross the nameless saddle (3,040 feet) between the **Funeral Mountains** and the **Greenwater Range,** and begin a long 20-mile descent to Furnace Creek Ranch. It is right easy to pick up a serious head of speed along here.

115 Miles   There is a turn to the left which takes you 13 miles up to **Dante's View.** Take it; it is a must-do.

119 Miles   The east (NO ENTRY) end of a one-way road through **Twenty Mule Team Canyon.**

Death Valley Junction

The place began its existence as the town of **Amargosa** in 1907, but after the **Tonopah & Tidewater** and the **Las Vegas & Tonopah** railroads arrived about 1914, it became Death Valley Junction. Population soared to 300. The railroad was used to haul borax out of nearby mines until 1928, and then things went into a slow decline. World War II came along, and the railway tracks were torn up and melted down to help the war effort.

In the middle of town is a large, one-story, U-shaped complex which was used to house railroad workers, and is now owned by Marta Becket, the ballet dancer. At one end of the U is the **Amargosa Opera House,** where Marta has been putting on superb performances since 1968, always on Saturday night, between October and May. This cultural event is not to be missed; call (760-852-4441) for full information. She also has a dozen rooms available in her **Amargosa Hotel,** which is in the complex. For restaurant food you will have to go seven miles north to the Nevada state line, where the casino serves up 24 hours a day (see Alternate Route).   ∎

Dante's View

Right after you turn you notice an operating mine off to your left. That is the **Ryan Mine,** just outside the somewhat gerrymandered national park boundaries, still producing borax. The road continues up **Furnace Creek Wash** into **Greenwater Valley.** After seven miles the road turns sharply to the right, with a parking area for trailers, and off to the left is the Greenwater Valley Road, 28 miles of dual-purpose dirt that will connect you with CA 178 just east of **Salsberry Pass.** It is an entertaining dual-purpose ride, climbing gradually to 4,050 feet about halfway, and then dropping slowly down to about 2,000 feet by the time you see pavement again.

The paved road starts a serious climb to **Dante's View,** first straight, and then winding through a delightful little canyon, followed by some serious squiggles to get to the top, and the view that Dante has. Of course you all know that Dante wrote The Divine Comedy, in which he describes visiting Heaven, Purgatory, and Hell—and this, according to some well-read namer of places, is his view of Hell. You are at 5,475 feet, directly above **Badwater,** right across from 11,049-foot **Telescope Peak** only 20 miles to the west, and Death Valley spread out to your left and right. It is a superior view, especially if you can catch it at dusk on a full moon, sun setting in the west, moon rising in the east. Perfect. Just watch out on your way down.   ■

121 Miles The start of the Twenty Mule Team Canyon drive; this is a well-maintained dirt road of a little less than three miles length, weaving through the hills; any good rider can do it. They say that if you are there in the evening as the land cools off, you can hear some sort of snap, crackle, and pop. By the way, the old 20-mule borax hauling wagons never came through here; it is just a catchy name.

122 Miles Ah, **Zabriskie Point.** Old man Zabriskie happened to be a superintendent at the borax mines a long time ago, and now his name lives on. Mobs of tourists come here, with huge buses in the parking lot full of French and Germans (though never in the same bus). Park the bike, climb the hill, and look out over an other-worldly scene. My advice is to skip it during the day when the crowds are around, and come up late on a moonlit night. Then it is purely ethereal.

Ah, yes, Dante's View, at 5,475 feet, is the best view in California, with Badwater below at –279.8 feet, and snow-capped Telescope Peak in the distance, at 11,049 feet.

123 Miles   Look for a small sign off to your right, ECHO CANYON, with a dirt road running off from **Furnace Creek Wash** toward the Funeral Mountains.

126 Miles   The road swoops around a couple of curves, and **Furnace Creek Inn** appears on your right. The building to your left used to be a garage that could actually do repairs, but that closed up about 15 years ago. Just beyond the defunct garage is the left turn down CA 178 to Badwater.

127 Miles   Arrive back at Furnace Creek Ranch.

For the Serious Dual-Purpose Rider

The nine-plus mile **Echo Canyon Road** is fun, but a skid plate should be considered essential equipment. I knocked a hole in the sump of a V65 Sabre a lot of years ago trying to get there, and once crunched, twice shy. But it is a great ride, about five rough miles up to the canyon, then a twisty trundle over a lot of smooth loose rocks as you go through the narrow, winding canyon; not for the faint of heart.

As you clear the canyon and come out into a small valley, a significant (i.e. you can't miss it) dirt road goes off to the left. Many years ago I found an old map of Death Valley, dating from 1951, and it showed a road going off from **Echo Canyon** and crossing over the **Funeral Mountains,** coming out at **Amargosa Valley** on the Nevada side. I had a KLR 650, with my bride-to-be on the back, and we went exploring. The only real problem, other than finding ourselves up a few dead ends, was an eight-foot dry waterfall, but previous passers had built a loose-rock ramp to get up, which could be negotiated with a good deal of care. Then we climbed to the top of the mountains, and came down a long, long dry wash into the Amargosa Desert, with a view of **Big Dune** from far off. It was the best 20-mile trip I've ever taken.

If you wish to try, do take a friend along on another bike; and some water. Just in case you get stuck out there.

Back in Echo Canyon, you can keep on going until you come to the site of the old **Inyo Mine,** very isolated and romantic, with a few decrepit old buildings slowly falling apart. Half a mile beyond the mine the road is barricaded as it disappears into the mountains.   ∎

Trip 26 Beatty, Scotty's Junction, Scotty's Castle

Distance *155 miles*

Highlights *This takes you out of Death Valley via Hell's Gate and east into Nevada, and you see that the park does cross state lines. Leaving Beatty, a working town with a little bit of gambling and a smidgen of prostitution, the road goes north across high desert, then west back to Death Valley.*

0 Miles TURN LEFT coming out of **Furnace Creek Ranch,** and go 11 miles on that fine paved road that runs through the center of the valley.

11 Miles TURN RIGHT at **Beatty Junction** (190 feet below sea level), and you are headed uphill in a rolling manner along Daylight Pass Cut-Off Road.

16 Miles There is a well-marked turn to the right, with a well-maintained dirt road going 2-plus miles up to the parking area at the **Keane Wonder Mine.** Begun in 1903, the Keane was worked into the 1930s, and now there are a lot of remains. This was no hole-in-the-ground operation, but a big-bucks investment.

The Antelope Valley (California) HOG chapter was out for a look at Scotty's Castle.

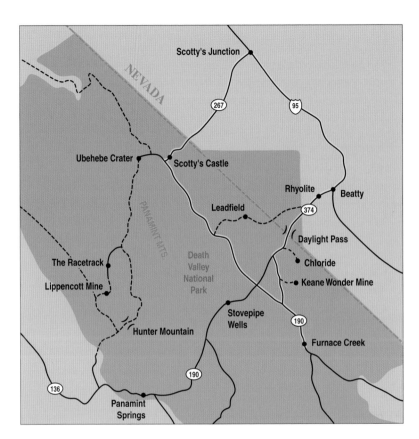

21 Miles STOP sign—TURN RIGHT as you come into the **Hells Gate** intersection, going up Daylight Pass Road. It has a few serious curves, and some terrified RVers who find the downhill a trifle steep for their smoking brakes.

24 Miles A dirt road to the right goes up to **Chloride,** where silver was being mined up until World War I. Good views of the valley from there.

27 Miles **Daylight Pass,** 4,317 feet. Back in the late Seventies some Young Urban Professionals from Los Angeles began an annual ride to Death Valley, and the Yuppie Run continues to this day, staying at Furnace Creek. On Saturday night everyone tears up to Beatty for a doctor-defying meal of red meat, and on the way back everybody stops at the top of the pass, kills the engine, and the coasting race begins. The hotshots have 70 pounds of air in their tires, and sewing-machine oil in their wheel bearings. Drafting someone with a dead engine can be an entertainment, especially when you grab the fellow's rear turn signal and pull yourself up alongside. Fun.

You are now entering **Nevada.**

Titus Canyon

The approach to the canyon is a one-way dirt road of some 24 miles, usually in pretty good repair as many small motorhomes go through. It is a beaut trip, but a bit rough on an Electra Glide or a Ducati, or for anybody who is fearful of riding on bumpy, rutted dirt; whether you are on a DR or a GL, you better know your way around dirt.

The first five miles go straight across the **Amargosa Desert,** then the road starts winding upward to the 5,250-foot summit; after that it drops twistingly down to the remains of **Leadville.** For a few brief months in 1920 gullible suckers came from all over the country, conned by a promotor who had convinced people there was lead in these hills.

After Leadville the road runs down into Titus Canyon, and the surface is made up of small, water-washed rocks. It is quite navigable on a bike if you are familiar with such terrain. At the end of the canyon the road suddenly opens out into Death Valley, and there are less than two miles of good, two-way dirt road to get back to the pavement 20 miles south of **Scotty's Castle.**   ∎

31 Miles You leave the park boundaries.

34 Miles The start of the road to **Titus Canyon.**

36 Miles A left turn takes you up to **Rhyolite,** where gold was discovered in 1904 and some 6,000 people eventually lived and dug for gold. The road dead-ends in about two miles, but it is worth a trip. An old railroad station has been fenced off, and there are local efforts to preserve the place, along with a caboose which hasn't seen any movement in half a century or more.

At the intersection you will see the remnants of a huge semi-mining operation which used to operate 24 hours a day until 2004, great floodlights illuminating the area at night, making it look like something out of a science-fiction film. Modern technology had made it possible to extract more gold from the old mine tailings, tailings being what is left after the gold was extracted with the methods employed in the early years of the last century. Everything lies dormant, waiting for gold to hit $1,000 an ounce, at which point a new process will probably sift through the tailings of the tailings.

Stay on the highway, wind over the hills, and drop into **Beatty.**

40 Miles You are at the intersection with US 95. Directly across the street is the **Exchange Club,** with gambling and rooms (775-553-2333). Should you take a right on US 95 South, in a hundred miles you will find yourself in Las Vegas. But you want to GO STRAIGHT, hooking into US 95 North, passing a Union 76 gas station on your right. Best to fill up.

41 Miles   The **Stagecoach Hotel Casino** is on your left, with **Rita's Cafe** (775-553-2419) serving casino-style food around the clock—no Michelin gastronomical stars awarded here.

Prostitution

Nevada, a sensible state which understands the need for a sound tax base, has realized the inevitability of prostitution, and decided to take financial advantage of the situation. This is a county by county decision, and the Houses of Joy are closely regulated by both the taxman and the medical profession. There are now 36 licensed cathouses in the state.

The customer base ranges from truck drivers to tourists to bi-sexual housewives. In these little compounds there is none of the glamour of the bawdy houses we see in movies, more of a Motel 6 approach to sex. Since the introduction of Viagra, the number of elderly gents visiting these establishments has greatly enhanced their profitability. ■

Angel's Ladies, a house of ill repute in Beatty, Nevada, has its own airstrip for the use of its patrons. Obviously the pilot of this plane was a little too excited at the thought of what was in store for him.

43 Miles   On your left, a few hundred yards off the road, is a brilliant pink house; this is **Angel's Ladies,** temporary home to some women of the world's second oldest profession. There is an airstrip out front, for the fly-in crowd, and a wrecked twin-engine plane as decoration.

50 Miles   All that is left of **Springdale** is a small house surrounded by a lot of valuable antiquities, or junk, depending on your point of view. But I did run out of gas there once, and the fellow cheerfully sold me a gallon.

Now you are crossing the **Sarcobatus Flats,** and it is a straight, fast ride.

72 Miles   And there is a bright yellow collection of trailers off to your right; a sign at the gate reads SHADY LADY. Competition for Angel's Ladies.

75 Miles   TURN LEFT at **Scotty's Junction,** where there is a little store

The Keane Wonder Mine produced a lot of gold from 1903 to 1916. It was occasionally mined after that, but hasn't seen any activity since the Thirties.

Scotty's Castle

Walter Scott was a cheerful braggart, rodeo rider, prospector, you name it, who made friends with a wealthy Chicago man, Albert Johnson, who wanted to bring his wife to the dry climate of Death Valley. Being a bit on the shy side, Johnson let Scotty be the front man for the house that he built at Grapevine Springs. Offically it was known as the Death Valley Ranch, but Scotty had no objection to having the place known as his castle.

The construction started in 1924, and when it was done the elaborate house had 18 fireplaces, a many-piped organ, and a 260-foot swimming pool. The house was never completely finished; Johnson died in 1948, and the money flow ceased. Scotty carried on for another six years, telling everyone who cared to listen that he had a secret gold mine. He died in 1954 and is buried on a hill overlooking "the shack," as he self-deprecatingly referred to the mansion.

Amongst the many curiosities, one is the huge stack of 120,000 railroad ties that were bought when the Tonopah & Tidewater Railroad was torn up; unfortunately, nobody thought to find out if the creosoted wood would burn well in a fireplace . . . it doesn't. Gas is usually available from 8:30 a.m. to 5:30 p.m. ∎

with rusty bits of this and that decorating the front, everything for sale. I've heard rumors that it does have "emergency" gas out of five-gallon cans, though I did not ask what the price would be. After the left turn you are on NV 267, and the road goes across the flats, past the ruins of a smelter.

86 Miles The **Bonnie Claire Dry Lake** is on your right, and if you have recently seen Anthony Hopkins in the movie *The World's Fastest Indian* and ever wondered what it would be like to tear across such a piece of uncluttered, unpoliced terrain at any speed your motorcycle is capable of, be my guest. Just turn off the road. But not if it has rained recently.

After leaving the flats the road goes deceptively downhill, and you can pick up a head of speed without quite being aware. Just as you enter the park boundaries, the road gets into some serious twisting as it follows the long-gone creek that created **Grapevine Canyon**. Be gentle, as there are big boulders right off the road which will bring an errant motorcycle to a swift and sure stop.

100 Miles Scotty's Castle, an appealing place that is worth a visit—as long as the wait is not too long (760-786-2392).

Ubehebe Crater & the Racetrack

Take the turn. After two-plus miles a dirt road goes off to the right, known as Death Valley Road, and going to **Big Pine.** It is 35 miles of good dirt, with about four miles of pavement in the middle, in **Hanging Rock Canyon.** It is usually well-maintained, and a Vulcan 2000 can get through with no problem—if the rider is familiar with loose-surface riding.

Another two paved miles and you are at the parking area for the crater. This was created by a volcanic explosion a few thousand years ago, and is half a mile across, 500 feet deep. The athletically inclined can walk to the bottom.

Right by the parking area is a sign indicating a (bad) dirt road that goes to the **Racetrack.** This is a helluva good ride for a competent dual-sporter, but do get a good map, as what I am saying here is not intended as a guide, just a titilation. First you have to battle your way up **Racetrack Valley** along a dry wash, with lots of stones. After 19+ miles you arrive at **Teakettle Junction**—and yes, there are a lot of tea-kettles hanging from the sign.

Keep on straight and in five more miles you are at the Racetrack, which is a dry lake on your left. Forty years ago and more, there were big rocks on the lake bed, weighing 100 pounds and more, which would move and leave trails behind, rather a bizarre geological sleight of hand—attributable to an extremely slick muddy surface and a very high wind. However, tourists have stolen all these rocks and taken them away, so don't expect to see anything.

In another five miles you are at the old **Lippencott lead mine,** and if you are really, really good on your d-p bike, you can ride down a very steep, rocky road for three miles, which comes out after four more miles to Saline Valley Road. From there you can go north 40 miles on good dirt to meet up with Death Valley Road, or south 30 miles on dirt to meet up with CA 190.

Now, back to Teakettle, if you turn left you go through **Lost Burro Gap** and into **Hidden Valley,** past a couple of old mine sites, then climb up over **Hunter Mountain** and drop down to meet with Saline Valley Road. That is a great ride, and not terribly difficult.   ■

Occasionally I do Death Valley on a dual-purpose bike; that is Kurt "Baja" Grife and myself, taking our ease in Rhyolite.

103 Miles   A paved road goes off to the right to **Ubehebe Crater.**
104 Miles   The ranger station will lighten your wallet by a five-dollar bill. The admission ticket is good for seven days.

Now begins a long, gradual descent, dropping over 3,000 feet in 50 miles. The road is good, the curves are benign, and the view down the valley is marvelous, with the **Mesquite Flat** sand dunes in the far distance.
122 Miles   A sign pointing to the left reads TITUS CANYON. It is a two-mile, two-way dirt road leading to the mouth of the canyon, and the start of the one-way road. If you have not cared to take your Nomad all the way down the canyon, ride up to the parking area and walk into the canyon for half a mile. It is impressive.
133 Miles   A very good dirt road to the right leads down to the sand dunes, which are the perfect place to take your dawn walk.
135 Miles   Daylight Pass Road goes off to the left, to Beatty.
136 Miles   STOP sign—TURN LEFT onto CA 190/178.
155 Miles   Arrive back at Furnace Creek Ranch.

Trip 27 Stovepipe Wells, Towne Pass, Wildrose Canyon

Distance *126 miles*

Highlights *Warning, there is a little bit of good dirt road on this loop, close to Wildrose Canyon itself. But this is a beaut loop that runs you over the Panamint Range, through the Panamint Valley, paralleling Death Valley, then back over the Panamints on another road.*

0 Miles TURN LEFT leaving **Furnace Creek Ranch** and stay on CA 190/178.

25 Miles **Stovepipe Wells Village,** with a store, gas, restaurant, bar, and 83-unit motel (760-786-2387), a bit cheaper than the Ranch, but there is not much to do there. The actual **Stovepipe Well** is about five miles northwest of here, across the dunes, and the well was long identified by an old bit of stovepipe travelers had used to prevent the hole from filling up with sand.

Behind me is old Dinah, a steam-powered tractor that used to haul wagons around in the valley in the early years of the 20th Century; the spokes on those wheels did not bend easily.

Now it is a long run up and over the **Panamint Range,** with lots of warnings to cars to turn off air-conditioners so the engines do not overheat. We motorcyclists don't need no stinking air conditioning.

34 Miles   As you pass **Emigrant Campground** a sign points off to **Emigrant Pass;** you will be coming back this way.

Panamint Springs

Ahead on CA 190 less than two miles is the pleasantly rustic **Panamint Springs Resort** (775-482-7680), a privately owned motel, campground, restaurant, et cetera. When Death Valley National Monument became a National Park a few years ago (it all has to do with federal funding), the boundaries were extended and **Panamint Springs** was included, though left in private hands. It has 14 rooms and is a nice place to stay. The food is generally good . . . at least the last time I ate there, but the chef might have moved on.   ■

40 Miles Towne Pass, at 4,956 feet. Wowzer! Now starts a beaut descent, the road swooping down through the mountains until suddenly the **Panamint Valley** is spread out before you. There are sand dunes to the north, a large dry lake in front of you, and off in the distance the sun glints off some buildings. It all looks as though it is right in front of you, but it takes forever to get down to the lake—the distances are big.

59 Miles TURN LEFT onto CA 178, where the sign reads TRONA, having just crossed the lake; you are on the Panamint Valley Road.

Panamint Valley Road/CA 178 heads south, is out of the park in a couple of miles, and rolls over undulating desert.

61 Miles STOP sign—TURN LEFT onto the Trona-Wildrose Road. CA 178 goes to the right, you want that left, toward Wildrose Canyon.

Connector
To Kernville
If you go right, following CA 178, you will be in **Trona** in 33 miles, and stay on CA 178 through **Ridgecrest** and **China Lake** and **Inyokern,** and it will eventually take you right over **Walker Pass** to **Isabella Lake** (Chapter 12). ∎

Climbing a bit, the park's limits are denoted by a large sign, and after seven miles the road begins to deteriorate, becoming dirt. Years ago the park used to keep this stretch paved, but every few winters the water rushing down the canyon would tear up the asphalt and leave a righteous mess. Finally some brilliant administrator decided to leave things as they were, and just run a dozer over the road in the spring if it were needed, leaving the surface dirt. You go through **Wildrose Canyon** proper on the dirt.

71 Miles STOP sign—TURN LEFT; to the right is **Mahogany Flat** and **Telescope Peak.**

From that STOP sign the road winds through a narrow canyon, breaks out into a small valley, then climbs again, crossing **Nemo Crest** at 5,547 feet, descending and then rising again to **Emigrant Pass** (5,318 feet); this is the way the **Jayhawkers** emerged back in 1849. Great fun on a bike, but questionable with ox-drawn wagons.

81 Miles The road levels out on the **Harrisburg Flats**, and a dirt road goes off to the right, six miles out to **Aguereberry Point.** The view from the point is superb, looking down on **Furnace Creek** 6,500 feet below. About a mile back down the dirt road you will see a locked gate on your left, and that is the beginning of what was once the road going down to **Trail Canyon** and the West Side Road. Park the bike and walk down it a short distance and

Mahogany Flat

The road out to **Mahogany Flat** is a mild roller-coaster; get six or eight bikes rolling along, run sweep, and the view is a delight as the motorcycles are constantly topping hillocks, disappearing, others appearing—grand video stuff. After five miles the road turns to dirt, and then these great beehives appear on your left, about 30 feet in diameter and 30 feet tall.

The ten beehive affairs are charcoal kilns. Few people today understand the importance of charcoal, but essentially if wood is turned into charcoal, it is far more transportable and turns out a higher heat. If you want to know about that heat thing, go back to your high-school chemistry book. But the charcoal was important for smelting the ore and extracting the gold and silver, because the gold and silver was a long way from where the trees were up on the mountainside.

A scrabbly dirt road leads up to Mahogany Flats, the highest place in Death Valley accessible by motorcycle (at least legally). From here, 8,133 feet, you can walk up to the top of **Telescope Peak** (11,049 feet) via a seven-mile trail; I've never done it, but I welcome those of you who do to write and tell me about.   ■

you will see why the road is no longer usable.

83 Miles A seven-mile dirt road goes off to the right to the remnants of the boom and bust town of **Skidoo.** Abandoned in 1917, not much remains.

The paved road starts dropping down through **Emigrant Canyon,** a beautiful run with a couple of deceptive curves.

92 Miles STOP sign—TURN RIGHT; you are back at the intersection by the **Emigrant Campground.** TURN RIGHT and head down the hill toward **Stovepipe Wells**—stunning views. And then on to Furnace Creek.

126 Miles Arrive back at Furnace Creek.

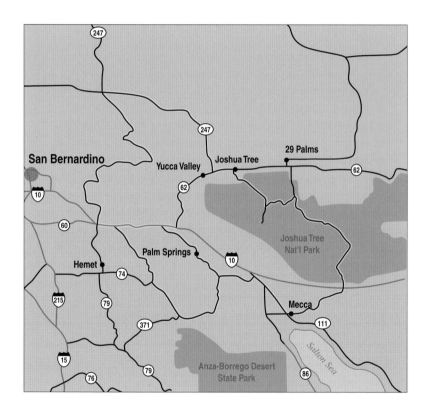

Palm Springs Alternative

Headquarters *Palm Springs*
Palm Springs Tourism Office *760-778-8415, 800-347-7746*
Best Time to Visit *All year, although you can find ice and snow in the mountains in the winter. Be wary if you want to haul over the San Bernardino Mountains or the San Jacinto Mountains in January.*
Getting There *Easiest way is just to head east out of the Los Angeles Basin on I-10. Or you might be coming in from Phoenix, Arizona, on I-10.*
Ground Zero *The following trips will start where Ramon Road crosses between Indian Canyon and Palm Canyon, convenient as Indian Canyon goes straight north to I-10 going west, Ramon goes due east to I-10 going east. And this is also the IHOP corner, so you can have breakfast there and plan the day.*

It's a long, lonely road coming into Joshua Tree National Park from 29 Palms.

In the curious geology that constitutes most of California, desert and mountains sit side by side, and you can be swimming down below and skiing up above. We've all heard of **Palm Springs**, where the rich come to play golf and die, the middle class come to party and leave, and the poor commute to work from **Indio**. Not many people might think of Palm Springs as being the focal point for great riding, but it is.

Nice town, thanks to a phenomenal amount of water deep down in the desert. Through the miracles of modern technology the local authorities pump it out at a great rate and keep 20 some golf courses green and healthy. The place has very much a live-for-today attitude, as nobody really wants to think about the inevitable day when the water gives out. The **Coachella**

That is General Patton and his dog, in front of a museum in his honor on Interstate 10, east of Palm Springs.

Valley, which is the long strip running from Palm Springs east to Indio, averages less than three inches of rain a year. But the date farmers use at least ten feet of water on their trees.

"Take the cash and let the credit go, nor heed the rumble of the distant drum." That's a thousand-year-old quote from a poet fellow named Omar Khayyam, which is still suitable.

Downtown Palm Springs is real nice on a quiet Monday afternoon. There are two wide, parallel, one-way streets, Indian Canyon Drive going north, Palm Canyon Drive going south, and the two miles between Alejo Road and Ramon Road is the place to be. There are a multitude of good open-air restaurants, shops and shopping centers, with a few museums thrown in for good measure. **Palm Canyon** is more the strolling side. For post office purposes, everything north of **Tahquitz Canyon** is referred to as North, and south of . . . etc.

For food, if you want Southwest cooking, go to the **Blue Coyote Grill** (445 North Palm Canyon, 760-327-1196). For all-American chow, try the **Burger Factory** (333 South Indian Canyon, 322-7678), where the one-pound "Kong Burger" is good for two people. Breakfast, in this land of food franchises, is best eaten at the **IHOP** (International House of Pancakes, for those who have forgotten) joint (471 South Indian Canyon Drive at Ramon).

Places to sleep are almost infinite, as greater Palm Springs has about 10,000 pillows to offer. Pricing structure is also quasi-infinite, ranging from mid-week low-season to weekend high-season. High scale is the **Hyatt Regency** on Palm Canyon (285 North Palm Canyon Drive), middle is the **Best Western Las Brisas** (222 South Indian Canyon, 325-4372, 800-346-5714). A favorite of the cost-conscious biking crowd is the quasi-omnipresent **Motel 6** chain—of which there are no less than four in Palm Springs; my choice is the one at 595 East Palm Canyon (760-325-6129) which is just a mile away from the action.

For local entertainment there are museums (I like the **Air Museum,** with all the WWII fighter planes), shows (**Liberace** wannabes are popular on the circuit), exertions (like how to learn rock-climbing and tandem sky-diving), and the great American pasttime, shopping. But I prefer to get on the road.

Trip 28 Joshua Tree National Park & Mecca

Distance *150 miles*

Highlights *This trip goes mainly through open, flattish country, going from low to high desert, and back, with lots of curvy pavement.*

0 Miles Head north on Indian Canyon Drive.

6 Miles Cross over I-10 and Indian Canyon Drive becomes Indian Ave.

10 Miles Pierson Blvd. crosses Indian Ave.; if you turn to the right you will get to **Desert Hot Springs,** where a dozen spas and resorts are located. This is where the Mafia heavies were reputed to hang out in the '30s, '40s, and '50s, the most famous place being the 56-acre Two Bunch Palms Resort; you need a reservation just to get in the gate—no looky-loos allowed.

11 Miles A gentle curve, angling off to the left!

14 Miles STOP sign—TURN RIGHT at intersection with CA 62. You are gaining altitude, going over a hill and dropping into the **Morongo Valley.**

25 Miles You have gained even more altitude and entered the town of **Yucca Valley** (3,256 feet) on the edge of the **Mojave Desert,** and on the right is **Dick Hutchin's Harley & HYKS** (Honda, Yamaha, Kawasaki, Suzuki) dealership (760-365-6311) and the **Harley Cafe,** open from 7 to 2 every day except Monday. Good food.

26 Miles Sign to PIONEERTOWN, pointing left. GO STRAIGHT.

26+ Miles John's Place is on your right.

These Boy Scout are getting set for a hike in the Joshua Tree National Park; that's a lot of gear they are carrying.

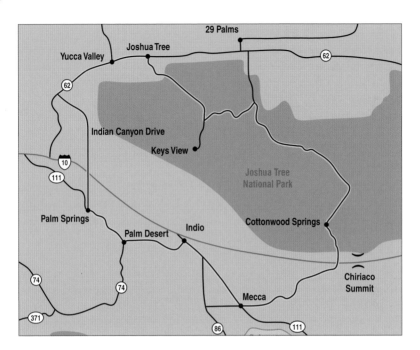

27 Miles STAY STRAIGHT on CA 62, a/k/a 29 Palms Highway, as CA 247 goes off to the left.

33+ Miles TURN RIGHT on Park Boulevard, where a sign indicates the way to JOSHUA TREE NATIONAL PARK. You are in the middle of the small town of **Joshua Tree.**

38 Miles The **West Entrance Station** to the park, where an attendant will take $5 and give you a map. This is high desert you are headed into, and a pretty spectacular place.

The park covers some 800,000 acres, and while there are jackrabbits, bobcats, and golden eagles in residence, what you will see most of are cacti, be they Joshua trees, ocotillo, cholla, or whatever. And a lot of very big rocks, often adorned with rock-climbers wearing bright shirts and shorts; geologists say that these rocks are officially known as **monzogranite intrusions;** they do look odd and other-worldly. The road is good, and quite curvy.

48 Miles Stay on the main road, Park Boulevard, goes leftish; if you want to get a fine view of the desert, take the right turn, which dead-ends after six-plus miles at **Key View** (5,185 feet)

59 Miles TURN RIGHT onto Pinto Basin Road.

Riding along Pinto Basin Road you find yourself dropping down from the high Mojave Desert to the low **Colorado Desert** . . . you can see for miles and miles into the basin. Go gently, as the road is a tad more than twisty, and tourists tend to clutter the narrow asphalt up. And you do not want to impale yourself on a cactus.

82 Miles   A dirt road, immediately splitting into two dirt roads, goes off to the left. For the adventuresome dual-purpose types.

89 Miles   Here is the ranger station and visitor center at **Cottonwood Springs;** the springs and campground are a mile east of the visitor center.

Now you go over **Cottonwood Pass** (2,800 feet) and down **Cottonwood Canyon** on a delightful stretch of road and leave the park boundary.

96 Miles   You arrive at I-10.

At that 96-Mile mark, cross over the Interstate and TURN RIGHT on to Box Canyon Road. The road goes through **Shavers Valley** and then drops down into **Box Canyon,** between the **Mecca Hills** and **Orocopia Mountains,** an excellent piece of riding.

111 Miles   Cross over the **Coachella Canal** into a sea of green and you are going below sea level as you enter the southern end of the **Coachella Valley.** This is very fertile land, as long as you have the water to make things grow.

114 Miles   Enter the small town of **Mecca** (Alt. -189 feet), now home to several thousand farm workers, where the American date industry started

29 Palms

If you are in no hurry, KEEP STRAIGHT, and after four miles you come to the **North Entrance Station** to the park. Another five miles and you are at the **Oasis Visitor Center,** the park's headquarters, is on your left, in the **Oasis of Mara,** in the town of **29 Palms;** it is just a few hundred yards south of CA 62.

Take a left right after the visitor center, and at 73950 Inn Avenue (don't ask me how they got to 73,000 on a very short street) is the **29 Palms Inn** (760-367-3505), offering hospitality since 1928. The place has over a dozen separate little residences, either adobe cottages or wood cabins, and a restaurant beside the swimming pool that serves lunch and dinner seven days a week, brunch on Sunday. It is a very nice place to lay back.

29 Palms itself does not have too much to offer, being an old Marine Corps town that has steadily been losing inhabitants, except that it has decided to revamp itself and has taken to calling itself the **City of Murals,** and lots of buildings have their sides painted.

Head back south into the park. Your ticket is good for seven days. Back to the intersection of Park Blvd. and Pinto Basin Rd.   ∎

General Patton Museum

An interesting deviation is to go four miles west on I-10 to **Chiriaco Summit** (1,705 feet) exit and visit the **General George Patton Museum.** Back in 1940 when **President Roosevelt** knew that entering the European conflict was inevitable, he had the army set up training bases in the desert in preparation for battling the Germans in North Africa. Every sort of World War II tank is parked outside the museum, and inside is an eclectic display of the equipment used by Patton and his troops.

Afterward, go back four miles and exit, back at the south entrance to the park.   ■

about 100 years ago. Nobody seems to know precisely how the town got its name, but presumably because many of the date palms were coming from the Middle East.

115 Miles   TRAFFIC LIGHT—and TURN RIGHT on CA 111, right after crossing over the **Southern Pacific** railroad tracks.

117 Miles   If you have a very sweet tooth stop at the **Date Garden Oasis** and have a date shake; an awful lot of sugar is in one of those babies.

Stay on CA 111 through the town of **Thermal** and on into the town of **Coachella.**

125 Miles   TURN LEFT onto Avenue 52, not very romantically named, but useful. Staying on Ave. 52 cross over CA 86 and HEAD STRAIGHT as the proverbial arrow toward **Indio Mountain.** Major farming here, but specialized, with dates and grapes abounding. Then you enter the new development town called **La Quinta,** with semi-expensive houses all looking just alike. The cross-streets all have presidential names: Van Buren, Jackson, Monroe, Madison, Jefferson. No Clinton, yet, nor Bush. Interestingly, this west end of Ave. 52 has new sidewalks, indicating that a lot of oldies who are buying these houses want places to walk—doctor's orders.

133 Miles   TURN RIGHT (north) on Washington Avenue.

136 Miles   TRAFFIC LIGHT—TURN LEFT onto CA 111; this little jog along Avenue 52 has avoided downtown **Indio,** a thoroughly avoidable place.

138 Miles   CA 74 goes off to the left, STAY STRAIGHT on CA 111.

146 Miles   STAY STRAIGHT on East Palm Canyon Drive as CA 111 goes right onto Gene Autry Trail; follow around the curve.

150 Miles   Arrive back at **Ramon** and **Indian Canyon.**

Trip 29 San Jacinto Mountains & Idyllwild

Distance *103 miles*

Highlights *Right above Palm Springs is Mt. San Jacinto. You can take an aerial tramway up, but it is much more fun to circle around the peak on a motorcycle. Even if it is hot down in Palm Springs, take some warm clothes as you will be going over 5,000 feet above the town, and it can be cool.*

0 Miles Head south on Palm Canyon Drive.

1 Mile CURVE LEFT, keeping to the obvious main road, East Palm Canyon Drive.

4 Miles Cross the southern terminus (love that word!) of Gene Autry Trail and East Palm Canyon also becomes CA 111.

12 Miles TRAFFIC LIGHT—and TURN RIGHT onto well-marked CA 74, a SHELL gas station on the corner. This is called the **Pines to Palms Highway** and is dead straight for the first five miles. Then it turns into Racer Road, known locally as **Seven Level Hill**. A beaut! It is back and forth for the next five miles, and you can take it slow and admire the vistas, or fast and scrape off excess metal from your bike.

The riding up CA 74 to the look-out on Seven Level Hill above Palm Desert is superb, as is the view over the Coachella Valley.

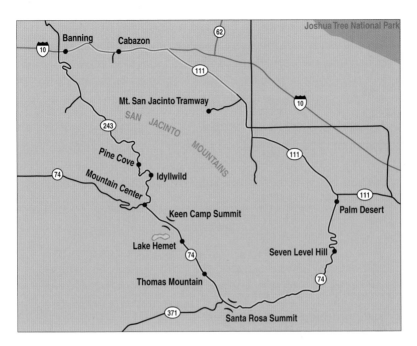

21 Miles   A big pullout and lookout is on the left side of the road, and on any weekend there will be motorcyclists there. And a great view of the **Coachella Valley.**

26 Miles   A fire station is on your right, a little restaurant on your left.

35 Miles   The road flattens out and you pass the **Pacific Crest Trail,** a hiking trail that runs from the Mexican border to Canada; I'd rather ride.

36 Miles   The **Santa Rosa Summit,** at 4,919 feet.

37 Miles   Intersection with CA 371, which drops down to **Aguanga** (see San Diego section). The **Paradise Corner Cafe** at the intersection is open most days (951-659-0730). Continue on CA 74, dropping gently into **Garner Valley,** past the growing community of **Thomas Mountain,** the road reasonably straight.

45 Miles   The general store at **Lake Hemet** (4,334 feet) has all the resources that the campers and fishermen at the lake need, like bait.

46 Miles   Over **Keen Camp Summit** (4,917 feet), and drop down twistily into **Mountain Center.**

48 Miles   TURN RIGHT at Mountain Center, onto CA 243, while CA 74 goes straight. In the center of the intersection is the **Mountain Center General Store,** with gas, and across the road is the sometimes-functioning **Mountain Center Cafe,** right next to the functioning post office. At the STOP sign, TURN RIGHT.

51 Miles   Enter the center of **Idyllwild,** a pleasant resort community.

CA 243 winds on to **Pine Cove,** sort of an adjunct Idyllwild, climbing to over 5,800 feet as it passes **Pine Cove Park.** This is excellent riding, through a landscape of pine trees, unless there is a lot of traffic on the road. The road is a twisty, double-yellow byway that offers little opportunity for legal overtaking.

68 Miles   Poppet Flat Road goes off to the left; stay on CA 243.

75 Miles   The descent to Banning begins in earnest, dropping over 2,000 feet in five miles. Good fun. The road curves down into the valley, and beyond the valley are the **San Bernardino Mountains.** Impressive.

Idyllwild

If you are tired of the Palm Springs heat, this is a great escape. The **Idyllwild Cafe,** on your right (951-659-2210), serves an honest breakfast and lunch (7 am to 2 pm) seven days a week. Smack in the very

center of town is **Jo'An's Restaurant** (951-659-0295), open for lunch and dinner through the week, breakfast as well on the weekend. For Mexican food, **La Casita** (951-659-6038) is the recommended place. Lodging is everywhere (www.idyl.com), from the funky fifties **Bluebird Hill Lodge** with 26 redwood cabins (909-659-2696; with motel-type rooms and cabins), or the **Idyllwild Inn** (888 659-2552), owned by the same family since 1904. If you want absolute silence, a mile from town is the genteelly shabby **Quiet Creek Inn** (909-659-6110, 800-450-6110); you can walk to any of the 15 restaurants in town, working up an appetite. ■

This totem pole sits on Village Center Drive in Idyllwild, right next to Jo'An's Restaurant, which is a good place to break one's fast.

76+ Miles TURN LEFT as you approach the Interstate. A sign indicates this is the way to get to I-10.

77 Miles TURN RIGHT, following Interstate signs, and in a quarter-mile you get on I-10 going east. Go past the huge **Desert Hills Factory Stores** on the north side of I-10 (unless you are in a buying mood).

84 Miles You are going through the **San Gorgonio Pass**, the dividing point between the **San Bernardino Valley** and **Palm Springs**. If you wish to see a concrete Jurassic Park, take the **Cabazon** exit, go under the Interstate, and behind **The Wheel Inn** (which serves a much, much better hamburger than the adjacent Fast-Food joint) are a very large brontosaurus and a tyrannosaurus rex; very good for a photograph.

This fossilized dinosaur is part of a concrete Jurassic Park behind the Wheel Inn at the Cabazon exit off I-10, west of Palm Springs.

89 Miles EXIT RIGHT onto CA 111, which will follow the south side of the dry **Whitewater River.**

97 Miles A large sign indicates that the PALM SPRINGS AERIAL TRAMWAY is to your left. Go three-plus miles up that road, climbing steeply to 2,643 feet, get in the gondola, and in 15 minutes you are up at **Mountain Station**, 8,516 feet. After which an hour's serious hike will get you to the top of **Mt. San Jacinto** at 10,804 feet. Grand views, but not nearly as much fun as motorcycling.

99 Miles **Palm Canyon** curves south, and right afterward CA 111 cuts off to the left, you STAY STRAIGHT on Palm Canyon.

103 Miles Arrive back at Ramon Road, Ground Zero.

Trip 30 Over the San Bernardino Mountains

Distance *181 miles*

Highlights *You can look forward to a lot of desert, a good deal of mountain, and a good ride which will last you the better part of a day. This has the same beginning as Loop 1.*

Looking up Mill Creek Canyon, you can see San Gorgonio Mountain, one of the San Bernardino Mountains, in the distance, standing 11,499 feet tall.

0 Miles   Go north on Indian Canyon, and follow the Loop 1 instructions for the first 26 miles, and about the only thing to remember is to TURN RIGHT at the STOP sign after 14 miles and continue on CA 62 into **Yucca Valley.**

26 Miles   TURN LEFT onto Pioneertown Road, going up through rocky, brushy country; pay attention to the dips in the road, because after a rain they may well be flooded.

30 Miles   Arrive at **Pioneertown**, a collection of old buildings and wagons, with some newer additions, such as a motel, to attract the tourist; part of the place was destroyed in a 2006 wildfire.

32+ Miles   TURN RIGHT at 4-way, middle-of-nowhere intersection onto Pipes Canyon Road; follow it, a winding stretch along **Pipes Wash** with scattered houses and a lot of horse activity.

These buildings are part of Pioneertown, sort of a Disneyland of the Old West out by Yucca Valley.

Alternate Route
Dirty Doings

A dual-purpose rider might opt to GO STRAIGHT at the intersection, headed for **Pipes Canyon Preserve.** The pavement ends in a little over a mile at **Rimrock,** then a rough dirt road continues past the **Farrington Observatory** for 17 miles (shortest version) to connect with CA 38 on top of the **San Bernardino Mountains.**

If you go left at the intersection another dirt road goes for 16 miles to meet up with CA 38 at **Onyx Summit.** Both versions have about a 4,000-foot climb, but are not terribly difficult.   ■

---

39 Miles STOP sign—TURN LEFT as **Pipes Canyon** ends at CA 247, also known as Old Woman Springs Road.

45 Miles You see signs for LANDERS, a desert community off to the right, where the mysterious **Big Tread,** or the Hairless Goldeman, is sometimes seen, a legendary creature that has never been photographed, only two known glimpses from local residents, and Kenda tracks in the desert. On your left you see what appears to be a row of statuary lining the road; that is **Moby Dick's** place. Dick moved out of The Big City (Los Angeles) in the late eighties, and has found happiness here in the high desert. He makes his mildly bizarre sculptures out of anything he can find, and one source is old motorcycle parts. He has a number of decrepit and cannibalized bikes neatly lined up, and boxes of nuts and bolts under a protective roof, and can probably find you a carburetor for a DT1, though it might be a little corroded.

CA 247 is now entering **Johnson Valley,** which looks rather barren, spread out between the **Big Horn Mountains** and **Iron Ridge.** People do live out here, but not many, and civilization as we know it has been left behind. Old Woman Springs is off to the left.

79 Miles   TURN LEFT onto Rock Camp Road at this remote intersection, with hardly a house or car to be seen.

84 Miles   STOP sign—TURN LEFT as Rock Camp slides into CA 18, with the huge Mitsubishi cement plant stuck in the hillside in front of you. What are the Japanese doing making cement in the California mountains? Obviously the global economy is beyond my comprehension. But CA 18 provides a great ride up the mountainside as you climb into the **San Bernardino National Forest,** with a sign warning of a 16 percent grade. For the trivia collectors, this was the second designated national forest in the country, signed into being by Prez Ben Harrison in 1892.

89 Miles   **Cactus Flats,** and a dirt road goes off to the right; had you come up from Rimrock you might have ended up here. Now starts a gentle descent down the **Johnston Grade** to shallow **Baldwin Lake,** whose surface is at 6,698 feet above sea level. These San Berdoo mountains are pretty high, and they stretch for over 50 miles east to west . . . though we are just going to cut across the eastern end.

In the middle of the mountains are several other lakes, Big Bear and Arrowhead being the best known, and the whole area is a resort so people can escape from the heat of the Los Angeles basin. Which means it is often crowded, and a lot of people have chosen to live up here all year around.

95 Miles   TURN LEFT as CA 18 enters a built-up area and meets head-on with CA 38, and both roads join to go to the right, south, on Greenway Drive.

96 Miles   STOP sign—TURN LEFT at the end of Greenway, following CA 38; CA 18 goes to the right, and if hungry, TURN RIGHT onto Big Bear Blvd. and go half a mile to **Thelma's Restaurant** (909-585-7005).

CA 38 is now the **Rim of the World National Forest Scenic Byway.** Follow CA 38 as it leaves civilization, angling right and going past the **Big Bear** suburbs of **Erwin Lake** and **Sugarloaf.** Now you are out in the forest, climbing slowly.

That's Moby Dick, a man in Landers who creates sculptures from old motorcycle bits; look for a retrospective of his work at the Guggenheim Museum sometime soon.

106 Miles   You are up on **Onyx Summit** now, at 8,443 feet the highest paved road in Southern California, which means that part of California which begins just north of the Los Angeles basin. To your left is the dirt road that could lead a d-p bike back down to Pioneertown. Up here high in the forest it is hard to imagine that you are just 100 eagle-flying miles from the crowded heart of Los Angeles and the sun-soaked Pacific beaches.

Now it is a steep descent to the stunning valley of the headwaters of the **Santa Ana River;** let me promise you, once that river reaches the city of Redlands, the romance is gone, but here in the wilderness it is a thing of beauty. To the south is **San Gorgonio Mountain,** the tallest peak in SoCal at 11,499 feet.

118 Miles   You have dropped 3,000 feet and are in the middle of **Barton Flats.** Glass Road goes off to the right, the pavement ending in a maze of dirt roads. Dozens of camps and private residences are scattered throughout Barton Flats, and in the summer it is virtually a city in the woods.

125 Miles   You are in the center of **Angelus Oaks,** which has a fire station, a general store, and a telephone, in case you want to reach out and touch someone.

130 Miles   TURN RIGHT, following CA 38, as the road comes down into **Mill Creek Canyon,** with a wide riverbed in front of you. If you TURN LEFT the road, Valley of the Falls Drive, dead-ends after four-plus miles in the community of **Forest Falls.** CA 38 goes down along **Mill Creek;** it is an impressive sight as it cuts down through the mountains.

And all of a sudden you are out of the mountains and the **San Bernardino Valley** is in front of you.

136 Miles   TURN LEFT onto Bryant Street, with the **Mill Creek Ranger Station** and a sign pointing left saying YUCAIPA 4.

141 Miles   TRAFFIC LIGHT—TURN RIGHT on Avenue F after passing through downtown **Yucaipa,** going down **Wildwood Canyon** and turning into Wildwood Canyon Road.

If you want to see how the other one percent lives, take a left on Avenue F and follow it west to the I-10, and you should see **"Angel's Roadhouse,"** a legitimate business owned and operated by the Hells Angels; it offers the best live music in the area, I have heard (909-795-0665).

145 Miles   Back in Wildwood Canyon, you come to a STOP sign. TURN RIGHT on Oak Glen Road, the road going alongside the **Little San Gorgonio Creek,** past the **Edward Dean Museum of Decorative Arts, Cherry Valley,** and due south to **Beaumont** (Beautiful Mountain in French).

151 Miles   You are at the intersection with I-10. Cross over and head east.

156 Miles   After the Banning exit you can pick up the last few miles from Loop 2, going past **Cabazon** and catching CA 111 back into **Palm Springs.**

181 Miles   Arrive back at Ground Zero, Ramon and Palm Canyon.

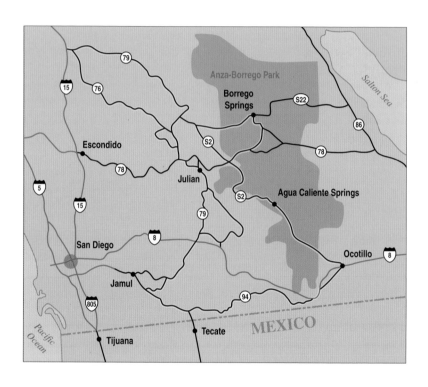

Eastern San Diego County

Headquarters *Julian*
Tourist Office *760-765-1857*
Getting There *Going north on I-15, take CA 78 east from Escondido; south on I-15, take CA 79 east from Temecula. If you are on I-8, take CA 79 north at Descanso.*
Ground Zero *The following loops will all start at the sole four-way STOP sign in the center of Julian, at the corner of Washington and Main streets.*

With lots of good mountainous country and a delightful strip of desert to the east, and great roads all over, **San Diego** is home to a lot of serious motorcyclists, and they know that they have some lovely roads to ride. If the **King of the Alps, John Hermann,** author of *Motorcycle Journeys through the Alps and Corsica,* chooses to live there when he is not gallivanting over the Passo dello Stelvio, you know there is some good motorcycling in the area.

Pleasant little town, is **Julian,** which will probably end up on the cutsey side of nice by the time the year 2010 rolls around. But no matter, it is a good base for superlative riding.

There is essentially one main street in Julian, cunningly called Main Street, and everything can be located from that half-mile stretch. The town is on the list of **"state-registered historical places,"** whatever that means, and tries very hard to maintain a hard-scrabble attitude, even though B&Bs flourish and Benzes and Volvos clutter the streets every weekend.

The place was named after one Michael Julian, a Confederate soldier from Georgia who had come west with some cousins in the late 1860s to try their luck at homesteading. But gold was found in them thar hills in 1870, and life changed drastically for a few years, until the gold petered out. Except for the gold in the tourist's pocket; the **Eagle** and **High Peak** hard-rock mines, at the north side of town, are open to visitors every day.

The miners went away, but people stayed to raise cattle and apples, and Julian has become known as **"Apple Pie City"** in recent times.

I first went there around 1981, and my legendary riding buddy, Fireball Stein, bought an apple pie for $76.50—$4.50 for the pie, $72 for the speeding ticket. Yes, California's finest do enforce the laws, expecially on the weekends.

Downtown Julian can get crowded on a nice weekend, what with all the tourists coming up to buy apple pie. (photo by Jasmine Kimura)

The place had the fortune (misfortune?) to be "discovered" about 25 years ago, and the population is slowly growing. During the week life is pretty quiet, but on a fall weekend it is controlled chaos, with the flat-landers coming up to eat apple pie and to buy apple pies to take home. A dozen pie shops line the main street to capitalize on that fact, and I would bet that some pies are not even made in Julian.

No never mind.

Julian's permanent population is about 2,000, and it sits at 4,200 feet in the **Laguna Mountains,** some 40 seagull flying miles from the Pacific Ocean. About 30 hostelries offer a place to lay your head, from tiny B&Bs with just one cottage to rent to middling sized establishments that can sleep 50 or more. There is nothing in the way of big resort accomodations in Julian, and certainly no chain motels.

At the high end of the financial spectrum is the **Orchard Hill Country Inn,** built in1994, a very well turned out hotel on top of, yes, Orchard Hill, two blocks east of the center of town on Washington Street. The owners, Pat and Darrell Straube, do have excellent taste. The lodge is all stone, with a lovely great fireplace in the foyer, and large, light-filled rooms; there are also four cottages for larger parties (760-765-1700, 800-716-7242). One note, there is a dirt drive up to the hotel, but German motorcycle tour groups use the inn frequently, and have no problem negotiating it.

For the historically inclined, there is "the oldest continuously operating hotel in Southern California," the **Julian Hotel** on Main Street. It has been around since 1897, when it was called the **Hotel Robinson,** and now is a delightful B&B, with afternoon tea included. All the rooms are individually appointed, and the Victorian decor throughout is worth the price of admission; there is also the separate **Honeymoon House.** No private parking, but the town is as safe a place to park your motorcycle that I know of. (760-765-0201, 800-734-5854).

On the conventional side is the **Julian Lodge,** a block off Main Street, with two dozen rooms (760-765-1420, 800-542-1420). If you are appreciative of Fifties funky, go to the **Apple Tree Inn** (a motel by any other name), in **Wynola** about three miles west of Julian center on CA 78/79. Sixteen units are spread around a pool in the best old motel tradition. Prices are quite good, depending on size of room and time of week. (760-765-0222, 800-410-8683).

Food is where you find it, especially apple pie, with half a dozen places like the **Julian Pie Co.** and **Mom's Pie House** along Main Street. My own preferred place for dinner is the **Julian Grille** (760-765-0173, 2224 Main Street) which does a very nice Porterhouse. For breakfast, the **Julian Cafe & Bakery** (760-765-2712, 2112 Main Street) does the sausage and eggs just right.

For drink there is lots of apple cider, but I recommend the very hearty Cabernet Sauvignon from the **Menghini Winery;** to get there, just take Main Street north, which turns into Farmers Road, which becomes Julian Orchards Drive.

Trip 31 One Lap Around Mt. Laguna

Distance *57 miles*

Highlights *This will be your half-day ride. Or stretch it out as long as you wish.*

0 Miles Head south on Main Street, past the Julian Hotel and the gas station.

1 Mile TURN RIGHT onto CA 79, with CA 78 going straight. Long smooth grade climbs into the wooded twisties, with quite a number of driveways going off left and right. Until you see **Lake Cuyamaca** in the distance in front.

6+ Miles TURN LEFT onto County Road S1, marked MT LAGUNA 15, with CA 79 going on straight. This road is called the **Sunrise Scenic Byway**, as it runs along the east edge of the **Laguna Mountains**, 4,000 to 5,000 feet above the **Anza-Borrego Desert** visible to the east. Lake Cuyamaca will be off to your right.

14 Miles This is the turn-off to the **Kwaamii Point** overlook, a few hundred yards to your left. On a clear day you will see the **Salton Sea** some 50 miles to the northeast. Stunning.

Residents up in the Laguna Mountains make a good bit of extra money selling healthy food to McBurger-eating city slickers.

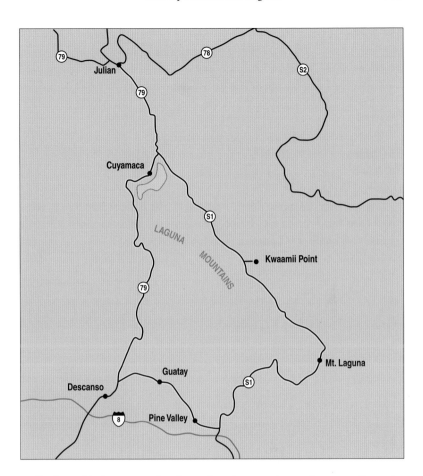

Back on S1 you are getting into nice pine woods, staying away from the eastern escarpment, the road swooping and leaning, very pleasant. Idyllic riding.

21 Miles Coming into the mountain community of **Mt. Laguna,** at almost 6,000 feet. Several cafes, a store, and the **Laguna Mt. Lodge** offering motel units and cabins (760-445-2342). An old garage sits on the left side of the road, but the owner allows as to how he does not have the expertise to work on motorcycles, preferring one-ton pickups with big V-8s. He might be able to do something with a Boss Hoss.

S1 peaks at a few feet above 6,000, then begins a descent toward **Laguna Summit** (4,055 feet) on Interstate 8. The road is usually clean and lightly trafficked and double-lined, and as it breaks out of the high forest it clings to the west side of the mountains, with a long drop should anyone be foolish enough to get overly enthusiastic.

29+ Miles TURN RIGHT where the sign to the right reads OLD HIGH-WAY 80 and PINE VALLEY 1. The Interstate (8) is straight ahead.

30 Miles Pine Valley, a main way-station before the Interstate appeared some 30 years ago, is a small but thriving community serving the traveler with gas and food available. And the **Pine Valley Inn Motel** (619-473-8560).

Old Hwy. 80 continues on through **Guatay.**

35+ Miles TURN RIGHT at the intersection with CA 79.

36 Miles A road goes off to the left to the farming community of **Descanso.** Keep on CA 79.

Now you are in **Green Valley,** irrigated by the **Sweetwater River.** Some smart folks heading via the southern route to the gold fields of California figured they could stay here and raise cattle and sell the beef to the miners, getting gold in return. The road enters **Cuyamaca Rancho State Park,** which covers a hefty 25,000 acres.

Anyone who wants to take a break from motorcycling can rent a boat and sit out in the middle of Lake Cuyamaca to contemplate the meaning of fishing.

CalTrans certainly does a good job with its signage in San Diego county . . . though road markers can be somewhat remiss in other parts of the state.

42 Miles A road off to the right goes to the **Cuyamaca Museum** and park headquarters. All this is part of the **Cleveland National Forest,** which has patches of forest all through San Diego County, If you wonder, "Why Cleveland?," it is because Grover signed the bill which began the national forest system in 1892. The museum building itself is in an old stone ranchhouse, with information on Native Americans, local history, flora, and fauna.

Back on CA 79 going north, it is a woodsy, winding, well-paved road, running through oak and pine. And then the view breaks as you come out on Lake Cuyamaca.

47 Miles The Lake Cuyamaca store and boat rental is to your right. The lake covers 110 acres, and is stocked with trout, bass, catfish, sturgeon, and other aquatic vertebrates.

50 Miles You are back at the CA 79 and S1 intersection.

57 Miles Arrive back in the middle of Julian.

Trip 32   Around Mt. Palomar & to the Top

Distance   *121 miles*

Highlights   *This is a fine country loop, and the climb up Palomar on S6 is one of the great short rides; this stretch has worn out a lot of footpegs, even put holes in pannier bags of more enthusiastic riders.*

0 Miles   **Julian** intersection; head south on CA 78/79.

3 Miles   Past Wynola Road turn-off, with the **Red Apple Inn** and several large fruit barns luring the tourist. Drop down the mountain, usually a good bit of traffic, the **Inaya Memorial Park** to the left, in honor of the firefighters who lost their lives in the great forest fire of 1956. Do be careful with flammables.

6+ Miles   TURN RIGHT, following CA 79 to the north. You have just dropped 1,200 feet and are in the **Santa Ysabel Valley,** where CA 78 and 79 split. If you are hungry, or the bike needs gas, fill up here, in the ZIP-coded community of **Saint Isabelle.** Of most fame is **Dudley's Bakery,** a hundred yards east of the intersection, which offers some 20 varieties of bread, including White Regular, Irish Brown, German Black, and Danish Apple Nut. A loaf of Jalapeno is a meal unto itself.

The Chapel of San Francisco at Warner Springs has been spreading the holy word since 1830, with services every Sunday.

8 Miles   Off to the right is the small **Santa Ysabel Chapel;** the original chapel built in 1818 as a mission outpost was supposed to make sure the local inhabitants got directions to Catholic heaven.

14 Miles   GO STRAIGHT on CA 79, ignoring the left turns to CA 76, curving to the right over **Carriso** and **Matagual** and **Buena Vista Creeks.** The flat land to the left is a broad valley that feeds **Lake Henshaw.**

18 Miles   Ignore the right turn on S2 and HEAD STRAIGHT, up and over a ridge which leads down to **Warner Springs** and a large resort. Crossing the **Pacific Crest Trail,** for the hikers amongst us.

22 Miles   Cross over the **Warner Springs Ranch Creek,** and right ahead on the hill is the old **Chapel of St. Francis,** built in 1830. As an animal-lover I appreciate old Saint Frank, and it is a handsome building.

24 Miles   CA 79 goes past the **Warner Springs glider port**—rides available any weekend, and often during the week if there happen to be pilots and a tow-plane around. I do recommend a glider ride at least once in your life; you will be surprised how much noise the wind makes.

The Officials in Green

There may be a **U.S. Border Patrol** station just a mile further up, and you may be asked to stop by the boys and girls in drab green. You will see a lot of these Border Patrol types in SoCal, driving in their green and white trucks and vans and sport-utes. Very simply put, their job is to prevent "undocumented aliens" from entering the wage markets of Los Angeles and the San Joaquin Valley. These uniformed types are usually pleasant enough, and have no direct authority to stop you for such mundane misdemeanors as speeding. However, if you are truly being irresponsible, "la migra" can stop you and discuss the weather until a California Highway Patrolman comes to write you up.   ■

CA 79 winds through scrubby semi-desert. Ahead you can see the **Palomar Observatory** atop **Mt. Palomar;** you'll be there in a couple of hours. In this terrain the U.S. Navy runs a **mountain survival school** for pilots who happen to get downed over such inhospitable real estate. Come up to the community of **Sunshine Summit,** with store, and just beyond that The Summit at 3,282 feet.

31 Miles   Dropping into **Dodge Valley,** the eponymously named **Dodge Valley Inn,** with cafe and saloon, is on your right.

34 Miles   Enter **Oak Grove** and see the only store, which was once a stage station for the old **Butterfield Overland Mail;** stagecoaches were running along here from 1858 to 1861.

42 Miles   Aguanga intersection, a right turn on CA 371 leads to **Palm Springs.**

45 Miles   **Radec** intersection, where the right turn on County Road R3 leads to Hemet. CA 79 then undulates through lightly civilized countryside until it crosses the **Temecula River** and enters **Pauba Valley.**

Oops! Lots of farming, lots of traffic, lots of buildings going up, the road widens, traffic lights—the suburban sprawl has taken over.

55 Miles   TRAFFIC LIGHT—TURN LEFT, with Pala Road/S16 clearly marked, going toward the Pala Indian Reservation. But you are now in the **Pechanga Indian Reservation,** with a huge casino on your right. The Riverside County part on either side of S16, romantically called **Wolf Valley,** is being highly developed, but as soon as you are back in San Diego County the build-up is over. The road drops steeply and twistily down between **Mt. Olympus** and **Tourmaline Queen Mountain** alongside **Pala Creek** to the **Pala Indian Reservation.** Watch out, as there are some tricky bits on that road, including a 240 degree right-hand corner that refuses to quit.

64 Miles STOP sign—TURN LEFT, down at the little community of **Pala**. Right on the corner is the **Mission San Antonio de Pala**, built in 1816—which claims to be the only one of the old missions that still is dedicated to the spiritual well-being of the Native Americans. If you turn right, you will get to the not-quite-so-huge Pala casino.

65 Miles STOP sign—TURN LEFT as S16 ends, merging with CA 76, which then rolls over hill and dale for some nine miles as it runs through **Pauma Valley**, thick with orange groves.

68 Miles And yet another casino, a mile off to your left, this one belonging to the Pauma Indians.

73 Miles STAY LEFT on CA 76 where S6 comes in from the right—and the going gets really good. The road winds delightfully through some orange groves, flat and smooth, an easy ride or a peg-scraper. Then it climbs up steeply, with a few very tight corners to a mesa.

78 Miles TURN LEFT onto the continuation of County Road S6, one of Caltrans' little offerings to the motorcycle community. It is nearly 7 miles and some 70 turns to the top, and on any weekend the sport riders are out in considerable force. There is no need to go fast, but there is the opportunity should you be of the knee-grinding persuasion. Several cattle-guards at inopportune moments will keep you honest. This, called the South Grade Road, should be ridden with caution until one has experienced it properly, and noted all the seriously gnarly turns. Guaranteed that your engine's temp gauge will go up. It is a great road, sure to rank high in Whitehorse Press's forthcoming 1,000 Best Motorcycle Roads In The World.

The 1920 Palomar Mountain Lodge was closed when I was up there in 2006, but I understand the owners are looking for a new manager.

Palomar Observatory

If you keep on up S6 another four miles beyond Mother's, you get to the **Palomar Observatory** parking lot. A short walk away is a smaller building housing a smaller telescope and gift shop, and then further up the hill the big observatory with the 200-inch telescope. The astronomers have been on Palomar for donkeys' years, but the increasing light pollution for all the building that goes on around the mountain has pretty much ruined the place for any serious exploration of the stars. But it is great for tourists.   ■

The dome of the Mt. Palomar Observatory crowns the top of the mountain in the distance.

85 Miles   TURN RIGHT at the intersection at the top (5,280 feet), heading down S7, East Grade Road.

But don't be too hasty, as you have your choices. TURN LEFT and immediately on your left is **Mother's Kitchen** (760-742-4233). On a bright Sunday morning a hundred go-fasters of all marques can be found, with the riders talking about aftermarket pipes, comparing the scrub marks on the edges of the tires, telling lies. The Kitchen, a veggie joint, is not an exceptional cafe, but the omeletes and coffee are fine.

Back at Mother's intersection, go right and head down the East Grade Road (S7).

85+ Miles   After a quarter mile you see Crestline Avenue going off to the left. That is where most of the local community lives. Go up Crestline to the end, and there is **Palomar Mountain Lodge,** based on a superbly retro log building built back in the 1920s. The place was closed in the summer of 2006, but locals said it would probably open again.

Back to the East Grade Road. It is a long, smooth, softly curved (for the most part) 11 miles down through **Dyche Valley** to the Lake Henshaw intersection, dropping 2,500 feet along the way. You go past the **Lake Henshaw Dam,** and S7 comes to an end.

97 Miles   STOP sign—TURN LEFT at the intersection with CA 78. The **Lake Henshaw Resort** is half a mile along on your right, mostly for the fisherfolk. Go past West Loop, a little bit of the old highway off to your right.

99+ Miles   TURN RIGHT at the street sign marked CENTER LOOP, and a large sign denoting the biker friendly **Hideout Saloon & Steakhouse,** open on weekends and by arrangement (760-782-3656). Just before you get to The Hideout is the sign for Mesa Grande Road, TURN RIGHT again. And start to climb steeply through the woods. Very tight road, and there can be a few leaves in the fall.

Pop out on top of the mesa, and for the next few miles the asphalt wends its way through farmland; watch out for tractors. Part of this is the **Mesa Grande Indian Reservation,** and I commend these folk for not having a casino. At the far end of the mesa the road drops down to the **Santa Ysabel Valley,** but this time the curvaceous descent is smooth and can be done at a goodly rate of speed.

112 Miles   STOP sign—TURN RIGHT, where Mesa Grande butts into CA 79, and head back on this previously traveled road to Santa Ysabel.

114 Miles   STOP sign—TURN LEFT here at **Santa Ysabel,** and start heading back up the hill.

121 Miles   Arrive back to Julian.

Trip 33 Mexican Border & Anza-Borrego

Distance *217 miles*

Highlights *This long loop goes south to the Mexican border, runs along CA 94 to the east, swings north to Anza-Borrego Desert State Park and Borrego Springs, and returns to Julian up the Banner Grade.*

0 Miles Head south along Main Street.

0+ Miles TURN RIGHT on CA 79; as you might have done in Loop 1. Stay on CA 79 for next 23 miles, past **Lake Cuyamaca** and **Cuyamaca Rancho State Park;** this section was dealt with, in reverse, in Trip #1.

23 Miles Cross under Interstate 8 and continue south on Japatul Road; a few houses on each side, sort of an exurban environment as this is within commute distance of San Diego.

28 Miles TURN LEFT on Lyons Valley Road; a large green sign indicates this is the way to BARRETT HONOR CAMP, where your delinquent second cousin once removed may be staying. Superb road, well maintained, swooping down and around the edges of **Gaskill Peak** as it drops down from 3,300 to 1,700 feet.

This rider is hustling up the Montezuma Grade, on County Road S22 west of Borrego Springs.

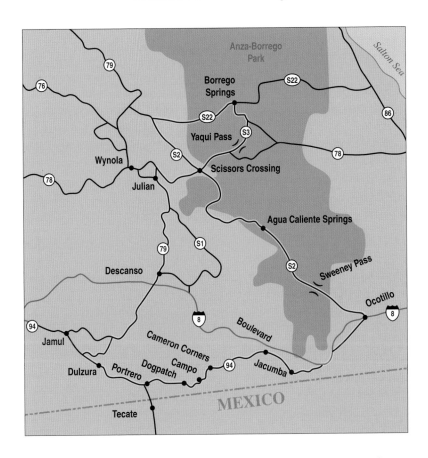

36 Miles TURN LEFT at a very country four-way junction, with just trees and grass and fields and an old water trough; you turn onto Honey Springs Road. Very rustic riding, through lush ranchland.

43 Miles STOP sign—TURN LEFT, as Honey Springs butts into CA 94, the southernmost state highway in California. You may well find a U.S. Border Patrol stop along here.

47 Miles Come into the small community of **Dulzura,** and there on the right is the **Dulzura Cafe,** open every morning at 8 a.m. for a good breakfast, or lunch (619-468-9591). Nobody seems to know quite when the original building was constructed, but learned commentary from the folk inside indicates it was probably in the late teens. It has been added onto and altered over the last 70 years, and is a small museum in itself. If you'd like to see the definitive collection of manual eggbeaters, it is there. Dulzura, for the etymologically challenged, means "sweet" in Spanish, and the name apparently comes from the good-tasting water in the **Dulzura Creek.**

Tecate, Mexico

If you have suitable identification and want to pop into Mexico proper for a brief visit, take CA 188 for all of two miles and it puts you at the **U.S. Customs & Immigration** office on the border, just on the edge of the town of Tecate. It is a very easy, and very lightly trafficked crossing, and three blocks south of the border is the town square, **Parque Hidalgo.** It's a good place to get your boots shined and some sustenance at the **Restaurant Jardin TkT** (that TkT is Spanish phonetics for "Tecate"). ■

CA 94 continues on through mildly mountainous countryside, with a gorgeous view of the **Cottonwood Creek Valley** as you come around **White Mountain** and over a ridge and see the road drop down, cross the valley, and go up the other side.

53 Miles At Barrett Junction in the middle of **Big Valley,** where Barrett Lake Road goes north from CA 94, is the **Barrett Junction Cafe & Fish Fry** (619-468-3416), an all-you-can-eat extravaganza most evenings of the week. Climb back up into the hills, and suddenly the narrow two-lane road widens. But not for long.

57 Miles Intersecton with CA 188 going off to the right, but you GO STRAIGHT, following CA 94, and the road goes back to narrow two-lane.

60 Miles Staying on CA 94, you pass through **Potrero,** with a general store and gas station.

65 Miles You pass the almost non-existent community of **Dogpatch,** which was once a railway-workers stop along the **San Diego & Imperial Valley Railroad,** now quite defunct. You pass beneath the old rail line and on along **Campo Creek.**

68 Miles Into **Campo,** best known as home to the **Pacific Southwest Railroad Museum** at the old depot. A few miles of track have been retied, and a steam or, more often, diesel locomotive will haul the tourists around; the park is in operation 9 to 5 weekends, and during the week by arrangement, but best to call (619-478-9937) to check.

Right alongside Campo Creek is the **Gaskill Stone Store.** A merchant by the name of Gaskill had built a store on that spot in 1868, along the old wagon road, but robbers burned the place in 1875, so the merchant rebuilt the whole thing in highly defensible stone. Further up the road is the old feldspar mill which now houses the **Motor Transport Museum,** a rusty collection of vehicles that is open to the public on Saturdays (619-478-2492).

70 Miles CA 94 goes up to **Cameron Corners,** with a gas station and hamburger joint on the corner with the southern terminus of S1. Keep on CA 94, over **Miller Creek** and under a high trestle for the SD & IV RR and on into the intersection at Boulevard.

82 Miles STOP sign—TURN RIGHT as CA 94 ends as it merges with Old Hwy. 80 going east.

90 Miles Old Hwy 80 comes into **Jacumba,** an old railroad town trying to figure out what to do in the 21st Century; back in 1925 15,000 people lived here, now the population is probably 500. There is a very fine old spa in town, the **Jacumba Hot Springs Spa,** which has a faithful clientele of San Diegoites and bicyclists who are on a cross-country run; the place has an excellent restaurant (619-766-4333).

Continue along Old Hwy 80.

95 Miles TURN RIGHT on Interstate ramp: Old Highway 80 butts into I-8 at the In-Ko-Pah entrance, and you head east on the Interstate.

Back on the Interstate you cross into **Imperial County** and wind through the **In-Ko-Pah Gorge** and then out into the **Yuha Desert.**

This couple was admiring the view at the Carrizo Badlands Overlook in the Anza-Borrego Desert State Park.

107 Miles   EXIT INTERSTATE at the OCOTILLO/IMPERIAL HWY/S2, and TURN LEFT. The little town of **Ocotillo** does not offer much except gas and basic sustenance. Head north on S2, a/k/a **Imperial Highway,** going toward Anza-Borrego Desert State Park. Go through town, such that it is, and watch out for that damn STOP sign (108.5 miles) out in approximately nowhere.

Desert View Tower

If you cross under I-8, TURN RIGHT onto a sort of frontage road, which soon disappears around a corner, and there the road dead-ends and in front of you is a very odd structure, a stone tower standing about 70 feet high. The ridge on the edge of the **Jacumba Mountains** where the **Desert View Tower** is situated is about 3,000 feet above sea level, and from the top floor of the tower a superb view is had of the **Imperial Valley** all the way to the **Salton Sea.** It costs $2.50 to go up to the top, and to the rock-animal caves, but it is money well spent. The tower was built between 1920 and 1922, but it never achieved any fame until I-8 was finished; now lots of tour buses make the stop here. Call 619-766-4612 for more info.   ∎

The cunningly named Desert View Tower offers a splendid view of the Anza-Borrego Desert.

115 Miles   You are at the Imperial Highway monument, the eastern edge of Imperial County. As you cross back into **San Diego County** the name of the two-laner changes to Sweeney Pass Road; you also are entering **Anza-Borrego Desert State Park,** the biggest state park in the country at 600,000 acres. It is a beaut ride, passing by the **Coyote Mountains,** past the **Carrizo Badlands,** over **Sweeney Pass** (at a lofty 1,065 feet) and **Egg Mountain.** Great names. Just past the **Well of Eight Echoes** S2 changes names again to the **Old Overland Stage Route.**

131 Miles   A road off to the left goes to **Agua Caliente Hot Springs** (a bit of bilingual redundancy), a little county park inside a state park. The **Agua Caliente Regional Park** is open September through May (too hot in the summer), and camp sites are available. The San Diego based Airhead BMW Club is often found out there, par-boiling brain cells. The outdoor pool is at a natural 96 degrees, the indoor pool is heated to 101. Enjoy.

S2 continues on through **Vallecito Valley,** on past the old **Butterfield Ranch** (a stopping point for the **Butterfield stage** of long, long ago), climbs past **Box Canyon** (pay attention here, as the road gets a little sharper than you might expect), and out into **Earthquake Valley,** where a small community has grown up.

154 Miles   STOP sign—TURN RIGHT here at **Scissors Crossing,** where S2 crosses CA 78. You can go left to Julian if you are tired, but take the right to **Borrego Springs** if you want to finish this loop in a grand manner.

CA 78 east goes down through **Sentenac Canyon** and out onto **Yaqui Flats,** where on a late winter day the wildflowers will be growing in glorious profusion.

161 Miles   TURN LEFT onto S3, with a sign for BORREGO SPRINGS, past the **Tamarisk Grove Campground,** and up over **Yaqui Pass** (1,750 feet). Then it is a long, straightish downhill shot into the desert town of Borrego Springs.

168 Miles   TURN LEFT at the intersection, with the left being the most direct way to Borrego Springs proper, such that it is. On the right is **La Casa del Zorro** ("fox") **Desert Resort** on your right.

West along Borrego Springs Road, curve north, and the metropolis will be far in front of you.

173 Miles   Enter **Christmas Circle,** the center of town, with several outdoor stands selling fruit around the circle. Palm Canyon Drive, going due west, is the main drag.

Back on the road, heading west on Palm Canyon Drive/S22.

175 Miles   S22 makes a left turn at the **Palm Canyon Resort;** if you go straight you end up in the parking lot of the **Visitor Center of Anza-**

Borrego Park Headquarters. Nice museum, nice views, and a short stroll along the Nature Path will show you as much about desert botany as most people will care to know.

S22 starts the climb up **Montezuma Grade,** which rates two stars as a motorcycling road from my jaded soul. It is a spectacular ride, especially taken early in the morning with the sun just coming up at your back. The road climbs over 3,000 feet in about six miles, and the views back over the desert are definitely worth a stop or two or three. Then you stretch your legs as the road drops into **Montezuma Valley.**

193 Miles STOP sign—TURN LEFT, as S22 T-bones into S2; go south. The next 12 miles go along **San Felipe Creek,** and can be traveled at a great rate of speed. Though the California Highway Patrol is aware of this, and often has a constable lurking in the bushes along there.

Borrego Springs

If you want to stay in **Borrego Springs** there are upward of a dozen places to lay your head, though if you arrive in wild-flower season you better have some reservations lined up, as horticultural enthusiasts flock to this locale. For lodging, on the simple side is **Hacienda del Sol** on Palm Canyon Drive, with six rooms, four cottages, and ten du-plexes, with no phones but coffee-makings are in the room; this is as close to the middle of town as one can find, not that the town has much of a middle (760-767-5442). Further up Palm Canyon is the **Palm Canyon Resort,** a modern place with all amenities which caters to a lot of motorcycle groups (800-242-0044). At the high end is the aforementioned **Casa del Zorro,** an old-fashioned place, with 60 rooms and suites, and 19 separate cottages, along with six lighted tennis courts and a commendable restaurant (760-767-5323; 800-824-1884).

This town is not really a sophisticated gastronome's delight, but the eateries prepare good fare. I like to hang out in the morning at the front side of the mall, the only mall, in the **Badlands Cafe & Market,** great for breakfast and lunch. At **Carlee's Place** (760-767-3260), on Christmas Circle, you can get all-American chicken, ribs, steaks, etc. for lunch and dinner. A popular place is out at the **Crosswinds Restaurant** at the **Borrego Valley Airport,** a couple of miles east of town (760-767-4546). Fancier dining is available at Zorro's. The sidewalks pretty much get rolled up in the evening, which is great for getting an early start. ∎

This is headquarters for the Pacific Southwest Railroad Museum in Campo.

205 Miles STOP sign—RIGHT TURN, back at **Scissors Crossing.** Go west on CA 78, 12 miles to Julian. First five are straightish, until you reach the store and campground at **Banner,** and start up the **Banner Grade.** The next four miles are very twisty, with a lot of downhill traffic taking more of the road than it should. Watch out.

213 Miles Wynola Road goes off to the right, which can provide an interesting back way into Julian. Just go up it a little less than a mile, and Farmers Road cuts to the left, with the **Menghini Winery** to the right. Take the left, and two miles later you are back at the center of **Julian.**

Or continue along CA 78.

217 Miles Arrive back in the center of town.

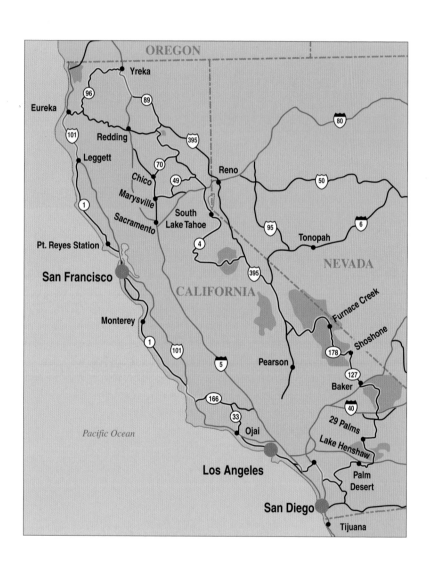

One Lap of California

As I said in Chapter 3, the previous baker's dozen (that's 13, for those of you not familiar with baking terminology) of chapters have more or less circled the state of California. Now you will have an opportunity to put them all together in one Grand Tour.

While the other chapters have been "in depth," this one is "in breadth." It all depends whether you want to focus on an area and get to see everything, or nearly everything, or lots, or at least a good deal—or take one big swoop around the state in which you touch on nearly all the previous chapters.

The minimum "lap" is 2,500 miles—and we will start from LA. If time is of importance, or your Jawa Californian 350 seizes solid along the route, you can cut the trip short at any time by going back to the starting point in Los Angeles—or to any place else in the state, for that matter.

If you want to know more about places I touch on here, refer to the appropriate chapter(s). We will hit 11 out of our 13 designated touring sites, leaving out only the Kings Canyon/Sequoia route and the Kernville area.

Of course, since you readers have good imaginations and excellent geographic sensibilities, you may have already figured that the whole thing could be tied together in some haphazard way, so you could go home and say, "Been to California, done the whole state, nothing left to see." Ha!

Anyway, for the Grand Tour types, this version of a lap of the Golden State hits many of the high points.

Trip 34 One Big Lap

Best Time to Visit *April through November*
Ground Zero *We will begin in Los Angeles, on CA 1 at Topanga Beach near Malibu (Chapter 3).*
0 Miles TURN RIGHT at the TRAFFIC LIGHT onto CA 27, Topanga Canyon Road.
5 Miles TURN LEFT at the fork in **Topanga** village, onto Old Topanga Canyon Road.
10 Miles STOP sign—TURN LEFT onto **Mulholland Highway.** Follow Mulholland through the **Santa Monica Mountains,** past the **Rock Store,** until you reach the coast.
40 Miles STOP sign—TURN RIGHT onto CA 1.
63 Miles MERGE with US 101 going north.
71 Miles EXIT US 101 onto CA 33 (Chapter 4).
84 Miles At the TRAFFIC LIGHT on the edge of Ojai, TURN LEFT, following CA 33.

We're atop Mt. Hamilton, looking west over San Jose.

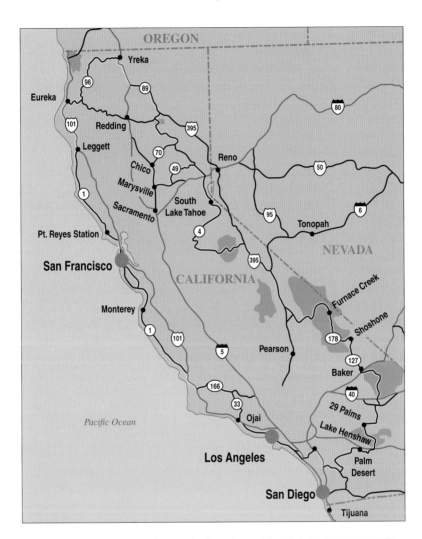

142 Miles At the STOP sign at the junction with CA 166, TURN LEFT.

207 Miles TURN RIGHT onto US 101 going north.

235 Miles EXIT US 101 onto CA 1, the **Big Sur Highway,** heading for **Morro Bay** and **Monterey** (Chapter 5).

371 Miles Arrive at **Monterey Peninsula;** continue on CA 1.

415 Miles Skirting the city of **Santa Cruz,** TURN RIGHT onto CA 9 headed for **Felton** and **Boulder Creek** in the **Santa Cruz Mountains** (Chapter 6).

442 Miles TURN LEFT onto CA 35 as you arrive at Skyline Boulevard and head toward **Alice's Restaurant.**

468 Miles STOP sign—TURN LEFT onto CA 92.

473 Miles   Arrive in **Half Moon Bay** and TURN RIGHT at the TRAFFIC LIGHT, onto CA 1 going north.

501 Miles   Arrive at the **Golden Gate Bridge** on CA 1/US 101.

507 Miles   EXIT US 101 onto CA 1 headed for **Stinson Beach** (Chapter 7).

508 Miles   TRAFFIC LIGHT—TURN LEFT at **Mt. Tam Junction**, headed for Stinson Beach on CA 1—and just follow your front wheel for the next 200 miles.

708 Miles   When CA 1 ends at **Leggett**, HEAD NORTH on US 101 . . . and after going north a few miles, take the well-marked **Avenue of the Giants** (CA 254) which parallels US 101 for 31 miles.

805 Miles   EXIT US 101 onto CA 299 going east toward **Willow Creek** (Chapter 8).

844 Miles   TURN LEFT onto CA 96, to go north and east along the **Klamath River.**

991 Miles   TURN RIGHT onto CA 263 headed for **Yreka.**

999 Miles   TURN LEFT to get onto I-5 going south.

1,038 Miles   EXIT I-5, TURN LEFT and head east on CA 89.

1,129 Miles   Pay $5 at the entrance to **Lassen Volcanic National Park** (Chapter 9).

1,220 Miles   STOP sign—TURN RIGHT onto CA 70, going down **Feather River Canyon.**

A foggy morning on Woodley Island, where the Humboldt Bay fishing fleet ties up.

1,282 Miles MERGE with the Chico-Oroville Highway, continuing on CA 70.

1,316 Miles TURN LEFT onto CA 20 at **Marysville,** heading east to **Grass Valley.**

1,351 Miles CA 20 will merge with CA 49 heading north.

1,355 Miles TURN LEFT at **Nevada City,** onto CA 49, heading for **Downieville,** for a stunning run up along the **Yuba River.**

1,428 Miles STOP sign—TURN RIGHT, CA 49 merging with CA 89.

1,433 Miles TURN RIGHT, staying on CA 89 in the middle of downtown **Sierraville** (pop. 85).

1,456 Miles TURN RIGHT onto I-80 going west toward **Truckee.**

1,458 Miles EXIT I-80, heading south of CA 89.

1,472 Miles STOP sign—TURN RIGHT, following CA 89 as you enter **Tahoe City** (Chapter 10).

1,500 Miles TRAFFIC LIGHT—TURN RIGHT, following CA 89/US 50 in **South Lake Tahoe.**

1,505 Miles TURN LEFT onto CA 89 just after the **California Agricultural Inspection Station.**

1,516 Miles At the STOP sign at **Picketts Junction,** TURN LEFT, following CA 88/89.

1,522 Miles TURN LEFT to follow CA 89, in the little village of **Woodfords.**

1,534 Miles GO STRAIGHT, moving onto CA 4 (CA 89 goes off to the left), over **Ebbetts Pass** (8,730 feet).

1,616 Miles STOP sign—TURN LEFT onto CA 49 toward **Sonora.**

1,651 Miles STAY STRAIGHT on CA 120, heading into **Yosemite National Park,** as CA 49 goes off to the right.

1,685 Miles Enter Yosemite and pay the $10 entrance fee.

1,694 Miles TURN LEFT at **Crane Flat,** following CA 120, as it were, heading up to **Tioga Pass.** (Now, if you want to eat the whole jar of pickles, you could stay straight, going into Yosemite Valley before heading south on CA 41, pick up CA 180 going east out of **Fresno** (Chapter 11), then go south to **Kernville** (Chapter 12), and head east over **Sherman Pass** or **Walker Pass** and on to **Death Valley.**)

1,754 Miles STOP sign—TURN RIGHT onto US 395.

1,876 Miles TURN RIGHT onto CA 136, at the south end of **Lone Pine,** heading for **Death Valley** (Chapter 13).

1,894 Miles GO STRAIGHT as CA 136 becomes CA 190.

1,980 Miles TURN RIGHT onto CA 178, opposite the **Furnace Creek Inn,** the sign pointing to **Badwater.**

2,052 Miles STOP sign—TURN RIGHT toward **Shoshone** on CA 127/ 178.

2,053 Miles STAY STRAIGHT on CA 127, as CA 178 goes off to the left.

2,111 Miles At the STOP sign in **Baker**, STAY STRAIGHT, and go under I-15, onto Kelbaker Road, through **Kelso**, and under I-40.

2,179 Miles STOP sign—TURN RIGHT onto Old Route 66, a/k/a **National Trails Highway.**

2,185 Miles TURN LEFT onto Amboy Road, having passed the one cafe/gas station/motel that is **Amboy** and gone over the railroad tracks; the sign will point toward 29 Palms.

2,233 Miles TURN LEFT onto Utah Road, which could catch you by surprise, but if you go on a mile to the TRAFFIC LIGHT on Adobe Road, you will figure things out (Chapter 14).

2,240 Miles Pay $5 at the entrance to **Joshua Tree National Park.**

2,244 Miles TURN LEFT at the three-way intersection, taking Pinto Basin Road toward **Cottonwood Springs.**

2,281 Miles TURN RIGHT onto Pinto Road after passing over I-10, heading for **Mecca.**

2,301 Miles TURN RIGHT onto CA 111, right after crossing over the railroad tracks.

2,324 Miles TRAFFIC LIGHT—TURN LEFT onto CA 74; you will be right in the middle of the town of **Palm Desert.**

2,349 Miles TURN LEFT onto CA 371, marked AGUANGA, while CA 74 continues on straight; CA 371 will drop 3,000 feet in the next 20 miles.

2,369 Miles STOP sign—TURN LEFT onto CA 79, as CA 371 ends at the Aguanga intersection (Chapter 15).

2,387 Miles TURN RIGHT onto CA 76.

2,391 Miles TURN RIGHT onto San Diego County Road S7, just past the **Lake Henshaw Resort.**

2,402 Miles TURN LEFT onto County Road S6 at the **Palomar Mountain** intersection.

2,409 Miles STOP sign—TURN RIGHT onto CA 76.

2,430 Miles TURN RIGHT onto I-15 going north.

2,459 Miles EXIT Interstate onto CA 74 and turn left, going west over the **Ortega Highway** (Chapter 4).

2,492 Miles TURN RIGHT onto I-5 going north.

2,503 Miles Take I-405 North.

2,556 Miles Take I-10 West, toward **Malibu.**

2,559 Miles I-10 will turn into CA 1, heading north.

2,565 Miles Arrive back at **Topanga Beach.**

Introduction: Baja

We're leaving Alta California and headed to Baja California; from a gardening point of view, I look on Alta California as being my front yard: rather well kept, lawn mowed and all that, whereas my back yard is less neatly maintained, good for teaching a kid to ride a dirt bike.

The Spanish gave to those two pieces of real estate these Alta and Baja designations. For a while in the 1500s the Spanish thought that California was actually an island. The Sea of Cortez is some 800 miles long, and the northern extreme could be difficult sailing; combine that with the huge Bay of San Francisco, and the lack of any Global Positioning System, and you can understand the mistake.

The official decision to separate Alta from Baja was an ecclesiastical one, made by the Franciscans in 1773. These brown-robed friars had the authority to proselytize and profit from their missions in Alta California, and wanted to keep the less fortunate white-robed Dominicans from encroaching on their turf, making sure they stayed south of the border down in the less populated and less fertile Baja.

This is a stretch of recently re-paved Mex 1—a very fine surface.

The highway curves alongside Bahia Concepcion for about 15 miles.

Which all comes to explain how the name "California" came about. It is a fiction, from the fertile mind of the 16th Century novelist Garcia Rodriguez de Montalvo. This writer, who apparently never left Spain, wrote a book called *The Adventures of Esplandian,* and at some point this fellow Esplandian visits an island which he calls California, inhabited by beautiful dark-skinned women. Nobody knows who the first person was to apply that California name on this part of the Pacific coast, but it stuck.

Having first ridden the length of Baja in 1975, and going back at least once, sometimes several times a year, I have become quite familiar with the place. Once you get beyond the confines of the northern tourist zone, Baja is indeed a rustic place.

Very few of us Norte Americanos actually go and see what the back yard has to offer. If you ride 500 miles north of San Diego you are in Sacramento, which is not all that dissimilar. Whereas 500 miles south of San Diego puts you in San Ignacio, an entirely different world. And well worth the visiting.

This is an abbreviated guide to Baja, really, as my trip plan is essentially designed for paved-road-riding motorcyclists, and never goes far from the famed Trans-Peninsular Highway, the 1,060-mile main artery along this peninsula that connects Tijuana at the top with Cabo San Lucas at the bottom. The trip is suitable for a Gold Wing or a Buell Ulysses—or anything in between. Adventurous types with adventurous motorcycles can take some of my side-trip tips, and go explore San Francisquito or the Westside Highway.

But the idea is to go . . . just go. You won't regret it.

General Stuff to Know

A VERY BRIEF LOOK AT GEOLOGY AND HISTORY

What we are primarily interested in here is the thin ribbon of asphalt, Mexico Route 1, which runs for over a thousand miles from the U.S. border at San Diego to the tip of this peninsula—but there is a whole lot more to this part of Mexico than 16 to 24 feet of pavement.

Lay out a map of North America. Run a line from San Francisco Bay southsoutheast down to the mouth of the **Sea of Cortez** (sometimes referred to as the Gulf of California, but I prefer the Sea of Cortez appellation), which separates Baja California from the rest of Mexico.

This is roughly the line of the infamous **San Andreas Fault** and, if geologists are to be believed, the separation of Baja from the mainland occurred about 30 million years ago when the fault had a major hiccup. Those who adhere to the teachings of Bishop Ussher, who maintained the entire universe was created in 4004 B.C., are free to disagree.

That thick finger of land, 58,000 square miles, that juts southeastwardly for 800 miles is not really blessed with much in the way of natural resources . . . at least the kind that kept people alive. It has a very dry environment most of the year, but there are many scattered sources of spring water to satisfy the wild animals and early Indian inhabitants. Then, when the rains come, there is often too much water. Every year or two a major storm blasts through some part of Baja and tears up everything. Flash-floods are always destroying roads and interrupting traffic. However, there is good weather reporting, and unless you are camping in some remote spot without benefit of radio, you will know when something big is coming. It is not anything to worry about . . . as long as discretion is observed.

Three big mountain ranges, and a lot of little ones, cover most of the middle of the peninsula. In the north is the **Sierra Juarez**, in the middle is the **Sierra Giganta**, in the south is the **Sierra Laguna**. A big desert, the **Vizcaino**, sits on the 28th parallel, right where the two states that comprise Baja join together.

Political note: Mexico is officially known as the **United Mexican States**, with 31 states and the Federal District (like our District of Columbia) of Mexico City. Baja was a territory until the state of **Baja California**, the northern half, was created in 1952; for clarification it is sometimes referred

This is the Mission San Ignacio, constructed in 1786 and still very much in use today.

to, incorrectly, as Baja California Norte. Twenty-two years later, just after the completion of the **Carreteria Transpeninsula** (Transpeninsular Highway), **Baja California Sur** became the 31st state.

The highway, known familiarly as Mex 1, is 1,060 miles of asphalt running from Tijuana in the north to Cabo San Lucas in the south. Without this highway, this section of the book would not have been written.

A smidge of pre-history: Baja has been inhabited for thousands of years, but the only sign of the earliest inhabitants are the many cave paintings that they left behind. The **Indians** that came after, and who greeted the exploring Spaniards, sometimes with open arms, sometimes with arrows, claimed no relationship to the cave painters. History, as preserved by the written word, began in 1534 when a Spanish ship sailed into the Bay of La Paz. Twenty-three of the crew were killed by Indians while seeking water; the rest sensibly sailed away.

Various explorers sailed up and down the coast, occasionally landing, for the next 150 years, but the first permanent **Spanish** presence did not occur until 1697, when a mission was founded in Loreto by the Jesuits. They brought not only their strange god, but also strange diseases that the Indians had no defenses against.

In 1734 the southern Indians, obviously celebrating the bicentennial of the first effort to keep the Europeans out, revolted and killed a few missionaries. A hundred troops came and restored order.

By the early 1800s mainland Mexicans became dissatisfied with the rule of Spain, as well as with the wealthy Catholic Church, and the colonials were in open revolt. A **Mexican Republic** was declared in 1823, and Baja was declared a territory in 1824.

After the Spanish departure, the **Catholic Church,** which had backed Spain and not the revolutionaries, found its power, and its financial position as lender of money to the rich in need, being eroded; understandably, as it held at least a third of the real wealth of the nation. In 1857 President Benito Juarez (many streets named after him) altered the constitution to force the Catholic Church to sell all its considerable secular property—though it could keep the churches. If you wonder why you don't see any white-collar clerics or black-cassocked padres in the the city streets, it is because they are forbidden by law from leaving church grounds in religious garb. The clergy are out and about, but in chinos and plaid shirts.

In 1846 the **Mexican-American War** began, and U.S. troops made a few minor forays into Baja. In 1848 the **Treaty of Guadalupe Hidalgo** ceded Alta California (and Texas and a few other places) to the Americans, and the California/Mexico border was drawn one league south of the entrance to San Diego Bay, going due east to the Colorado River.

By the 1880s only half a dozen mission fathers (Dominican) were left in all of Baja, and the population of the entire peninsula was less than 50,000. The Mexican government was actively looking for foreign investment in Baja in an effort to make a little money off of the place, and was willing to lease, or even sell, land to foreigners, as in Santa Rosalia and San Quintin.

The 20th Century **Mexican Revolution** began in 1910, landless poor against the rich, and in 1917 the government announced the *ejido,* or common land, act. This would take the land from the plutocrats and give it back to the people, and roughly 70 percent of Baja became owned by the mixed-blood (mostly Indian and Spanish) mestizos who lived there. You will see signs for Ejido Uruapan, Ejido Bonfil, hundreds of *ejidos,* little communal villages, mostly agricultural, with a few houses and perhaps a store *(tienda).*

During Prohibition border towns like Tijuana offered a place for California to go and drink legally, and do a little gambling while they hoisted their whiskeys. Then World War II came along, and red-light districts catered to U.S. servicemen about to go overseas. A benign approach to sin kept the border economy going through the 1950s, when tourism experts figured out there was more money in family vacations than the single male. The northern quadrilateral prospered, and then in the 1970s the government sank a lot of money into the southern tip, specifically Cabo San Lucas. That area, too, has prospered.

Today Baja is really two different and entirely separate worlds. In the very north and the very south are the areas frequented by tourists, populated by hard-working, profit-oriented locals, while the huge middle area tends to be more traditional rural Mexico. Outside of the tourist zones, Bajaeneos tend to be a quiet lot, and friendly. In the back country I have always been treated with the utmost courtesy when stopping to ask directions or for water, while along Highway 1 the *tienda* owner is helpful, even if she doesn't speak a word of English.

The tourist meccas in the north and south of Baja are fun, but the real pleasure of Baja is, for me, to be found in the hundreds of miles in between.

COMMON SENSE

Don't leave home without it. I remain bemused by the fact that a lot of people think that once outside of the United States and safely on the foreign soil of Baja California, anything goes. This unfortunate attitude is most apparent in the Tourist Zones, the Tijuana Quadrilateral in the north, and the Cabo Corridor in the south.

The truth is that once outside the U.S. you should be more polite, more considerate, and more careful. Common sense also dictates that you make sure your motorcycle is in good condition and that the tires have a lot of wear left.

MONEY

Money is good. Dollars are good. Pesos are good. The current rate (summer, 2006) of exchange is about 10.5 pesos to one dollar, subject to minor fluctuation. In the tourist zones dollars are always acceptable, although you may be slightly shorted in the change department. Pesos are more useful in the big In-Between; stop at a roadside *tienda* to buy a bottle of water, and the elderly lady running the place will be glad not to have to figure out exchange rates. When purchasing gas with dollars, attendants might well offer a slightly lower rate of exchange than you can get at a bank, which gives them a little added profit. Change some money at the border.

Credit cards are usually accepted in the tourist zones, and at many of the middling to better hotels in between, but cash is king. ATMs are everywhere in the far north and deep south, and in the larger towns in between.

PAPERWORK
After 9/11 things at the border changed. Going into Mexico is still no problem, and most motorcyclists are just waved on through, but coming back can be a different story. As of January, 2007, Americans will have to show either a passport or an approved photo-ID card; sorry, the old driver's license just does not do it anymore.

If I am going down south of Ensenada, I adhere to Mexican legal protocol and have a Tourist Card. The law reads that if you are going to be in Baja more than 72 hours, or going beyond the northern tourist zone, this Tourist Card is required. These TCs are available at any border crossing, and need to be stamped there as well. They are also available from AAA offices, Mexican tourist offices, Mexican consulates, as well as many travel agents.

For the motorcycle, carry a registration, and having a copy of your title is never amiss. However, for anyone planning on going to the Mexican mainland, either by ferry boat or via Sonora, proper and extensive paperwork for the bike is essential.

Since your U.S. insurance is not valid in Mexico, it makes sense to buy some Mexican insurance when you go to Baja.

Note: If you are going to do a loop via ferry boat back through the Mexican mainland, you must have a Tourist Card and a Temporary Vehicle Import Permit; these will be checked. To get the permit you must show proof of ownership of the vehicle, and that requires that you have the original document, nothing photocopied. It is a hassle, but this is what is required . . . and don't say I didn't tell you. You will also need a credit card, and to pay a $30 fee, in order to get the TVIP, which provides the Mexican government a guarantee that you will re-export the motorcycle from mainland Mexico. All this is due to the fact that at one time it was popular for Norteamericanos to drive deep down into Mexico, have a good time, sell their vehicle for a small profit, and fly/train/bus home. The Mexican bureaucrats want to make sure they get their tax cut these days.

INSURANCE

The Mexican insurance industry has a great scam working, and your U.S. insurance company cannot cover you in Mexico. Around any border crossing are well-advertised agents that will sell you a policy for a day or more. You should have liability insurance, just in case you do get involved in an accident. Mexican law reads that if you are in an accident, and cannot produce proof of liability insurance, whether you are right or wrong, off to the slammer you go. Current liability rates are about $14 a day, less for longer policies.

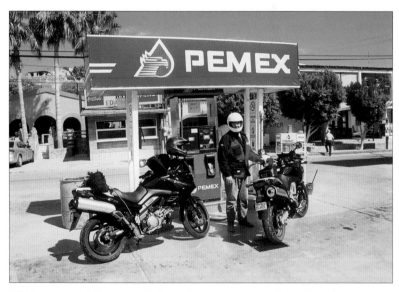

All Mexican gas stations are PEMEX, and the green pump indicates lead-free gas.

The company I deal with, Instant Mexico Auto Insurance Services about a mile north of the Tijuana crossing, will also write the motorcycle for fire, theft, and collision, with a $5,000 deductible: hardly worth it. IMAIS can be contacted at 800-345-4701, and their offices are at the San Ysidro Avenue exit from I-5, at 223 Via de San Ysidro. They can also fax you a policy.

There are two Baja clubs, mostly geared to the motorhome types; if you join, which costs a fair bit, these can provide less expensive liability insurance. One is the Discover Baja Travel Club (800-727-BAJA), the other the Club Vagabundos del Mar (800-474-BAJA). They are both headquartered near San Diego, and calling up to get their information packets is worthwhile.

GAS

Don't worry about gas . . . unless you're running some highly tweaked, 100-octane motor. Gas is a state monopoly, and all gas stations are called PEMEX (PEtroleos MEXicanos). You will generally see a blue pump and a green pump. The blue is regular leaded, with an advertised octane rating of 80. You want the green pump, or Magna Sin (unleaded), which claims 92 octane; I think that is a bit on the optimistic side, but I have run all manner of modern bikes, from Harleys to Hondas, BMWs to Triumphs, on Magna Sin, and never had a problem.

On the main roads, the only lack of PEMEX might be on the 200 miles of Mexico 1 between El Rosario and Villa Jesus Maria, and as my Mileage Log for that stretch explains, there are ways around that if you don't have a 200-mile tank. As a matter of course, I always carry a few feet of siphoning hose with me—just in case.

MOTORCYCLE REPAIR

If your bike is in good shape, it should not need any repairs for the next couple of thousand miles. If it is not in good shape, you are a fool. Once you leave Ensenada, there is no franchise shop for the next 850 miles. Down in La Paz, the major Japanese manufacturers all have big shops, and there is a Harley outfit in Cabo San Lucas. However, the famous "shade-tree" mechanics in Baja tend to be pretty resourceful, should you be in need. More concern should be given to the possibility of flat tires, and since most Bajaeans run on discarded U.S. tires, tire repair shops (llanteros) are everywhere. But I would also highly recommend that you have the expertise and equipment to fix your own tire.

ROADS

Riding in Baja is not like riding in the U.S. of A. Interpretation of the basic rules of the road tend to be more liberal. If a car pulls off to the right, he may actually be turning right, or preparing to make a U-turn in front of you. Caution is advised. Driving at night is downright foolish. As my Baja guru, Kurt Grife, is wont to say: "It is hard to see a black cow lying on black asphalt on a black night."

This trip is set up to be on pavement, but Baja asphalt can change from a smooth, newly laid, 80-mph surface to wheel-busting potholes in the blink of an eye. Many miles of Baja roads do not have what we call shoulders; the only way to pull off the pavement is to go down a steep embankment. Which means if a truck breaks down, it will sit on the road, day and night. When there is a pull-off, five layers of asphalt may have created a five-inch drop from pavement to dirt. Baja roads tend to be narrow, expecially in the great In-Between. Oncoming semis will slow to 15 mph to pass each other on a narrow stretch, but when it comes to passing a motorcycle, they will blow by at 70 mph. Pay attention to road signs, especially the diamond-shaped ones which mean something hazardous lies ahead. The two most

I am parked on a big yellow tope, *and you can see the arrow pointing down to it.*

This is the fish taco place in Plaza Corona in Mulege—get there before noon.

common problems are *vados* (dips for allowing water to cross the road) and *topes* (speed bumps). Usually these are sign-posted beforehand, but not always. Arriving at a dip at speed can create some serious problems as you fly through the air and your front tire smacks the far side. Speed bumps are most often found in villages and small towns, and range in height from minor to major. The town of Maneadero, just south of Ensenada, is nicknamed Tope City, and only about half are marked.

Along the length of Mex 1 you will see occasional green and white trucks, known as the Green Angels. These trucks, and their drivers, are part of the Mexican tourist services, and offer free service to stranded motorists of the tourist variety. They are good at fixing tires and providing gas, and all have training as mechanics, but fortunately I have never had the need to check their motorcycle expertise. They do give one a nice feeling of security, which is the intent.

HELMET LAWS

Both states in Baja California (BC and BCS) have helmet laws on the books. Enforcement is entirely arbitrary. One day in Cabo San Lucas when riding with the wind coursing over my bald spot I was stopped, escorted to the police station, paid a 35-peso fine, and sent on my way—still without a helmet.

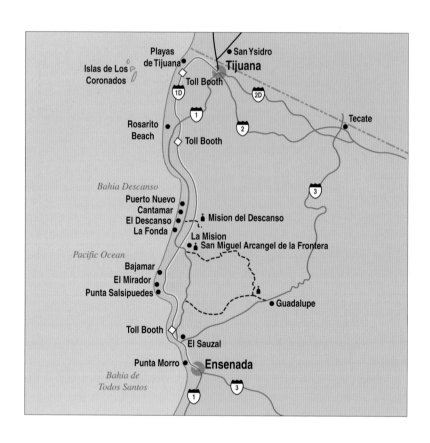

Playas
de Tijuana
Islas de Los
Coronados
Toll Booth
San Ysidro
Tijuana
1D
2D
1
Rosarito
Beach
Toll Booth
2
Tecate
Bahia Descanso
Puerto Nuevo
Cantamar
El Descanso
La Fonda
Mision del Descanso
3
La Mision
San Miguel Arcangel de la Frontera
Pacific Ocean
Bajamar
El Mirador
Punta Salsipuedes
Guadalupe
Toll Booth
El Sauzal
Punta Morro
Ensenada
Bahia de
Todos Santos
1
3

Tijuana to Ensenada

No big deal. You pop over the border, get on Mex 1-D (the toll road), and you're there in **Ensenada**. Easy as pie.

Well . . . maybe a little explanation is good for the soul. At least for my soul, as I am responsible for getting you from the frontier to deep within the United Mexican States.

The **Tijuana** entry is quick, simple, efficient—and some 15 million American tourists use it every year. For many of you, this may constitute the first time you have left the United States of America. But nothing dramatic happens.

You are cruising down I-5 into **San Ysidro**, California, ten lanes wide, border coming up, last turn-around sign goes by, and there in front of you are a dozen toll booths. Usually there is nobody in the booths, but brown-uniformed border officials may be standing to the far side, waving you on. Trucks stay over to the right, you move to the left.

The guy will just look at you with half an eye, and wave you on. You're in Mexico! Hurrah!

Now what?

If you are going further south then Ensenada, you want to get your tourist card stamped and paid for here; pull over to the right and ask for **Migracion**. You will be directed to the official who gives out tourist cards, and he will direct you to the bank next door where you pay your $22, come back with the receipt, and you are legal all the way to Cabo San Lucas. Don't complain about the money; a Mexican pays more than twice that to get a visa for the U.S.

Lots of people hang about here, from insurance touts to taxi drivers to police and officials. They're all very pleasant, understanding that tourism is the main business of this city of well over a million people.

An arch (**Puerta Mexico**) reaches over the road not a hundred yards from the toll booths, and the **Tourist Information Office** is at the right side, in case you wish to clutter up your tankbag with a few hundred brochures.

Mexico Highway 1-D, the Toll Road from Tijuana to Ensenada: 66 Miles
Mile 0 Head away from the border. Big signs overhead show the way to the TOURIST CENTER, ENSENADA CUOTA, and RIO TIJUANA. Pay atten-

Olé!

Bullfighting is the local equivalent of our heavyweight boxing. I make no judgement as to the ethics and morality of this sport, and have seen a dozen such events in Mexico and Spain. A bullfight well done is a drama, and can be an impressive occasion; it is up to the matadors, toreadors, and picadors to provide a graceful complement to the actions of one thoroughly angry bull. A bullfight usually has six separate fights, involving six bulls and three matadors, each matador dispatching two bulls. Granted, it is not a fair fight, with the bull's chances of getting out alive being very slim indeed, as he has to dispatch all three matadors, but there can, and should, be grace in this execution. I can't really recommend the Tijuana fights too much, as they are put on with second-rate matadors and third-rate bulls. The major bullfight season is in the fall, with a minor season in the spring.   ■

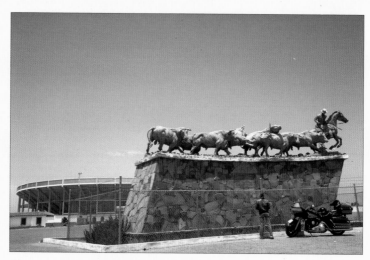

The most popular bullring in Baja is the Bullring-by-the-Sea.

tion, sticking to the middle route to **Ensenada Cuota** (Cuota = Cost, as in toll road), which makes a complete circle, passing under itself, and taking you along Avenida Internacional, the road paralleling the frontier.

This is the easiest way out of TJ. Ensenada Cuota, also referred to as ENSENADA SCENIC ROAD on many signs, was built to help siphon the Ensenada-bound gringos right from the border to the sea, and on down the coast.

Ave. Internacional is not a very pretty sight; rather tatty, in point of fact. To your right is a bleak fence made of vertical sheets of iron, a very unprepossessing international boundary. The road is four lanes wide, with traffic pulling in from and going off to the left. It often floods in heavy rains, and suffers many potholes. The "avenue" goes straight, starting to climb steeply, and you get views over the boundary fence to the U.S., a large estuarial expanse, with the occasional green U.S. Border Patrol vehicle roaming about in the distance.

Mile 3   As the road crests the hill it turns to the left and descends, becoming the northwest end of **Libramiento,** the half-circular loop road that circles around the south of Tijuana. It can't go north, thanks to the border.

Mile 3+   You want the first exit to the right, well marked as ENSENADA CUOTA.

Staying on Mex 1-D, the four-lane road goes up and over the **Cerro de Piedras Grandes,** and then the **Pacific Ocean** is in view.

Mile 5   This is the well-marked exit to **Playas de Tijuana,** a beachside suburb. It's main attraction is the bull ring.

Mile 5+   First **toll booth,** and you will be freed of 26 pesos, or $2.35, either currency equally acceptable. (Two more booths are awaiting you further down the road, all asking for the same amount.) Rest rooms and a small tourist office await you. To save the costs of lots of toll booths and salaries, the 55 miles of Mex 1-D between Playas de Tijuana and Ensenada have about 15 exits, but collect tolls only at the beginning, in the middle, and at the end.

The toll road has two lanes in either direction, and is reasonably lightly trafficked, as most locals, and especially truckers, don't want to spend the money. But there can be occasional stray dogs, bicyclists, pedestrians, and unexpected construction sites. Be sensibly wary when traveling this road.

You've paid the fee and are hurtling southward, past a humongous number of seaside developments. The whole coast from Playas de Tijuana to Bajamar is being built up at a frantic rate, mostly for gringo consumption.

Out to sea you will see the **Islas de los Coronados,** a small uninhabited group of islands about seven miles off-shore.

Pass the **Real del Mar** exit, the **San Antonio del Mar** exit, the **Oasis Resort** exit, and see great industrial smoke stacks and a station generating power as the road curves inland a bit.

Mile 17   **Rosarito Beach North,** where Mex 1 Libre (= Free) crosses 1-D.

Mile 21   Rosarito Beach **toll booth.**

Mile 32   **Cantamar** exit.

The Tourist Alternative

If you want to see a long line of tourist businesses, exit at Cantamar. If you TURN RIGHT on the free Mex 1 and go north a mile, there is the gourmand's delight, **Puerto Nuevo** (Newport, for the linguistically impaired), with over two dozen restaurants offering their culinary delights, all of which are much the same. Lobster predominates on every menu. Hotels are available for those who dissipate too much.

For those interested in Baja history, the site of the **Mission del Descanso** (meaning "a place to rest") is just south of Cantamar. Go south on Mex 1 a mile, and a dirt road crosses under Mex 1-D and goes up along the streambed to the mission. Nothing of the old mission really remains, but locals have erected a new chapel on the old site. Apparently the padres liked the area because the well-watered land in the **Descanso Valley** was good for viticulture—and wine was important to the sacraments.

A mile further along on Mex 1 is the **Half-Way House**, selling food and spirits to the Ensenada-bound travelers since 1922. Still do turn out a fine meal.

Another five miles provides access back to Mex 1-D, right between **Hotel La Mision** and **Hotel La Fonda**. Good spot, the La Fonda, the place being seriously funky—sort of a redundant name, as "fonda" means inn. But nicely funky, with 27 rooms, right on the cliffs over the sea. And great food, with great ambience. You can tuck the bikes in close to the place, and not have a worry as you stuff yourself with lobster crepes and retire to your room to sleep.

From here the adventurous can take the free road, Mex 1, as it goes under Mex 1-D and inland to the village of **La Mision**, and the remains of the mission of **San Miguel Arcangel de la Frontera**. From there it is 18 miles up and over a mesa and back to the coast near Ensenada. ■

Mile 39 La Mision exit

Mile 46 **Bajamar** exit, with hotels, golf, shops, and all the stuff of a major resort. South of here the coast is a bit gnarly for developing, with steep cliffs, and the reason why this stretch of road was put in less than 30 years ago, and sometimes washes away in a storm, like parts of California 1.

Mile 50 El Mirador, a scenic stop overlooking the ocean at **Punta**

Llantera is the universal sign for "tire repair," and these shops are everywhere.

Salsipuedes, with restaurant, shops, and the always essential bathrooms.

Mile 60   **Ensenada tollbooth.** You've just spent some seven bucks for the privilege of not interacting with much local traffic.

This main road between the toll booths and Ensenada is four lanes wide, with a median strip, and a good deal of traffic. Much of which makes U-turns across the median.

Mile 61+   A major road goes off to the left, marked TECATE MEX 3.

The Tecate Egress

When the time comes to leave Baja, you can go back the way you came, through Tijuana, but a much better choice is to take the 66-mile road to Tecate. At the Tijuana frontier you may wait for an hour or more to get through the U.S. officials, whereas Tecate is generally done in 15 minutes or less. The Tecate road is also a lot more scenic. Crossing the border at Tecate puts you on CA 94, about 35 miles from San Diego.

■

A Word About the Word "Gringo."

It is a Spanish word from Latin America which generally denotes somebody who has blonde hair, and in Mexico has become broadened to mean anybody who comes from the U.S. or Canada. It used to have a mildly pejorative connotation, but now has come into common parlance and is used by gringos and Latinos alike to indicate Norteamericanos. One of Mexico's leading authors, Carlos Fuentes, wrote an excellent novel called The Old Gringo, which was critically acclaimed on both sides of the border and made into a very good movie.   ■

Mile 65 The highway splits, with SAN QUINTIN, MEX 1 and ENSENADA ORIENTE to the left, ENSENADA CENTRO to the right.

Stay to the right at the intersection, and head down to the port of **Ensenada** and the center of town.

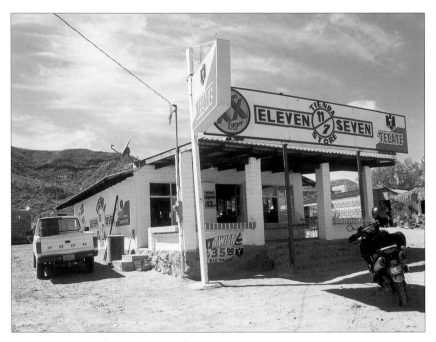

Some tiendas *have truly inspired names.*

Ensenada: The City by the Bay

Not many natural mooring spots exist along the California coast, and when the Spanish explorer Juan Cabrillo sailed his square-rigger into this gorgeous bay on St. Matthew's day in 1542, he gave thanks to the saint by naming the place in his honor.

Sixty years later, in 1602, another intrepid adventurer, Sebastian Vizcaino, anchored, and decided to expand the role of the honored and changed the name to "Ensenada de Todos Santos" (Bay of All Saints). And the fishing village that grew up there become known simply as **Ensenada** (The Bay); people were too busy earning a living to do any more renaming. Now the secluded body of water is often referred to as Ensenada Bay, a bilingual redundancy if there ever was one.

Nothing much happened until 1870, when gold was discovered in the area, and life perked up. Then it became the capital of northern Baja California in 1882 and acquired a small importance as a bureaucratic stronghold. A publican named J. D. Hussong set up his cantina a few years later, 1892, and he and his descendants have prospered ever since.

That is the civic plaza on the malecon *in Ensenada, and I promise you that that flag is huge.*

For many people, going to Ensenada demands a trip to Hussong's Cantina, in business for more than 100 years and now making lots of money off the tourist trade. It's a dive, but a mildly interesting dive if you enjoy loud gringo drunks.

Now it is a major port, and tourist center, and home to some quarter-million residents. Tourists love it; get on a cruise ship in San Diego, sail down the coast, spend a day strolling the trinket markets along **Avenida Lopez Mateos,** and back on board to sleep in clean gringo sheets. A pretty dull way to travel, in my mind. Far better to arrive by motorcycle.

If you follow the ENSENADA CENTRO sign, you will make a left turn by the docks, and then come to a traffic light. Go right; that is a broad, divided avenue called either Boulevard Costero or Blvd. Lazaro Cardenas (makes no matter—*costero* meaning coastal, Cardenas being a president back in the 1930s) going in front of the fish market, the sport-fishing terminal, and the civic plaza.

The locals are in the process of developing malls and such along Cardenas to lure money out of the tourist pocket, but the real pleasure is going into the fish market. A seriously fishy place, with the tuna, albacore, and red snapper fresh off the boats. All around are taco joints, serving up pretty good fish and shrimp tacos. And hawkers hawking every sort of souvenir imaginable.

Parallel to Cardenas, one block inland, is the main Tourist Alley, Avenida Lopez Mateos (Mateos being president in the 1960s). Once you get situated on Mateos, everything is accessible.

My recommendation for a place to stay, suitably downtown, is the **Bahia Resort Hotel** (local 646-178-2101, U.S. reservations at 888-308-9048), fronting onto Mateos, with hotel parking having a 24-hour guard. From here you walk to wherever you wish to go.

Other choices are two Best Westerns, both on Mateos. One is the **Casa del Sol** (U.S. 800-525-1234, local 646-178-1570) and the other is the **El Cid** (646-178-2401). A couple of blocks further south along Mateos, after crossing over the (generally) dry **Rio Ensenada,** at the intersection with Avenida Guadalupe, is the **San Nicolas Resort** (646-176-1901). Behind that is the **Hotel La Pinta** (646-176-2601, U.S. 800-336-3942), one of a small chain of six rather boring hotels in Baja between Ensenada and Loreto. Many other hotels are in the area.

Food is all over, from corner taco vendors to expensive white-tableclothed restaurants. Upscale Ensenada folk like to breakfast, lunch, or dine at **Bronco's Steak House,** at the corner of Mateos and Guadalupe. Mexican food done to American taste is a specialty of **Cafe Hussong,** upstairs in the Hussong Plaza, on the corner of Mateos and Ruiz, a couple of doors down from **Hussong's Cantina.** American fast-food franchises are moving in, just in case you can't bear to be away from Pizza Hut.

For those who like the taste of the grape, the **Santo Tomas** winery has a tasting room, **Bodega de Santo Tomas,** about six blocks east of Mateos, at Ave. Miramar 666, which is a continuation of Ave. Macheros. The tasting room is also a wine-bar, **La Esquina de Bodegas,** which offers a good selection of all Baja wines.

Ensenada gets several million tourists a year. Of course a good time can be found.

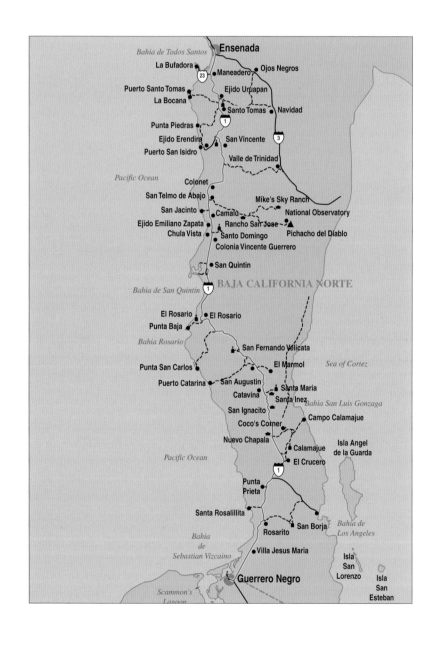

Ensenada to Guerrero Negro

Through Baja's Bread-Basket and the Boojums on Mex 1: 382 Miles

Americans might not think that the earth is flat, but may tend to believe that all reasonable signs of 21st Century civilization stop a few miles south of Ensenada. I would guesstimate that of the 15 to 20 million Norteamericanos who cross the border into Baja California every year, probably less than 20,000 ever go further south than a few miles beyond Ensenada.

Ensenada being such a sprawling city, it is hard to figure out a place to zero your tripmeter. However, since we took you to the Blvd. Costera along the waterfront, the *malecon,* as this pedestrian walkway is referred to, we'll start from there, in front of the Civic Plaza where the gigantic Mexican flag is flying—you can't miss it.

Mile 0 Plaza Civica. Just head south on Costera.

Mile 1 TURN LEFT at TRAFFIC LIGHT onto Calle Augustin Sangines.

Mile 1+ TRAFFIC LIGHT—Gigante supermarket on the corner, TURN RIGHT onto Ave. Reforma, which is Mex 1 going south.

Mile 2 A PEMEX is on the right. And the city just continues on. Some suitably disreputable apartment buildings are lined up along the road, with graffiti-covered walls. The occasional traffic light prevents the traffic from going pedal-to-the-metal for the dead straight nine miles to the Maneadero intersection. You pass the military base, and military hospital, and then the airfield, shared by civilian and military alike.

Mile 5 The well-marked turn to the **Estero Beach Resort** (646-176-6230); this is a full-service resort much frequented by gringos, including jet-skiing, fishing, and laying on the sand. Mex 1 goes from four-lane to two, and the housing build-up seems to cease at the bridge over the **Rio San Carlos.** On the east side of the road are 20 or so palm-fronded stalls dedicated to catching the returning day-tripper, selling hot peppers in jars, olives, corn on the cob, tamales, strings of garlic, all that gorgeous-looking condiment.

Mile 9 **Maneadero** comes up, looking very tatty. The name, which translates as "rein-maker," is said to derive from the fact that a man who made harnesses lived here many years ago; maybe, maybe not. Watch out for the *topes* (speed bumps), of which the town has about eight. They are not all

A Trap for Trippers

A Maneadero a sidetrip to the local tourist trap is in order if you have a spare hour. At the only TRAFFIC LIGHT in town TURN RIGHT, onto State Route 23 going off for 14 miles to the west, to the overly touted (in my opinion) **La Bufadora** (buffalo's snort).

BC 23 curves pleasantly through flat, estuarial land, with more road-side stands flogging the local produce. After six miles there is a paved turn to the right to the **Baja Beach & Tennis Club,** an attempt at building a resort hotel. Rumor has it that the building was begun in the early 1980s with the notion that gambling would be legalized and this would become a casino. That has not come to pass, and the place is rather vacant, and you have to wander around to find someone who will serve you a drink in the bar.

The road goes by the **La Jolla Beach Camp,** with camping on the beach and a very eccentric five-story structure looming over the road. There are a number of small houses, mostly owned by Americans, and a large camping area along the seawall. On a weekend it tends to be noisy, but weekdays are delightfully quiet. A Russian emigre began this little empire long ago, and it is now a very old-fashioned, and delightful, place. Yes, the sign does say you have to push your motorcycle, but that is only true for noisy little dirtbikes.

A half-dozen tamale vendors are set up on the other side of the road.

Continuing along BC 23, the road climbs up around **Pico Banda** (1,264 feet), and then curves around and starts dropping into a small bay, with many houses on the far side, a few boats in the water. At the top of the hill is a square water tank; turn off onto the bumpy dirt area, and 200 yards ahead is the edge of a cliff, which looks down on La Bufadora from above. That may be your best view of the place.

A **blowhole** is merely a hole in a rock where the tide can surge underneath and send a spout of water up through the hole and into the air. I like the legend that a baby whale swam into the underground cavern when he was very small, and has grown up inside unable to leave, and the blowhole is his spouting. Although it does tickle my claustrophobia.

Twenty-five years ago there was nothing out here but the blowhole, a couple of stands selling souvenirs, and a small restaurant. Now it has been turned into the Mexican version of Old Faithful, with half a dozen restaurants and a carefully constructed strip of some 50 shops that you have to go through to get to the blowhole—which is now accessible only through a relatively new complex, with pay toilets and all the rest. Access is free, but please do not try to go there on a weekend.

The best thing about La Bufadora is having an evening dinner at **Cecilia's Restaurant** (the fried whole sea bass is highly recommended) and then riding back over the mountain and seeing the 20 miles of shoreline of the **Bahia de Todos Santos** all lit up. It is a sight.   ■

A Sunday afternoon at the beach, a horse, a bottle of beer—ahhh!

marked, but the vehicle in front will let you know when one appears. Maneadero used to be a small junction community of a few hundred people and one PEMEX, and now has 10,000 inhabitants and three gas stations. Most of the population is involved in farming.

Back at the Maneadero intersection, GO STRAIGHT on to the south. The mile-long row of shops, garages, et cetera, is set back from the two-lane road, with roaming vehicles sending up clouds of dust from the expanse of dirt between pavement and stores. The old immigration checkpoint closed down 15 years ago. Bump on over the *topes,* past the last PEMEX, and soon you are free of commercialism.

Mile 11 You might well find a semi-formal **inspection station** manned by the Federal Police and the army. No worries. I've never been stopped going either way. I slow way down as I come through the orange cones, and get waved on by whoever is standing at the stop sign. But I do have my tourist card, just in case.

These impromptu checks are most thanks to our Uncle Sam, who has leaned on the Mexican government to try to cut down on the amount of illegal drugs heading toward our border. Noble thoughts, but I doubt that any smuggler with an IQ of over 60 has ever fallen afoul of these cops, except as a routine shakedown of a trucker without proper papers. I look on these occasional roadblocks as a window into the fictional "bandito" past.

The road starts swooping through the hills and enters a small valley.

Mile 22 The turn-off to **Ejidio Uruapan.**

Now Mex 1 climbs up and crosses over into **St. Tom's Valley,** with a delightfully steep descent, including one monstrous downhill U turn. The valley was the beginning of the **Santo Tomas** winery, and still grows grapes and olives. We can thank the padres of yore for the grapes, as they had to have wine to celebrate the sacraments.

Mile 26 Signs pointing right indicate the way to **La Bocana** and **Puerto Santo Tomas,** this dirt road is 16 miles long, follows the **Rio Santo Tomas** and ends at the sea where there is a small fishing community and a number of gringo houses.

Mile 28 You are in the village of **Santo Tomas.** The **El Palomar** has the tourist trade sewed up, with PEMEX, a ten-room motel (646-178-2355), restaurant, store, and RV camp. Warning: it is a noisy place because of truck traffic.

If you go down into the RV area, on the east side of the road, go to the end and TURN LEFT through the olive grove, heading toward three very tall palm trees, you will find the remains of the Mission of **Santo Tomas de Aquino,** operating from 1791 to 1849. Not much is left, just three clumps of adobe, and little is being done to protect it. As well as letting history be washed away, the El Palomar owner is missing a bet by not advertising, and protecting with a roof, his little bit of history.

Going south on Mex 1, the road climbs gently out of the Santo Tomas valley and drops into the valley of the **Rio San Isidro.**

Mile 51 The sign indicates a TURN RIGHT to the ruins of the **Mission of San Vicente Ferrar.** Little remains except for some adobe bricks, but for the half century the mission was in use, 1780 to 1833, it had a rough go. The local Yuma Indians were not happy with this papist invasion and enjoyed tormenting the padres and the small military contingent that protected them.

Mile 52 The village of **San Vicente** has PEMEX, several stores, and two motels of unknown quality; I'd say, cheap.

The road again crosses a low ridge as it goes from valley to valley, this one watered by the **Rio San Antonio.** As you come over the ridge you will see a line of mountains to the southeast (looking over your clutch lever), and that is the **Sierra San Pedro Martir.** On a clear day you can make out the **Picacho del Diablo**, which stands over 10,000 feet; that is some 45 miles away.

The Green Angels are to be found the length of Baja; they are funded by the Baja Departments of Tourism and offer basic support for tourists with troubles.

Mile 76   Entering the town of **Colonet,** and beginning a 40-mile stretch through heavily farmed land. On the right is a PEMEX which is erratically open. On the left is the **Restaurant Magui,** the town bus terminal. Inside it is clean, with 1950s chrome and formica, and a menu of rural Mexican gastronomical delights is prepared by several cheerful women in the back. They claim the place is open from 7:30 am to 8 pm daily.

Mile 84   Coming into **Ejido Diaz Ordaz,** also known as **San Telmo de Abajo,** a dirt road goes off to the east, 66 miles to the observatory near the top of Picacho del Diablo.

Room With a View

The road to the **National Observatory** is a long 60 miles of generally well-graded dirt. However, after the road starts climbing up into the **Parque Nacional Sierra San Pedro Martir,** there is a gate at Mile 54 and the fellow in charge will probably turn you away. No motorcycles allowed, which can be blamed on the dirt bikes which send up clouds of dust that hover over the mountain top and obscure the lenses on the telescopes in the observatory. At times there is no guard, but that is a small chance.

About the 6,000-foot level you come into heavy pine forest, and the road makes a few switchbacks, going up to about 8,000 feet before running into a barrier. The observatory personnel live here, and commute the rest of the way to the top, on a paved surface. Tourists have to walk up this stretch. The road ends at the observatory, at 9,184 feet above the sea, only 33 linear miles away to the **Sea of Cortez,** 44 to the **Pacific Ocean.** There is informal camping near the barrier, in the **Viacitos** meadows; bring your own water. At the top of the mountain are two small peaks about a mile apart, one reaching to 10,154 feet, the other two feet lower. These were not climbed until 1911.   ■

Back on Mex 1, going south.

Mile 89   A large sign shows the dirt road to **San Jacinto,** a little over three miles to the west. It's a good road, but be warned that a thin layer of drifting sand can make the handling a bit queasy. A most remarkable sight is on the coast, where the land curves out to **Punta San Jacinto,** where a straggling of trees is scattered about a seldom open restaurant and trailer park, and lying on its side just 150 feet off the shoreline is an old coastal freighter that ran aground in 1981, the *Isla del Carmen.* A few pangas belonging to the local fishermen are drawn up on the shore, protected by the wrecked vessel. The whole scene makes a modernist romantic seascape, especially when some surfers are out catching waves in the bay.

Mile 95   The farming community of **Camalu,** with PEMEX

Mile 101+   You've come through **Ejido Emiliano Zapata,** then **Chula Vista,** then the white and green **Baja Cafe, Restaurant & RV Stop** is on your left, rise over a hill, and at the top is a small cement bus stop with MOTEL ORTIZ advertised on top. Just beyond is a dirt road to the left that goes out to the remains of the **Mission Santo Domingo,** along the **Rio Santo Domingo;** it is a five-mile ride through rustic farming country feeding off some good ground water. The mission remains are by a new chapel and school up at **Red Rock Canyon;** if you are there on August 4th, it is major fiesta time.

Back in the 1960s, Mama Espinoza acquired a deserved reputation for the lobster burritos she served at her little restaurant in El Rosario; she has long since retired, but her establishment continues on.

Mile 102 Colonia Vincente Guerrero stretches along both sides of the road, with PEMEX, several small motels (the **Ortiz** and **Sanchez**, neither of which I have sampled) and cafes, and all other signs of a successful agricultural community.

The highway now goes dead straight for the next 15 miles, across endless well-worked fields; when you see your well-stocked produce department in your local supermarket in the winter, the veggies might well come from here.

Mile 114 An elegant **Ministry of Tourism** office sits by itself in the fields—it may or may not be staffed when you go by. Mexico is well-known for allotting money to build a project, but nothing for maintenance or staffing.

Mile 115 The start of **San Quintin**, with a big sign advertising the HOTEL LA PINTA 20 K. further on. And right opposite the sign on the left side of the road is the **Restaurant Mision Santa Isabel,** which is run just like any such place between Texas and Southern California. Clean, efficient, uniformed waitresses, and a menu in Spanish and English, though occasionally the English is slightly flawed, as in "onion liber" (liver with onions). If you are there for breakfast, the farmers are in discussing weather and wages. Most will be eating menudo (tripe stew), which the locals prefer to ham and eggs. In the corner might be a couple of local big shots, with a sycophant or two hanging on. It is good-old-boy stuff with a Mexican accent, open from 7 a.m. to whenever the clients go home.

The town has PEMEX. At the south end, just before the bridge, is the **Motel Chavez** (616-165-2005) cheap, clean, and quite nice with the **Restaurant Quintin** attached. Across the road is the **Hotel Reale de Cora,** and a block behind that is the **Motel Los Cirios.**

Mile 121 A big sign advertises the **Old Mill Motel & Resort** (616-165-3376, U.S. 619-428-2779), but it is three miles along a dirt road going west to **Bahia San Quintin.** If it weren't for the occasional sandy bits, I would say this is a "must stop." The old mill refers to the mill that a British-based consortium, the Lower California Development Company, built to process the wheat that they were going to make a fortune off of. Back in the 1890s they had leased the entire San Quintin area from the Mexican goverment, thinking it was perfect for wheat; they even built a short railroad to get goods to the bay. However, four years of drought spoiled that idea, and they pulled up their railroad tracks and went home. The Old Mill has lovely new rooms, and an excellent restaurant and fine bar housed in an old fish cannery that was active until the 1960s; it has been thoroughly cleaned up, I might add.

Mile 124 The road splits, the main Mex 1 angling slightly off to the left, sticking to the high ground, the secondary, which used to be the main some years ago, to the right. The old road got properly washed out in 1993, and the crossing of **Rio Santa Maria** is close to a mile of dirt; the two roads meet again after six miles.

Mile 129 A large sign indicates the **Hotel La Pinta** (616-165-9008; U.S. 800-800-9362) off to the left, down two miles of paved road to the **Bahia Santa Maria.**

Now Mex 1 is tearing off into the undeveloped world. The sea, and several fishing camps, is off to the right, and the land becomes less fertile as you go south, with scrub and rock and sand taking over. The road climbs up onto a small plateau, and then starts a seriously steep, twisting descent into the valley of the **Rio del Rosario;** the sign CURVA PELIGROSA (dangerous curve) says it quite well. All sorts of strange things can happen on that hill, with trucks trying to get up, stalling and blocking half the road, and trucks going down losing their brakes. Not likely to happen on your watch, but a look down in the gullys can be sobering.

Not much romance in this shipwreck at San Jacinto, but it makes a great photo backdrop; the small freighter Isla del Carmen *ran aground here in 1981 and was left to die.*

Tourist or Traveler?

This next stretch of road is what separates the tourist from the traveler, or so some pundit stated years ago. If a hundred thousand people go to Tijuana, and five thousand to Ensenada, not a hundred pass past El Rosario. Perhaps I exaggerate a bit, but you get the point.

Today the highway south from El Rosario to Guerrero Negro is generally good asphalt, but it wasn't like that until 30-some years ago. The road was paved as far as El Rosario in the 1960s, but beyond that were hundreds of miles of rough dirt. Any number of motorcyclists challenged that road on Harley Panheads, BMW twins, and AJS singles, but it was not a trip for the timid.

Then, in that marvelous Mexican manner the decision was made to complete the highway from Tijuana to the tip of the peninsula—lay asphalt, and the tourists shall come. They paved, finishing the task in 1974, and lo, the tourists did not come. At least not in the droves that the **Mexican Tourist Commission** had hoped for. There is a small amount of heavy-truck traffic, and those big boys only give way for each other; slow way down when you see one coming.

Nothing much happens over the next 200 miles; El Rosario is supplied from the north, Guerrero Negro from the south, via Santa Rosalia on the Sea of Cortez. In between is an entrepreneurial no-man's land, with one major hotel, one small one, two official gas stations, half a dozen unofficial ones, a couple of dozen places to eat, and a number of *tiendas* where you can buy anything from bottled water to canned beef.

While this stretch provides superb motorcycling, it is time again to remind you that Baja is quite intolerant of riding beyond one's abilities.   ■

Mile 160 Entering **El Rosario** (The Rosary), with PEMEX on the left. This town has never been out of gas in my years of going through, so fill up, even if there is a line at the two pumps.

Just downhill from the gas station is the excellent **Baja Cactus Motel** (616-165-8850), which has new rooms with all modern conveniences, including air conditioning, hot water, and good water pressure. An added plus is that it is the shortest of walks to the well-known **Mama Espinoza's Loncheria**, famous for its lobster tacos. The place has been around for over half a century, and Mama has long since retired, but the tradition goes on, and the prices go up.

Mile 161   Mex 1 makes a hard left, while the dirt road to the right goes out ten rough miles to the fishing and surfing spot at **Punta Baja.** This corner will be the start of the next section, El Rosario to Guerrero Negro. A quarter mile up from the corner is the **Sinai Motel** (616-165-8818), with a good restaurant, the **Bocana Beach,** right across the road.

Mile 166   The road turns south, crossing over a long bridge, and then starts to climb up on the **Pitahaya Mesa.** It is a superb motorcycle road, running along ridges, dodging in and out, the occasional *vado* to keep your mind alert. This is not a road to mess with; if you go off the edge, it is a rock and cactus landing zone.

Mile 176   A bad dirt road goes off to the right, some 40 miles to **Punta San Carlos,** where there are often a lot of gringo wind-surfers.

Mile 193   The **Loncheria Descanso** (Cafe Take A Break) is at the **Rancho del Descanso,** with a great big parking area for the long-haul trucks. All of these highway cafes have big, dusty pull-offs, as feeding truckers is their business. As well as good food, this one has a superb *sanitario* (toilet), with two stalls and a sink outside.

Mile 199   To the right is the turn to the few remains of the **Mission of San Fernando Velicata,** three miles down a bumpy dirt road. Those who follow the religious squabbling inside the Catholic Church in the 18th Century may be interested in the fact that this is the only Franciscan-built mission on the peninsula.

Mile 209   A turn to the right for **Puerto Catarina,** a seasonal fishing camp some 20 miles down a bad dirt road

Mile 217   The little village of **San Augustin,** where the failed promise of this highway can be seen in the abandoned PEMEX station: just not enough traffic to make a go of it

Mile 218   To the left is the turn for **El Marmol** (The Marble), an old onyx mine 14 miles down a dirt road. The **Southwest Onyx & Marble Company** was operating from 1900 all the way to 1958, and still to be seen is an onyx building (whether it was a jail or schoolhouse depends on whom you talk to), a graveyard (local necessity), and some rusted mining equipment that was not worth hauling away.

Mile 221   You have now entered the "**Desierto Central de Baja California Natural Area,**" which is about 15 miles wide and 100 miles long, and is home to a lot of vegetation you will never see anywhere else. Including the cirio cactus, in botanical terms, *Idria Columnaris,* also known as the boojum tree; obviously the botanist who came upon these had been reading Lewis Carroll's "The Hunting of the Snark." This plant, which can reach 60 feet in height, is found only in this small part of the world. The landscape

For the ecclesiastically curious, the mission San Fernando Velicata was founded by Padre Junipero Serra in 1769, before he moved off to proselytize Alta California.

along the highway is really quite bizarre, with great boulders and a dozen varieties of cactus covering the entire horizon. To get the full effect of the weirdness, pitch a tent on a full-moon night.

Mile 237 The oasis of **Catavina**. Watch out, as on both sides of this place are *vados* across the highway which tend to have a trickle of water most of the year and slimy green stuff underneath. Many a motorcyclist has been surprised.

Catavina itself has a **Hotel La Pinta** (646-176-2601; U.S. 800-800-9632) on the right side of the road, with a PEMEX pump for the hotel clients, although sweet-talking gringos with a bribe in hand can often get to use it. However, it usually is not operating between 9 a.m. and 4 p.m., when the hotel's electric generator is turned off. On the other side of the road is a large, dusty PEMEX station which is generally out of gas.

If you can't get gas here, don't worry, we'll fill you up down the road.

Next to the gas station is an abandoned cafeteria, which was originally intended to feed the hordes that would come off the buses—sorry, never happened. A small *loncheria* takes care of the inner man or woman.

A half-mile beyond the gas station is the **Rancho Santa Inez,** a few hundred yards down a paved road to the left. Before the highway was paved, this was the stopping place on the dirt road, and the ranch offers several rooms, hot showers, camping, and excellent food. Several notches up on the Pinta in terms of ambience, romance, and all those indefinable qualities that make up good traveling.

From **Santa Inez** a very bad dirt road goes off for ten or so miles to the ruins of the 1767 **Mission of Santa Maria de los Angeles,** the last of the Jesuit-built missions. In the 18th Century this place was resupplied from **Bahia San Luis Gonzaga** on the Sea of Cortez, and the trail has virtually disappeared; it must have been a hellish trek.

Mile 244   The **Rancho San Ignacito,** with a trucker's roadside restaurant, has its little footnote in history, as a small monument on the west side commemorates the completion of the **Transpeninsular Highway.**

Mile 255   The road passes an old landmark, **El Pedregoso** (The Rocky Place), a pile of boulders just to the right of the road that goes up over 3,000 feet above the distant sea. Several miles further on the road comes out on the long run that passes on the west side of **Laguna Chapala.** This is a dry lake most of the time, but can have very sticky mud beneath the crusty surface.

Mile 271   A left turn for the corrugated dirt road to **Gonzaga Bay** on the Sea of Cortez and north to **San Felipe.** On the right side is a *llantera* and *loncheria;* go behind the buildings where sit a dozen 55-gallon drums full of gas. They like to sell in ten-liter amounts, as this is the size of the can they use; the price will be about 25 percent higher than at a PEMEX, but I figure

When you travel the back roads, it is good to be wary.

that into haulage. And do not worry about the gas being watered; the main clients are locals, and the fellow would not be in business if he did that.

Mile 272 Rancho Nuevo Chapala is on the right, offering truck stop food.

Five more miles and you are out of the **Laguna Chapala Valley** and descending through an army of large cardon cactus.

Mile 288 This is The Cross (El Crucero), with several abandoned buildings, where a bad dirt road goes off to the left to the remains of the short-lived **Mission Calamajue**; lack of water doomed it early on.

Mile 302 The **Bahia de los Angeles** turn-off, often referred to as the **Punta Prieta** junction, though the actual village of PP is really a few miles further on. An abandoned PEMEX is on the right side, a very large automotive junkyard on the left. And there is often a benign military presence. Sometimes a local with a pickup can be found at the defunct gas station with drums of gas in the back; he is looking for the likes of you, the nervous tourist, and his markup might be a good deal higher than 25%.

A Trip to Angels' Bay

This is a 42-mile excursion, and worth the hour. Following World War II this place became a minor fly-in destination for fishermen, and following the completion of Highway 1, a good many motorhome people have shown up. PEMEX is readily available. A half dozen motels have set up business, from the original 1950's **Casa Diaz** at the south end of town to the more modern 40-room **Villa Vitta**. Half a dozen restaurants offer excellent fish dishes.

Rugged dual-purpose types can leave town by going south on 80 miles of rough dirt road to **San Franciscquito**, and then heading west on more dirt to catch Mex 1. Most of us will take the paved road back. However, 14 miles along you will see a major dirt road off to your left, which is the back way 20 miles into **Mission San Borja**; if you have the right bike and good dirt-road competence, the mission should not be missed, a large stone edifice. The hardpacked dirt square in front of the mission covers about an acre, and off to the side are only half a dozen little houses. Lady Maria Borja, the Duchess of Gandia, obviously felt that her soul was in danger, and gave a lot of money to the Jesuits to build some missions. When the Jesuits signed off on the place in 1767, they claimed 621 cattle, 1,108 sheep, 232 horses, 722 goats, and 1,618 Indians. From there it is another 20 miles to Rosarito on Mex 1. ■

Mile 321 The roadside community of **Punta Prieta** has food, both in cafe and grocery forms, and little else.

The road is easing through some low hills, comes up on a ridge, and you can see a serious expanse of scrub and desert in front of you. This is the beginning of the great **Vizcaino Desert** that stretches for the next 130 miles.

Mile 334 The village of **Rosarito** is off to the east of the road, and a failed PEMEX to the west. There are also signs to **Mission Borja.**

Mile 361 Entering the village of **Villa Jesus Maria,** a rural PEMEX is to the left; in my experience it has always had gas, as this station is supplied from the south. The tamale stand by the road provides tasty food.

Fifteen more miles down the road and something large starts to loom on the horizon. What is it? Is it a monolith? An abandoned skyscraper? A giant bird?

Mile 380 Yes, it is a giant bird, a modernistic, metallic interpretation of an eagle, standing about 140 feet tall. This statue marks the **28th parallel,** the division between Baja California (Norte) and Baja California Sur. A minor police and military presence keeps things spiffed up, and you may be

The eagle is the symbol of Mexico, featured on the Mexican flag. This 140-foot high, highly stylized bird sits on the state line between Baja California (Norte) and Baja California Sur, at the 28th latitude north.

That is a boojum tree, or cirio cactus, in Baja's Central Desert Nature Park.

asked for your tourist card. There is also an agricultural inspection station; since no fruits nor veggies are supposed to come into BCS from the north, or vice versa, they may spray your motorcycle with insecticide and charge you a buck for the privilege.

Just south and west of Big Bird is the **Hotel La Pinta** (615-157-1300; U.S. 800-800-9632), 27 rooms out in the middle of not much. And the mandatory PEMEX Green pump. I'd head on into **Guerrero Negro**.

Mile 382   The road forks, the left going on across the desert, the right into the charming (I joke) company town of **Guerrero Negro**. Take the right which goes along Blvd. Zapata.

Guerrero Negro: The Quintessential Company Town

The town of **Guerrero Negro** exists because the **Exportadora de Sal S.A.** (ESSA) exports about five million tons of salt every year; the salt is produced by solar means, the sun evaporating the salt water in over 100 square miles of salt pans south of town. The community, dependent on ESSA paychecks, stretches for some two skinny miles along Blvd. Emiliano Zapata. The name came from an American whaling ship, *Black Warrior,* that wrecked on this coast in 1858.

The big draw of the town is the whale-watching it affords at nearby **Scammon's Lagoon,** which is why there are a number of motels . . . many of which offer whale-watching services.

A mile along Blvd. Zapata, on the right, is the **Malarrimo Restaurant & Cabanas** (615-157-0100); these cabanas are really individual trailers, and are quite comfortable. Further along is the **Motel El Morro** (615-157-0414) with restaurant. Behind the El Morro is the **Motel Las Ballenas** (615-157-0116), clean and cheap. For food I sometimes go to the Malarrimo, more often to **El Figon de Sal** (a "figon" is a "cheap restaurant"); it is not a fast-food place, and service can take a while, but it is good.

The town itself is pretty minimal, with an uninspired collection of bars, cafes, stores, garages, and several PEMEX stations. And a bank with an ATM. If you head all the way through town, keeping to your left as you pass over a small causeway, you will be on the five-mile hard-packed dirt road to the old wharf on **Laguna Guerrero Negro;** it is a nice ride, and a nice view, and birdwatchers can find 100 species in the area. The lucky few might see a grey whale floating along in January or February.

The company town of Guerrero Negro is now over half a century old.

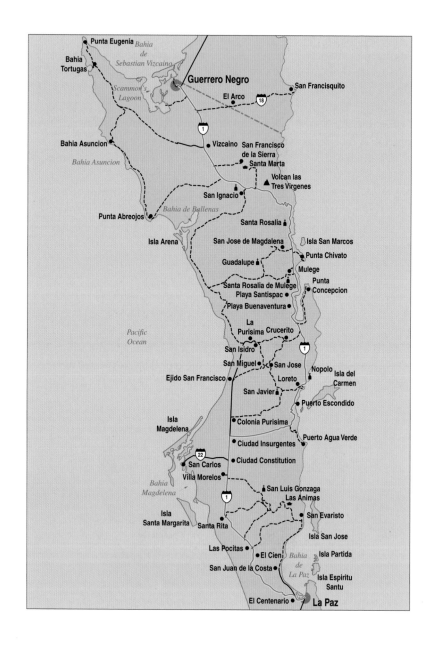

Guerrero Negro to La Paz

The First Half, to Loreto, is the Best Part of Baja; the Second Half, Loreto to La Paz, is Pretty Boring. Mex 1: 466 Miles
This next stretch, by my humble reckoning, encompasses the best of Baja. Some people like the heavily touristed northernmost section, others like the southern Cabos—me, I'll take the middle. It has stunning scenery, lots of history, adventurous roads—everything a good traveler looks for.

Mile 0 Here the road coming out from Guerrero Negro meets Mex 1. We're on the northwest edge of the **Vizcaino Desert,** which has now been ecologically labeled **El Vizcaino Biosphere Reserve.** I must admit, the place does not appear to be useful for much else, with over 5,000 square miles of desert and mountain covered by sand and rock and cactus. Not to say there is not a good deal of activity out there, with ranching and mining and fishing, but on the whole I find the desert delightfully inhospitable.

However, if a 40-mile-an-hour wind is blowing at right angles to the road, I sometimes think otherwise about the delightful part.

Mile 6 There is the well-marked turn-off to the **Parque Natural de la Ballena Gris** (Grey Whale) 16 miles away; this is quite a little cash cow (whale variety) that is successfully milked. It's a dirt road, generally good but with an occasional bit of shifting sand that might hinder a Gold Wing rider who is not familiar with dealing with soft stuff. You head out to the whale-watching area, paying a nominal entry fee at a small shed, ending up on a beach on **Laguna Ojo de Liebra** (Hare's Eye Lagoon or Jackrabbit Spring; there are a dozen versions of where these names came from, which I shall not repeat here), but it is more popularly known, at least among Americans, as **Scammon's Lagoon.**

If you are at the lagoon in the winter months, you can see the whales from the shore. If you want to be guaranteed a place in one of the licensed sight-seeing boats, you should arrange for that at one of the places in **Guerrero Negro,** the Malarrimo or Morro motels being the easiest. However, if there is a boat going out that is not full, you can negotiate a price and have a look at these aquatic mammals at close quarters.

Back on Mex 1, the road travels headlong into the desert. As you cruise along at 80 mph on the generally straight, little trafficked, occasionally pot-holed, two-laner, warning signs will state: PRECAUCION: NO ES UN

CAMINO DE ALTA VELOCIDAD (Warning: This is not a high speed road). Fancy that.

Mile 44   The junction community of **Vizcaino** has PEMEX, two motels, a restaurant, and several stores. From here is the take-off for the 109-mile paved, gravel and dirt road that goes west through the **Peninsula de Vizcaino** to the fishing town of **Bahia Tortugas** (Turtle Bay) and **Punta Eugenia.**

Heading south on Mex 1, there is more desert; nothing dramatic, many old plastic bags hung on barbed-wire fences by litterers and the wind. Baja California Sur has moved into the consumer era, but the garbage collecting is still back in the Dark Ages.

The desert soil is not only dry, but saline, and only the hardiest of vegetation can survive. There are creosote bushes, and a lot of opportunistic jumping cholla.

Mile 60   To the left is a turn to the village of **San Francisco de la Sierra,** which is a recommended sidetrip for dual-purpose bikes. It is 23 miles to the village, the road climbing up on the eroded volcanic mesas; coming down from the mesa the view is directly across the Vizcaino Desert to the **Sierra Santa Clara** on the Pacific side.

Mile 72   You go past the right turn to **Punta Abreojos,** marked by the **Crucero del Pacifico Restaurant** and parked trucks. Punta Abreojos is 50 corrugated miles away, on the Pacific coast.

Now the road starts twisting a bit. At the 80-mile point, watch out for a deep arroyo; the approaches are steep on both sides, with turns, and the bottom collects its share of wrecks.

Mile 87   The most delightful town in Baja, by my humble estimation, is off to your right, **San Ignacio.** When the padres came tromping through a quarter-millenium ago, they found a steady supply of water in this little oasis. The word of God could be spread from reasonably comfortable surroundings.

A Visit to Saint Ignatius

The road into town, which is about a mile off the highway, goes past a small lagoon and a large grove of 80,000 date palms, and enters into a dusty *zocalo* (town square), with the mission church on the west side. A small museum, with a good deal of information on the cave painters, is off to the left side. The mission was begun by the Jesuits in 1728, and was finished by the Dominicans many years later, and claims to have been in continuous service.

Accomodation and food is readily available. Alongside the

lagoon on the way into town is the **Ignacio Springs B&B** (646-173-4141), which has a number of separate yurt-like cabins, and a dock to dive off into the water. A quarter mile beyond is the **Hotel La Pinta** (615-154-0300; U.S. 800-336-5454). A couple of blocks off the square is the small **Posada San Ignacio** (615-154-0313), and since there are not too many streets in San Ignacio it is not difficult to find. The inn was founded by a German sailor, Frank Fischer, who jumped ship in Santa Rosalia about 1900 and moved up to San Ignacio; his descendants still own the place. A good place to eat is **Rene's Bar,** close by the town square, where both locals and tourists mingle.

Along the highway, just before you get to the San Ignacio turn-off, is a PEMEX station on the left, and a big sign announcing **Ricardo's Rice & Beans,** off to the right; the place has nice rooms and good food.

■

He Made a Killing

Charlie Scammon was a whaling-ship captain back in the days of President Buchanan, and in 1857 he sailed into these quiet waters and realized he had a fortune at hand. In those times people lit their homes with oil lanterns, and whale oil was the primo stuff to burn, and the purpose of whaling was to fill all the barrels on board with this whale product. In the lagoon, the whales, never having been molested by man before, just floated around while the sailors slaughtered them.

Scammon returned to San Francisco, laden to the gunnels, and aroused much curiosity as to how he had been so successful in such a short time. The crew was sworn to secrecy. Next year he returned to the lagoon and repeated the process, but this time he was followed, and the year after that other whalers appeared in droves and virtually wiped out the breeding grounds. So much for the nobility of man. ■

West Side Highway

Before Mex 1 opened up in 1974, what little traffic there was going the length of Baja stayed on the Pacific side from San Ignacio to Ciudad Insurgentes, euphemistically called the **West Side Highway.** It is 35 rough miles down to Laguna San Ignacio, then 60 miles on either the "high" road, dirt and sand, or the beach road south to **San Juanico,** another 30 miles to **La Purisima,** and 64 miles of pavement to **Ciudad Insurgentes.** It's a rough go in parts, but any competent type on a dual-purpose bike can do it. As did the drivers in their 18-wheelers.   ■

Back on Mex 1 at Mile 87. Soon you are crossing over the mountain range which runs the length of Baja, and start descending to the **Sea of Cortez** side. To the north you can see the **Three Virgins Volcanos,** three distinct peaks on the horizon. The tallest one is 6,299 feet, and while not very active this trio does provide the heat for a geo-thermal power project a little to the east. Watch the descent, as the corners should be taken seriously. If you want to admire the ocean views, stop.

Mile 139   You are entering **Santa Rosalia,** a somewhat scruffy town; its main business being the ferry for those wanting to cross the Sea of Cortez to Guaymas on the mainland—but you better have your paperwork in order.

As you ride along the waterfront, everything is covered in a dingy brown, a residue of more than 100 years of mining and smelting. It's a working town, not a vacation spot. A small, shabby park is home to a collection of mining equipment, though the casual passerby might think it was a junkyard.

Mining types first found the copper deposits in the 1860s. The ore came naturally in little balls of copper carbonate and oxides; the **Compagnie de Boleo,** the French outfit that moved to exploit this resource in 1885, bailed in 1954, and the operation was taken over by Mexican concerns. But it pretty much shut down work operations in the 1990s.

The French connection is why the town church, **Santa Barbara,** is a metal pre-fab structure, designed by A. G. Eiffel (of Eiffel Tower fame), and transported here in pieces in 1897.

Mile 141   A little locomotive sits in a little square to the right. The town proper is in a little arroyo between two mesas, a skinny 50 blocks with bank and bakery and all the merchandise you can hope for. Plus great tacos at the outdoor stand on **Avenida Alvaro Obregon,** just a few doors down from the bank.

Conception Bay is a most attractive place, even though the norteamericanos seeking southern sun seem to have cluttered up the beaches a fair bit, like here at Playa Santispac.

Mex 1 goes straight south, far enough inland so as not to see the water. Past a bleak prison, climb through a few hills, and the road descends into the valley of the **Rio Santa Rosalia,** better known as the **Rio Mulege.**

Mile 177 Houses on both sides of the road, a bridge ahead, a turn into the town of Mulege on the left. Nice place. Up river is the old (1705) **Mission Santa Rosalia de Mulege,** and on top of the hill is the old prison (now a museum, and brilliantly whitewashed). A captive of the church or a captive of the state, take your pick.

Mile 179 Two miles south of town is a large PEMEX, and a small grocery store, and a place to send and receive faxes; the modern world has come to Mulege. But the road goes on, slips into a few hills, and then you come on a most beautiful sight, **Bahia Concepcion.** The bay, bounded on the far side by a mountainous peninsula, is almost 25 miles long, and three to five miles wide. It is a haven for sailors, and for motorhomes, with the beaches often cluttered with palapas and Winnebagos.

Mile 190 You are at **Playa Santispac.** If you are in the camping mode ask the chap at the gate for a palapa, which runs maybe $6; you can buy food and water at the two little restaurants which serve the residents.

Mile 202 A small tourist complex has been built here at **Playa Buenaventura** at the south end of the bay, with the **Hotel San Buenaventura** (615-153-0408), restaurant, satellite TV, and all amenities.

Mulege

Mulege is tucked along the north shore of the "only navigable" river in Baja, and that is just for half a mile at high tide. The town has a small *zocalo* (Plaza Corona) with the Hotel Hacienda on one side, a supermarket on another, and the best fish tacos in Baja (by my own unprejudiced opinion) sold from a tiny shanty on wheels between 8 a.m. and noon

The **Hotel Hacienda** (615-153-0021) is a low-bucks affair, built as a traditional wealthy family's house over a hundred years ago, with a courtyard inside. There is a fenced-in parking area, but if you are paranoidally concerned, you can push your bike into the courtyard. At the entrance to town is the much newer and more conventional **Hotel Mulege** (615-153-0416), a two-story motel built around a courtyard.

The south side of the **Mulege River** is basically Gringoland, with houses and trailers along the bank. Down toward the mouth of the river is the very pleasant **Hotel Serenidad** (615-153-0530), complete with its own airstrip and a pig roast on Saturday night.

For dining, the Serenidad is good, as are the downtown eateries—with fewer than 5,000 inhabitants Mulege does not have a very extensive downtown nightlife. The **Restaurant El Candil** on Calle Zaragoza close by the *zocalo* is fine, as is **Los Equipales** on Calle Moctezuma. If you have any questions about Mulege, stop in at **La Tienda** on Calle Martinez, which sells everything from guide books to diving equipment, and owners Miguel and Claudia are a wealth of local information. ∎

Mile 222   A dead-straight dirt road, well marked as SAN ISIDRO, goes off to the west (your right) and La Purisma/San Isidro, about 36 miles of corrugated surface. This connects you with the old West Side Highway, but it is a bumpy ride.

Mex 1 tears south over rocky, brushy landscape, with nothing but an occasional abandoned store or scrawny cow to indicate the presence of people.

Mile 249   You have arrived at **Loreto Junction**, gateway to the first Spanish settlement in the Californias. Mex 1 skirts the town, and at the obvious sign you will turn east to go into the center. As you come down the avenue, a PEMEX will be on your left, and on the right the rather basic **Motel Salvatierra** (613-135-0021).

Back to **Loreto Junction**, and south. Most of the next 200 miles are rather dull, so we will get you through in the shortest time.

Mile 250 A well-marked dirt road goes off to the right to the **Mission of San Javier**—which is well worth seeing except that the 20 miles are pretty rough.
Mile 264 A road to the left goes to **Puerto Escondido**, which was to be part of the greater Loreto tourist complex.
Mile 271 Your last view, in your mirror, of the Sea of Cortez for a while.

Loreto

Loreto was founded in 1697 by Padre Salvatierra (Father Save the Earth), and served as the capital of Spanish Baja until the town got thumped good and proper by the hurricane of 1829; that plus some politicking got the seat of government moved to La Paz. To add insult to injury, Loreto was pretty much destroyed by an earthquake in 1877.

Not that you would know it today. The **Mission Nuestra Senora de Loreto** has been rebuilt, the city looks quite clean, and the *malecon* is a delight to stroll along. A small fishing fleet still makes its home along the embarcadero, but mostly the harbor looks for rich people on pleasure boats. Not many come.

Any number of hotels are available, as Loreto once had aspirations of being Baja California Sur's tourist mecca. But, as with the moving of the capital in the last century, shortly after the construction of a major resort hotel was completed in the 1970s, politics caused the Mexican government to become more interested in developing the Cabos, and Loreto's development fell into a financial backwater.

The airport is technically an international one, but only half a dozen flights a week come in, not enough to support a major tourist economy.

The **Hotel La Pinta** (613-135-0025; U.S. 800-336-5454) is at the north end of the *malecon,* while the **Hotel Oasis** (613-135-0211) is at the southern end. If you want luxury, check into the **Hotel Posada de las Flores** (613-135-1162), close by the mission; it is an old building, gorgeously redone, with 15 elegant rooms—and a bar with 250 different tequilas.

Food is all around. **Cafe Ole,** right on the plaza east of the mission, is good morning and afternoon, and all you have to do for dinner is to walk upstairs (no elevator, sorry), to the **Restaurant La Terraza** for an excellent dinner.   ∎

Mile 284 A dirt road goes 25 miles to the **Puerto Agua Verde** fishing village. A couple of miles further on Mex 1 comes out of the mountains onto the **Magdalena Plain.**

Mile 322 You are at the southern end of **Insurgent City** (Ciudad Insurgentes), and Mex 1 makes a left, going south, straight as the proverbial arrow for 50 miles. A PEMEX station is up to your right, about 300 yards. This is the south end of the old West Side Highway.

Mile 339 Enter **Constitution City** (Ciudad Constitucion), a major farming center atop a giant aquifer.

Mile 372 At the village of **Santa Rita** the road finally makes a 30-degree jog.

Mile 408 The village of **El Cien** (The Hundred—100 km from La Paz), with PEMEX. Soon you will be able to glimpse the **Bay of La Paz.**

Mile 463 A huge sculpture sits beside the road; whether it is a whale's tail or a dove is up to the viewer to decide. The road curves slightly left and heads straight into the city along Calle Abasolo.

Mile 466 Intersection with Calle 5 de Febrero, and a PEMEX, a sign indicating that Mex 1 goes sharp right. GOING STRAIGHT runs you directly into the city of La Paz, turning right onto 5 Feb. puts you in the Cabo direction.

The entrance to La Paz: Is that a whale's tail or a dove of peace?

La Paz: Nicest City in Baja

This is the nicest city in Baja; it is big, with over 200,000 inhabitants, and getting bigger. But the center of the city, the area which backs onto the *malecon,* the seaside promenade, is a real pleasure to walk through, with a big market, a cathedral built in 1861, a good museum (free), and the **Library of the History of the Californias** found in the 1880 **Government House.** The place is good for strolling.

I recommend riding into town, finding a hotel, parking the bike, getting a room, and just laying back. If you GO STRAIGHT at that aforementioned intersection Abasolo becomes Calle Alvaro Obregon and you will soon arrive at the bayside drive and pass the **Hotel Los Arcos** (612-122-2744, U.S. 800-716-8644) and then the **Hotel Perla** (612-122-0777, U.S. 800-716-8799), both with safe parking. I prefer the Perla, which has been around for over 60 years; I love the open-air La Terraza restaurant on the ground floor, where I can look at the elegant people promenading along the sea front during the evenings.

At the other end of the financial spectrum, but just four blocks from the *malecon,* is the **Hosteria del Convento** (612-122-3508), a nunnery turned into an inexpensive hotel. Each small nun's "cell" has its own shower and toilet, and the little courtyard often has a couple of motorcycles in it.

Food? Everywhere. **La Terraza** has great ambience, and the foodstands at the **Mercado Municipal Madero** provide delicious fare. The city offers everything from McDonald's to sushi to clam tacos.

If you want to go to the beaches, you continue along the bayfront road toward **Pichilingue,** and half a dozen beaches are along that road. Pichilingue is also where the ferry to the mainland leaves from.

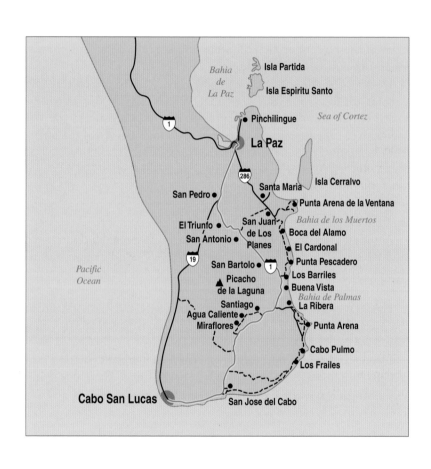

La Paz to Cabo San Lucas

The Final Dash on Mexico 1: 133 Miles

Get back along the waterfront to that PEMEX at the corner of Abasolo and 5 de Febrero. I know this urban mapping is a misery, but you gotta do what you gotta do.

Mile 0 Head south on 5 Feb., which is Mex 1, and go 15 blocks; don't bother counting the blocks, unless you enjoy the precision; your heads-up comes after passing a large sports complex on your right.

Mile 1 Angle right on the 45 degree turn, which is Mex 1. The Carretera al Sur, officially known as Blvd. Forjadores, is large and well-marked, with signs pointing the way toward Cabo San Lucas.

Mile 1+ Mex 1 goes straight, pointing to SAN JOSE CABO; there are two Cabos, **St. Joe** and **St. Luke,** a mere 17 miles apart, so you are on the right track. A well-marked turn to the left goes to **San Juan de los Planes** and the **Bay of the Dead** (Bahia de los Muertos) on State Highway 286.

Mile 4 Curve to the left; no chance of going wrong. Then it is over a low rise and a long, straight run across the **Plain of La Paz.**

Mile 20 A three-way intersection at the south end of the village of **San Pedro.** Mex 1 goes straight, while Mex 19 goes off to the right. They meet up again in Cabo San Lucas. Stay straight.

Mex 1 is now entering the **Sierra de la Laguna,** this mountain range that fills up most of the tip of Baja. The highest peak, **Picacho de la Laguna,** is over 7,000 feet tall; no road up there, as it is a natural reserve, although you can hike the trails. The **Mountains of the Lake** got their name because a lake used to exist south of the peak, which ran dry a hundred or more years ago.

The asphalt of Mex 1 provides a delightful motorcycle road, full of twisty bits—which means you should take a good deal of care. A lot of four-wheeled wrecks can be seen along the way, decorating the arroyos.

Mile 34 Entering **El Triunfo,** a splendid little mining town which hasn't seen the smelter working for many a year. But lots of photogenic brick structures. If you turn at the little church, you can wind your way down several dirt roads to the huge brick smokestack, nicknamed **La Ramona,** as it was inaugurated on **St. Ramona's day.** Silver was discovered in 1862, and gold soon after, and within 15 years the place had become an industry, with over 10,000 people living here. The mines began to play out after the turn of the century, and by 1925 the place was down to a couple of hundred inhabitants. Now the government sees the wisdom of keeping a bit of history intact in order to lure the tourist, and has restored the old city hall (Casa Municipal) along the main road. Close by, the **Restaurant Las Glorias** will provide good Mexican fare.

Mile 39   San Antonio is another old mining center, this one begun back in the 18th Century. It is now a small agricultural community, with a PEMEX down where the road curves around the dry river bed. Almost opposite the PEMEX is the dirt road that leads down along the riverbed for 15 miles to the Bay of the Dead.

Mile 56   The village of **San Bartolo** is a little tropical haven, watered by a spring further up the canyon. Roadside stands sell mangos and avocadoes, and more complete meals can be had at the several restaurants in town. This is often a Sunday-drive destination for La Pazians.

Mile 64   The turn to the left to **Los Barriles** and **Bahia de Palmas**. Mex 1 now goes close to the seaside, with the hotels, RV camps, and fishing boats of the **Buena Vista** (Good View) area to your left. And then the road starts to climb again and the sea disappears. Back in the hills.

Mile 74   A paved road to the left goes seven miles to the village of **La Ribera**; if you have a dual-purpose bike, you can do a delightful 58-mile loop, including a lot of dirt and sand, around **East Cape** to **San Jose del Cabo.**

Mile 79   A paved road goes to the right a mile or so to the town of **Santiago,** founded back in 1723 with the building of the **Mission of St. James the Apostle.**

Mile 81   Here it is, your official passage into the **Tropics.** Here at 23 degrees, 27 minutes north of the equator, you have crossed over the line demarcating the **Tropic of Cancer.** Here the sun is directly overhead at noon during the **Summer Solstice** (and directly over the **Tropic of Capricorn** during the **Winter Solstice**); so every point within the tropics receives the perpendicular rays of the sun at least one day of the year, in case you wanted to know the astronomical definition of "the tropics," a/k/a "The Torrid Zone." Unfortunately, this is not a very romantic spot, merely a scrubby pull-off by the side of the road; a large graffiti-covered concrete ball symbolizes the earth.

Mile 87   A PEMEX on the highway and a paved road going right to the village of **Miraflores.** The place has a small, deserved reputation for making tack, all that gear used in riding horses, as well as the more touristy stuff. One tannery is on the road into town, with a small sign, LEATHER SHOP.

Mile 105   The **Los Cabos International Airport** is to your right, a very busy place thanks to tourism, and access is via a toll road. The highway you

The San Jose Church was built in 1940 on the site of the 1730 San Jose del Cabo mission.

stay on, Mex 1, becomes four lanes as it begins to skirt San Jose del Cabo.
Mile 111 A paved road angles off to the left, past a PEMEX, and this is the northerly approach to San Jose, along Calle Zaragoza. Do head into town, and you will get lost, and have a good time.

Staying on Mex 1, we are sweeping past San Jose.

Mile 113 The turn to ZONA DE HOTELES and the Paseo San Jose. Now begins **The Corridor,** 18 glorious miles between **San Jose del Cabo** and **Cabo San Lucas,** dedicated to The Tourist; this four-lane highway was completed in 1993, was immediately washed out by a hurricane, and just as quickly repaired. There are over a dozen hotels along here, all costing at least $300 a night, and all designed to keep you in that hotel, spending money in the hotel.

Mile 115 The turn to **Hotel Palmilla** (624-146-7000; U.S. 866-829-2977), my favorite amongst the slew of expensive resorts along the coast—though I have never had the money to stay there. This one was built in 1956, when Cabo tourism was in its infancy, and had a $80 million upgrade in 2004, but is pleasantly old-fashioned and pricey. Cobbled drives and lots of palm trees make it very welcoming.

San Jose

San Jose is an entertaining town, established by the Spanish in 1730 due to its good source of water. Today it has some permanent 30,000 inhabitants, and two-thirds of the place is genuinely Mexican, the other third, mostly down on the coast, is dedicated to separating tourists from their money. I like it better than San Lucas.

Calle Zaragosa will bend a couple of times, but take you right down town, past the church of San Jose and the *zocalo,* where the locals tend to hang out. Take a right turn onto the divided Boulevard Mijares, and that is where low-key tourism can be found. **Mijares,** to alert the politically correct types, was named for Lt. Jose Antonia Mijares, who died fighting against the Americans here in 1847.

The twin-steepled church was built in 1940, on the site of the 1730 mission. Over the doors is a mural portraying the killing of one Padre Tamaral in 1734. Tamaral had had the temerity to declare the local Indian custom of polygamy illegal, and since such high-handedness irritated the locals, they sacked both this and the mission at Santiago. Reminds me of our battles with the Mormons over that same subject.

On Mijares is the **Tropicana Inn** (624-142-0907), with a sidewalk cafe where lots of people hang out; this is very nice, and as gringo as the town gets. On the north end of Mijares, close to the *zocalo,* is the city hall, with a collection of art and artifacts in the courtyard.

A favored eatery is the **Ristorante Damiana,** on the northeast corner of the *zocalo.* South along Mijares, in a corner of a big empty lot where fairs are held, is **Mariscos El Muelle,** an outdoor restaurant which is open early in the morning until late at night.

Down on the shore, along the **Paseo San Jose,** are half a dozen fancy hotels, anchored by the 400-room **Presidente Intercontinental Los Cabos Resort** (624-142-0211; U.S. 888-567-8725); their busy season is around Christmas, and the rest of the year you can usually negotiate a better rate. But best to leave these to the fly-in tourists. All Cabo hotels have seasonal rate fluctuations. ■

Todos Santos

You can do a nice loop to get back to La Paz via Mex 19 and Todos Santos—as a matter of fact, this way is 30 miles shorter than via San Jose. Take that right, follow your front wheel, and in 46 miles you will be entering **Todos Santos** (All Saints). This little agricultural community, and artists' colony, has about 5,000 inhabitants and half a dozen hotels. A nice place to stay is the **Hotel California** (which has nothing to do with the Eagles' song—612-145-0525), right in the middle of town. Keep on Mex 19, and in another 32 miles you are back at Mex 1 at the San Pedro intersection. ∎

Mile 117 The antithesis of the Palmilla is the **Westin Regina Beach Resort Los Cabos** (624-142-9000; U.S. 800-937-8461), a huge, pink, modernistic structure with 240 rooms high above the sea. This joint reputedly cost $200 million to build in 1994. More hotels follow along the road.

At the marina in Cabo San Lucas, with yachts owned by wealthy Americans.

Post Script

If you are among the very wealthy and business needs attending to, you may have your corporate jet fly down to Cabo to pick you up, and drop off a favored underling who will be very glad to ride your bike back north—on company time. If not, you and your motorcycle will be headed back north—and everything is different. Even the flat Magdalena Plain. Gives you a new perspective. You will also have the knowledge of some good places to eat and sleep, and hope you will be passing Mulege late in the morning, in time to get some of those fish tacos at the Plaza Corona.

A thousand miles later you are arriving at the Tecate border crossing. Good trip. But you are ready to go home. However, in a month or two, you may start thinking about doing it again.   ■

Mile 122 A suitably ugly monument is in the middle of the road, commemorating the highway's completion in 1993. More hotels between the road and sea, and then the beginnings of an urban zone.

Mile 132 The alternate road to La Paz, via Todos Santos, is Mex 19, going off to the right. For the full benefit of Cabo San Lucas, GO STRAIGHT ahead.

Mile 132+ TURN LEFT at McDonald's if you want to go to **Playa El Medano** and the beach hotels.

Mile 133 "Cabo San Lucas, I have arrived!" The traffic is terrible!

Cabo San Lucas

Kentucky Fried Chicken, Domino's Pizza, condo salesman on every corner, the Giggling Marlin, Harley-Davidson rentals, Hard Rock Cafe, Haagen-Dazs ice cream—Cabo San Lucas, this is the gringo playpen! The center of town is around the marina, where a huge mall called **Puerto Paraiso** tries to offer everything that a tourist might want.

This is a tourist town, pure and simple. The local economy is based entirely on supporting the tourist industry, and there is not much in the way of cultural or historic interest.

If you want to stay in town, near the "action," **the Siesta Suites Hotel** (624-143-2773, U.S. 602-331-1354) on Calle Zapata is convenient, as is the **Hotel Santa Fe** (624-143-4403; U.S. 866-448-4623), on the corner of Zaragoza and Obregon; both have secure parking.

If you want beach living, I would head for the **Hacienda Beach Resort** (624-143-0063; U.S. 800-733-2226) on **El Medano** beach.

Looking across Bahia San Lucas to Land's End—the very tip of Baja.

Weather

CALIFORNIA

The weather in California is generally very good. But on occasion it can be very bad. We get snow in the mountains, and the temperature (we'll deal strictly in Fahrenheit here, as it sounds so much more impressive) can reach 120 degrees in the summer desert.

Since the state of California is so big, the weather can vary a lot. At the beginning of a chapter I sometimes put in a little line on weather, which indicates what months may be the best time to go to Eureka, or Julian, or wherever.

But do not take my word for it. You should not try to project a September weather pattern in June, even if you've brought up all the weather channels in the universe, cross-referenced all the information as applicable to Lat. 39.56N and Long. 120.56W (Quincy) . . . the forecast might just be terribly wrong. An easier way to do it, if you are sitting in San Francisco, say, and are thinking of going up to Quincy, you can always buy the *San Francisco Chronicle,* which usually has a five-day forecast. Which is only wrong half the time.

The best approach is to call the telephone number of the local chamber of commerce or tourist bureau, also listed at the start of each chapter, and ask the person at the other end to look out the window. That's a start.

If said person truly deserves the job of representing the town to foreigners, of promoting its scenic beauty and historical significance, of bringing in free-spending yokels from Los Angeles or Boston or Paris, then that person should also have scrutinized the local weather report that morning, and can tell you if a nor'wester is blowing in and about to dump ten inches of rain, or a tropical high is expected to keep the temperature between 70 and 80, with humidity at 64 percent. And the wind always at your back.

You just can't tell. I got rained on in Death Valley at Thanksgiving in 1981, all the passes being closed due to mudslides and snow. I've alternately roasted and frozen in Redding, which can be one hellaciously hot sumbich in summer, one cold misery in winter—and you never know which way spring and fall are going to go. I've found mountain passes closed by snow as late as July.

The Pacific Coast can be really foggy all through the summer; in Mark Twain's mortal words, "The coldest winter I ever spent was summer in San Francisco." Conversely, it may be 80 degrees when crossing the Golden Gate bridge. You never can tell. Los Angeles can be awash in rain more months than not in the year, and if you stay in Bear Valley in November, you might find a foot of snow on your motorcycle seat in the morning.

And if that's not enough to deter you, think of earthquakes opening up the road in front of you, forest fires sweeping through your campsite, hailstones battering you at Mono Lake, and extra-terrestrials kidnapping you for a few experiments. California has it all.

But mostly we have benign weather. Yes, it rains a lot up north, but that's what rainsuits are for. And the mercury can boil in Palm Springs, but that is why motels are air-conditioned. No guarantees on the weather, but anytime of year somewhere in California there is better motorcycling weather than in Massachusetts in the winter, or Florida in the summer.

And since my routes can take you anywhere from below sea level to nearly 10,000 feet, bring layers of clothing accordingly.

In truth, there is not much you can do about the weather. Except to dress appropriately.

BAJA

When is the best time to go to Baja? Just about anytime, I would say, but best in spring and fall. The Pacific side generally stays cool, even in summer, thanks to the ocean air. On the other side of the peninsula the Sea of Cortez is balmy from the end of September to the beginning of June, and damned hot during the summer. Of course the odd tropical storm or hurricane can come in any time, but that's just the luck of the draw; long-range forecasters usually have these plotted a week or more in advance. Down at the southern tip, around the Cabos, the infamous *chubascos* occasionally rip in and deluge the place for an hour or a week; these are most often seen between May and November.

Motorcycle Rental Companies

Quite a few companies are trying to make a buck from renting bikes. Which on the surface does not seem that hard to do. Buy a Harley Big Twin for $15,000, rent it out for $150 a day, and it's paid for in less than four months. However, the company does have to worry about insurance (which can be very expensive indeed), repairs, maintenance, et cetera. As well as what happens when the motorcycles sit unrented.

There are some very reputable rental outfits, which give you bikes in good condition. I've also heard that you can get real junkers. I can't tell you which companies are the best ones, because I don't often need to rent a bike in this state.

If you do make a long-distance arrangement, and have to put down a deposit, make sure that you get all the particulars on what you are paying for in print. So that when you expect a BMW R1200RT, and the guy offers you a Bridgestone 350 GTR instead, you have some recourse.

The following is a partial list of motorcycle rental outfits that have sites in California; I expect that several of these may have gone out of business by the time you read this, and new ones will have appeared. If you have a computer, run up a search engine, type in something catchy like "motorcycle rentals in California" and see what the screen says.

Blue Sky Motorcycle Rentals: San Diego, Ventura, Newport Beach
866-340-4294, www.blueskymotorcyclerentals.com
Harleys, Hondas, Triumph and, Wow!, the Boss Hoss

California Beemin'—San Jose
1886 West San Carlos Street, San Jose CA 95128
408-295-0205 rentals@sjbmw.com
BMWs out of a BMW dealer

California Motorcycle Rental—San Diego
1838 Caminito Ascua, La Jolla CA 92037
858-456-9577 www.calif-motorcyclerental.com
BMWs

Dubbelju Motorcycle Rentals—San Francisco
689 Bryant St., San Francisco CA 94107
415-495-2774, www.dubbelju.com
H-D, Triumph, and BMW

EagleRider: a dozen locations in California
11860 La Cienega Ave, Hawthorne CA 90250
800-501-8687, www.eaglerider.com
H-D, Honda, BMW

Harley-Davidson Authorized Rentals: all over the state
Lots of Harley dealers are signing up for this program.
www.hdrentals.com

Harley Owners Group Fly & Ride: All over the state
You have to be a HOG member to take advantage of this, but if you are,
dial 411-343-4896 for all the particulars.

Moturis Motorcycle Rentals—Los Angeles, San Francisco, and other U.S. sites
400 West Compton Blvd, Gardena CA 90248
877-MOTURIS, www.moturis.com
H-D, Honda, BMW; you can ride one way and drop the bike off.

Route 66 Riders Motorcycle Rental—Los Angeles
4161 Lincoln Blvd, Marina del Rey CA 90292
310-578-0112, www.route66riders.com
H-D

San Francisco Bay Area Motorcycle Rentals
757 Lincoln Ave, #18, San Rafael CA 94901
888-812-9253 www.motorbikeusa.com
H-D

Organized Motorcycle Tours

Running tours to the Alps or the Andes is one thing, running tours in the two Californias is quite another. A lot of riders are perfectly happy to pay the extra money for an organized tour, for having a guide along to show the way, for knowing that a good bed is waiting each evening. Not to mention having a van carry your luggage, and not worrying about the possibility of a break-down.

To be guided or not? In Alta California the roads tend to be well-marked, and it is generally not difficult to find a place to sleep—unless you are in Borrego Springs in wildflower season. In Baja there is essentially only one major road, so it is difficult to get lost—unless you leave the pavement; but gas stations are less frequent. A guided tour is certainly not a necessity, but it does add a certain cachet to a trip, and riders or passengers who tend to be fretful will certainly fret less.

If you want to fly into Los Angeles, be met at the airport, whisked off to a nice hotel, introduced to your motorcycle, meet some pleasant strangers who will soon be friends, and then go and explore the high passes in the Sierra Nevada mountains, or the beaches in Baja, then an Organized Motorcycle Tour may well be the way for you to go.

More than a dozen OMT companies offer tours in the Californias, and here are a few that I have found; it is definitely an incomplete list. Any company with Baja in the name usually means it is focusing on dual-purpose or dirt-bike tours. Give them a call, or, better yet, look at the websites and get the particulars. I'll put a city down to show where a business is headquartered, unless it has several locations. Or again, run up www.moto-directory.com on the insidious Internet, which has a huge list in its North American touring section.

Ad-Mo Adventure Motorcycle Tours—Los Angeles, Las Vegas
800-944-2356; www.admo-tours.com

Baja Bound—San Diego
888-664-2252, www.bajaboundmoto.com

Baja Off-Road Adventures—San Diego
877-677-BAJA, 714-256-0875, www.bajaoffroad.com

California Motorcycle Tours—San Diego
888-408-7631, www.ca-motorcycletours.com

EagleRider Motorcycle Tours—several locations
800-514-6777, 310-536-6777, www.eaglerider.com

Edelweiss Bike Travel—several locations
800-582-2263, www.edelweissbiketravel.com

Moto California—Los Angeles
949-606-6655, www.motocalifornia.com

Moto Discovery—San Diego
800-233-0564, www.motodiscovery.com

Moto Mexico Tours—San Diego
888-668-6639, www.motomextours.com

Pashnit Motorcycle Tours—Northern & Central California
530-391-1356, 209-609-3216, www.pashnittours.com

Rebel Harley-Davidson Tours—San Diego
858-292-6200, www.rebelusa.com

Ride Free Motorcycle Tours—Los Angeles
310-487-1047, www.ridefree.com

Top Shelf Motorcycle Tours—San Francisco
877-870-7062, www.topshelfmotorcycletours.com

Trail Boss Tours (Baja)—San Diego
888-228-6878, www.trailbosstours.com

Index